Government Procurement Management

1985 Second Edition

Stanley N. Sherman
Professor of Business Administration
George Washington University

Wordcrafters Publications
Gaithersburg, Maryland 20878

WORDCRAFTERS PUBLICATIONS
15804 White Rock Road
Gaithersburg, Maryland 20878

International Standard Book Number ISBN
0-941448-01-0

Library of Congress Catalog Card Number
84-052711

Printed in the United States of America

Preface

Three years have passed since publication of the first edition of this book. They have been years filled with public debate, legislative action, and regulatory reform in the procurement area. In the preface to the original edition I made the statement that the art of management for procurement is similar to that in other fields--it requires dedication, sensitivity to people and organizations, and deep understanding of the system and its environment. With the activity of the last three years, I have mixed emotions with respect to that expressed sentiment. The challenge to managers of procurement programs is as great as ever, but the complexity of decisionmaking and the impediments to creative action have increased rather than decreased for participants in the government's acquisition programs.

The cost of procurement by the United States grew from $94 billion in fiscal year 1979 to the 1983 level of $168 billion because of the rise in defense expenditures, inflation in the economy, and increased levels of contracting out activity on the part of government agencies. As its overall volume of activity expanded, the system's newsworthiness has increased and emphasis on trying to improve it redoubled. The rise in the amount of defense acquisition activity, coupled with deep concern over the amount of the national resources being expended for defense, has been a central factor in generating intense criticism of wasteful (or apparently wasteful) procurement practices.

Some of the notable events of the last three years have been: 1) issuance of the first presidential executive order dealing with procurement (E.O. 12352) on March 17, 1982; 2) approval of the Prompt Payment Act (P.L.

97-177) on May 21, 1982;   3) approval of the Small Business Innovation Development Act (P.L. 97-219) effective
on October 1, 1982;   4) approval of a Small Business Act
amendment to increase the requirements for publication of
procurement opportunities (P.L.   98-72)   on   August   11,
1983;   5) reauthorization of the Office of Federal Procurement Policy with reinstatement of its regulatory
powers (P.L.   98-191), approved December 1, 1983;   6)
implementation of the Federal Acquisition Regulation on
April 1, 1984;   7) approval of the Competition in Contracting Act of 1984 (CICA) (Title VII of P.L. 98-369) on
June 23, 1984;   8) approval of the Defense Procurement
Reform Act of 1984 (Title XII of P.L. 98-525) on October
19, 1984; and   9) approval of the Small Business and
Federal Procurement Competition Enhancement Act of 1984
(P.L. 98-577) on October 30, 1984.

These and other procurement related events have sig-
naled important philosophical and practical change in government procurement, the most dramatic of them occurring
in 1984. The events have received mixed reviews by leaders in the field. This measured response results from
difficulty in assessing the impact of the actions; some
are clearly beneficial, others are questionable because
they add complexity and administrative delay. Unfortunately, changes that seek procurement reform tend to
carry mixed blessings. On the positive side, management
attention to the procurement process has been increased,
for example, by the establishment of agency procurement
executives. There is an increased consciousness on the
part of government managers of the benefits of good procurement practices, and attention has been paid to the
need for improving the skills of the procurement work
force and to the management environment within which it
plans and executes its responsibilities.

My objective for this book continues to be one of
explanation, however, policy changes have made that
objective difficult. Although the procurement process
remains stable, the probable impacts of the changes are
significant and need to be studied by those involved. It
is hoped that this book will contribute to an understanding of the practices employed and fill some part of the
void in the literature of procurement. It seeks to
capture interest in how the federal system operates to

achieve the award of some twenty-one million contracts annually.

Three new chapters have been introduced with the second edition. Chapter six provides an analysis of the Competition in Contracting Act. This special treatment is called for by the important, perhaps historic, legal and philosophical changes introduced by that act. Chapter seven, a comparison of private and public sector make-or-buy decisionmaking, has been added because that subject regularly generates comment and controversy, and because the issues associated with it are fundamental to effective organizational performance. Chapter nine treats automation of procurement by suggesting several ADP applications that are currently feasible, by reviewing selected major operational systems, and by summarizing the status of current ADP applications in government procurement offices based on a recent survey by the author. In addition the second edition has been revised throughout to reflect policy actions, to improve readability and to address specific management or policy issues not covered in the 1981 edition.

Much credit must be given to my students at George Washington University for their diligent research that has helped build the information base from which this work is drawn. I should also like to acknowledge the contributions of Joseph Zimmer, David Musio, and Curtis Cook who read portions of the manuscript. For the most tireless worker of all and for her editorial expertise and kindness in correcting the worst of my errors, I give thanks to my wife, Helen. Responsibility for those that remain is mine.

Table of Contents

1. **Introduction   1**

   Procurement Management Objectives and Contributions
   to Organizational Effectiveness/ Comparison of
   Private Sector and Public Procurement/ Integrated
   Materials Systems/ Materials Management and
   Procurement/ Materials Management Objectives/
   Inventory Policy Management and Control/ Statisti-
   cal Summary of Federal Procurement/ Planning
   Concepts and Strategy for Procurement Action.

2. **Procurement Objectives and the Federal
   Environment   22**

   Procurement: A Tool and a Field of Management/
   Proposed Uniform Federal Procurement System/
   Objectives for Acquisition and Assistance Programs/
   Federal Authority for Procurement Action/ Delega-
   tion of Authority/ Limitations on Actions of a
   Contracting Officer/ Freedom of Information Act/
   Ethical Problems in Procurement/ Public
   Acquisitions Categories.

3. **Procurement Functions   45**

   Policy and Procedure Development/ Personnel Training and Development/ Procurement Action Review/
   Legal Review/ Buyer and Negotiator Units/ Technical
   and Price Analysis/ Procurement Operations and Con-
   trol/ Advocacy Offices/ Source Identification and
   Qualification/ Source Selection, Planning and Con-

trol/ Procurement and Contract Management Review/
Contractor Procurement Systems Review/ Contract
Administration and Quality Assurance/ Contract
Audit/ Contract Adjustment/ Contract Appeals

✓ 4. **Organization of Government Procurement**   65

Congressional Actions Affecting Organization/ Procurement-Related Functions in Government/ Organizational Concepts and Choices in Federal Procurement/
Method of Procurement/ Commodity or Service Cate-
gory/ Organizational Level and Type/ Industry/ Func-
tion/Role Performed in the Procurement Process/
Geography, Installation and/or Magnitude/ End
Result/ Illustrative Government Procurement Organi-
zations/ Navy Organization for Acquisitions and
Contracting/ Environmental Protection Agency/
Goddard Space Flight Center

5. **Policy Formulation**   99

The Report of the Commission on Government Procure-
ment/ The Congress/ Office of Federal Procurement
Policy/ Rulemaking and Policy Development/ The Federal Acquisition Regulation (FAR)/ The Comptroller
General/ The Procuring Agencies

✓ 6. **A Statutory Cornucopia**   118

Keynote for Government Procurement/ The Paperwork
Impacts/ Congressional Urging and Policy State-
ments/ CICA Innovations/ Sealed Bidding/ Competi-
tive Proposals/ Noncompetitive Procedure/ Exclusion
of Sources/ Synopses/ The Advocate for Competition/
Protest Procedure - Comptroller General/ Special
Protest Procedure for ADP/ CICA Definitions and/or
Detailed Guidance

7. **Make-or-Buy**   141

Comparison of Personal and Nonpersonal Services
Relationships/ Elements of the Make-or-Buy Decision
In Industry/ Factors Which an Organization May

Consider in Make-or-Buy/ Government Make-or-Buy, an
Evolving Productivity Enhancement Tool.

8.   Procurement Management   160

The Procurement Manager/ Problems With Procurement
Management/ Improving Procurement Management/
Functional and Project Concepts of Management.

**9.   Applications of Data Processing In
Procurement   179**

Management, Statistical and Operational ADP Applica-
tions in Government Procurement/ Potential ADP
Applications in Procurement/ Survey of Automatic
Data Processing Applications in Government Procure-
ment Operations/ Operations Measurement/ Document
Generation/ Acquisition Management Information/
Purchase Analysis/ Source Listing/ Supplier Perform-
ance/ Purchase Planning/ Communications/ Price
Comparison Data Base/ Workload Planning/ Inventory
Analysis/ Purchase Order Generation/ Contract Pay-
ments/ Source Research/ Selected ADP System
Description: AMIS.

10.   Planning and Funding   197

Setting Objectives and Securing Resources/ Planning
Factors/ Specifications and Work Statements/ Budget
Execution/ Contract Funding/ Contract Finance.

11.   Models and Strategies   216

Models of the Procurement Process/ COGP Model/
Generic Procurement Model/ A-109 Model/ Procurement
Strategies/ Price-Directed Strategy/ Classical
Competitive Procurement Strategy/ Limited Source
Procurement Strategy/ Technological/ Conceptual
Strategy/ Procurement Process Interrelationships:
Cyclical Analysis.

√12. **Price Directed Sourcing** 238

Sealed Bid Model/ Criteria for the Use of Sealed
Bid Procurement/ Historical Summary and Policy
Considerations/ Formality of Sealed Bidding/ The
Firm-Bid Rule and Award to the Low Bid/ Contract
Types Used in Sealed Bid Procurement/ Constraints
on Communications Between the Parties During Sealed
Bidding/ Processing Bids/ Acceptance, Rejection,
and Award/ Mistakes/ Two-Step Sealed Bid Procure-
ment/ Suboptimization Problems With Sealed Bidding/
The Auction/ Life-Cycle Cost.

√13. **Competitive Negotiation** 260

Competitive Negotiations Overview/ The Statutory
Authority for Negotiations/ Affirmative Guidance
for Negotiations/ The Competitive Range/ Cost and
Pricing Data Requirements/ Dual Negotiations/
Models Developed for Competitive Negotiations/
Pre-1962 Model/ NASA Model DOD Model/ Scope of Nego-
tiations/ Deliverable Item Description/ Technical
Description of Work Requirement/ Schedule/ Co-
Contractor and Subcontractor Relationships/ Govern-
ment-Furnished Material, Data and Approvals/ Manage-
ment Planning and Systems/ Specialized Personnel
Capabilities/ Cost, Price and Funding/ Terms and
Conditions-Type of Contract.

14. **Noncompetitive Negotiation** 283

Specialized Sourcing Procedures/ Leader Company
Procurement/ Architectural and Engineering Serv-
ices/ Provisioned Item Orders/ Policy Directed
Sources/ Foreign Military Sales Agreements/
Specific Acquisition of Rights in Technical Data/
Unsolicited Proposals/ Classic Success Story: The
XA4D-1 Aircraft/ Solicited Noncompetitive
Proposals/ Second Sourcing/ Change Orders/
Regulated Industry Purchases.

15. **Technological/Conceptual Strategy**   303

Overview--Technological/Conceptual Strategy/
Historical Techniques for Securing Competition in
Complex Acquisitions/ Technological/ Conceptual
Strategy in Brief/ Specific Elements of A-109
Policy/ DOD Acquisition Policy Developments.

16. **Formal Contracting Arrangements**   318

Contract Type Historical Notes (1960-1980)/ Func-
tion of Contract Types/ The Need for Alternative
Types of Contracts/ Alternatives Available to the
Purchasing Manager/ Bases for Classifying Contract
Types/ Form of Acceptance of Work, Logistics
Needs/ Pricing Arrangement/ Fixed-Rate Contract
Types as a Group/ Fixed Price Contract Types as a
Group/ Cost versus Fixed Price Contracts/ Cost
Contracts as a Group/ Contract Type Utilization
Statistics/ The Process of Selecting Contract Type/
Criteria for Contract Type Selection/ Current State
of the Art/ Current Stability of the Technology/
Nature of the Contract Specification/ Program Objec-
tives/ Program Importance/ Program Stage/ Duration/
Motivational Factors/ Past Performance of Contrac-
tor/ Legal Constraints/ Production Potential/ Con-
tract Management Complexity/ Independence of Action
During Performance/ Administrative Costs/ Use of
Government Furnished Property/ Availability of Cost
and Pricing Data/ Accounting Systems/ Summary.

17. **International Procurement**   344

Buy American Act/ Balance of Payments Program/ The
Agreement on Government Procurement/ Objectives and
Potential Impact of the Agreement on Government
Procurement/ Transparency/ Method of Government
Assistance/ NATO RSI.

18. **Socioeconomic Issues**   365

Socioeconomic Programs/ Competitive and Noncompetitive Procurement/ Qualifications of Contracting

Personnel/Professional Status of Buyers.

APPENDICES   388

Appendix 1   388
Categories of Services Regularly Publicized in the
Commerce Business Daily

Appendix 2   389
Categories of Supplies, Equipment, and Material
Regularly Publicized in the Commerce Business
Daily

Appendix 3   392
Presidential Executive Order 12352 Federal
Procurement Reforms

Appendix 4   395
Structure of the Federal Acquisition Regulations

Index   405

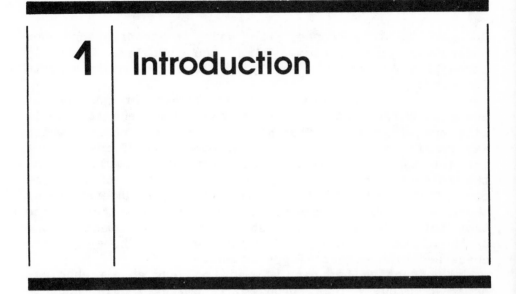

1 | Introduction

On October 15, 1984, <u>Business Week</u> published an article, "The Pentagon Steps Up Its War On Shoddy Workmanship." The article summarized several examples of poor quality in products built under government contracts. It is cited here only because it is one of the most recent of a long running series of media reports on deficiencies in government procurement. The first edition of this book was published in September, 1981. The media series was already in progress at that time reporting on numerous and now infamous purchases of furniture, plastic caps, hammers, coffee pots, chips and other items. The reports dealt with various forms of overpricing or deficient quality. A few of the reports reflected fraudulent acts and cases that were litigated. Most involved poor judgment or poor management.

The media reports have been accompanied by congressional investigations and reactions such that the 98th Congress was probably more active respecting procurement matters than any previous Congress. In excess of 150 procurement-related bills were introduced to it, and several important new statutes resulted. In general the statutes attempted to address and correct perceived system deficiencies.

Does the government have a good procurement system?

Do government personnel who work in contracting jobs understand the system? Are the problems more in perception or are they really as bad as the media reports indicate?

There are weaknesses in the government procurement system. Unfortunately, the symptoms that generate publicity are often far different from the real problems which may remain masked while short sighted "fixes" are devised for the apparent problems. The system is complex beyond the tolerance of most observers. Correction of problems can result only if the system is fully understood by those who seek to improve it. It is the author's hope that this book will bring about some improvement in the depth of understanding of procurement by those who are concerned with effective government.

Contracting has been viewed too long as a technology or as a uniquely legal problem, receiving little recognition as a management discipline. This view is especially dominant in government; it is reinforced by the expanding statutory and regulatory prescriptions created to improve the effectiveness of the system. Much of the redirection has occurred during 1984. A major thesis of the author is that better management and increased attention to work force capabilities would bring about more real improvement than increased detail in the statutory and regulatory foundation for carrying on the work.

This chapter examines five topics selected to familiarize the reader with the general subject matter. Initially it suggests several objectives of procurement management and its contributions to organizational effectiveness. Next it draws comparisons between private and public procurement, showing that there are many similarities as well as differences.

The third major section of the chapter introduces the concept of materials management. The purpose of this section is to place procurement into a proper framework as one of the several materials management functions. The fourth section provides a statistical overview of government procurement. The numbers give insight into the magnitude of federal procurement and rank the major agencies in terms of volume of procurement activity. In the final section of the chapter certain planning concepts, strategies and new terminology are introduced.

Efforts to improve the management of federal procurement began with the Second Continental Congress in 1775. They have taken several forms, among them commissions, boards, reorganization statutes and interagency task reviews. The most recent major effort in that direction began when the Congress appointed the Commission on Government Procurement (COGP) in 1969. Although the COGP completed its work in 1972, its report initiated a reform process that has continued into 1984. Actions of the 98th Congress in 1984 may have brought the reform process to a conclusion, but that seems unlikely because government procurement continues to generate criticism.

Public confidence in the procurement process is low. Media reports of misfeasance and malfeasance tend to reinforce public doubts about it and it has become a politically lively subject. Doubts arise because the institutional environment of government does not appear to consistently encourage efficient and effective expenditure processes. Political attention to apparent deficiencies, coupled with efficient media, generate negative public images. This book describes the federal system of procurement, examines its strengths and weaknesses, and attempts to clarify how the system works.

Procurement Management Objectives and Contributions to Organizational Effectiveness

In organizational life, "general management" has become a familiar term, denoting the roles filled by those designated as chief executive officers, chairmen of boards of directors, secretaries of government agencies and similar titles. Also, members of commissions and boards of directors exercise many of the powers and perquisites attendant to general management. These individuals are charged with overall leadership for the purpose of giving the organization an effective and successful life. General management works through functional or staff subdivisions to achieve its objectives. This book will examine one of the functional subdivisions--procurement. In corporate life, it is one of several management functions analogous to finance, marketing, production, engineering, and so forth. In government, the functions include administration, financial management, personnel, and various directorates or offices related to the agency's mission. Staff offices might include general counsel, legislative liaison, industrial relations, and planning groups.

Procurement's role is becoming more evident as the increasing complexity of our economy forces organizations to seek external resources and capabilities beyond their own capacity. Decisions begin when objectives are established and make-or-buy questions arise, but the procurement function is recognized best through its role in securing external capabilities that meet organizational needs. We can approach its definition by recognizing that procurement performs an interface function: it must interact with a part of the organization's environment, suppliers and contractors, and it must interact with an organization's internal functions and activities. To achieve its overall objective, procurement's principal managerial role is that of negotiation, through which it establishes agreements making external sources a part of the organizational system, using the contract or purchase order as its principal tool. Procurement management must develop a contractual system upon which organizational operations can rely. This contractual system is vital to achievement of organizational objectives.

An effective procurement manager will deal regularly with many internal managers. The vitality of procurement depends on internal relationships that generate information and support for the performance of external sourcing, negotiation, and contract administration responsibilities. Traditionally, procurement has encountered difficulty gaining stature among its internal organizational contemporaries. It has had a problem establishing its identity within the organization even though its responsibilities and contributions are vital.

The procurement manager's role in the strategy of organizations is to help convert objectives and broad concepts into workable plans of action. Its processes cause the translation of mission statements and technical goals into concrete schedules and costs. It does this primarily through the interactions associated with the solicitation and award process.

Much of the work carried out under the guidance of

procurement can be characterized as either complex and detailed, or routine and repetitive. Either way, the work requirements in procurement offices entail high volumes of information flow to which precision and accuracy are vital. Journeyman buyers and negotiators work under time pressures dictated by production or project schedules that generally tend to be optimistic. One must look beyond this daily work effort, however, to discover the principal contributions and the broad mission of procurement as a managerial discipline.

Procurement is universally practiced in organizational life in public and private sectors, yet continues to search for its central mission, its identity, in the business system. To address this issue, procurement managers must lay aside their immediate tasks and come to grips with strategic questions. These strategic matters require integrative thinking that encompasses market trends, economic forces, public policy developments, source availabilities, source development, competition and productivity issues, technological change, ethical concerns, economy and efficiency of the process, and the general problem of information flow across organizational boundaries. One theme of this book is that procurement's mission in the strategy of organizations is productivity gain. Procurement plays a vital role in achieving economic efficiency, by generating productivity benefits for the organization and the economy as a whole. Its contributions in this matter are twofold. First is its ability to advance competitive practices through encouraging tradeoffs between in-house and out-of-house acquisition of needs through make-or-buy analyses. Second is its ability to mobilize external resources. These contributions powerfully stimulate economically agressive behavior. In light of these factors, procurement is defined as a business function charged with source research, plus the formation and administration of agreements with external sources for the purpose of obtaining material or services to support the work of the organization.

Comparison of Private Sector and Public Procurement

Chart 1-1 compares several aspects of federal and

Chart 1-1

COMPARISON OF PRIVATE
AND FEDERAL PROCUREMENT

Topic	Private Industry	Public (Federal)
Status of the parties	Equality of supplier and buyer as legal entities. Size and financial strength differentiate	Sovereignty of buyer affecting: rule-making, ability to change its mind
Account-ability	General standards, compliance with law and precident, ethical conventions	Public oversight of funds, compliance with political stan-dards, legal proce-dures, public infor-mation policies
Process complexity	Relatively simple and practical, individual corporate procedures for contract award and documentation of contracts, claims	Detailed procedural guidance dictated by public oversight, concern for "equity" in public decisions, social policy issues
Operational objectives	Production support, nonproduct pur-chases, commercial resale	Consumption or use by agency, public use and benefit
End objectives	Profit and loss standard, enhance competitive posture	Primacy of objec-tives unclear, multi-plicity of objec-tives evident, sub-jective measurement of success, economic efficiency one of many objectives

N/A
N/A
Rare
Limited

Reps & Certs
Flow Down Clauses
Audit
Contract Admin/oversight

private procurement. With respect to the fundamental
solicitation and award processes, they are generally
similar, but differ in several areas as shown on the
chart. The processes are discussed more fully in
subsequent chapters.

Differences between private and federal procurement
are largely qualitative and appear to fall into the five
categories set forth in Chart 1-1. The first category
concerns the status of the parties involved. The chart
reflects one of the fundamental objectives of public policy in the United States--to maintain equality of status
of private parties in terms of legal standing. Nevertheless, size, economic strength, technical knowledge, and
other factors often differentiate buyers and sellers.
These differences could give advantages to either party.
The federal government, as buyer, has the advantages of
size and economic strength. Superior technical knowledge
could be held by either party. However, the government,
as sovereign, is the rulemaker in virtually all circumstances. Its capacity to write contract clauses, procurement regulations, and management procedures is nearly
unassailable. It acts through statute, executive order,
agency regulation, and management instructions. Additionally, the government can change its corporate mind at any
time before, during or after contract award. Its changing perceptions and policies affect procedures, clauses,
technical content, costs, and desired procurement results. While negotiations provide for adjustment for
change, the change itself is unilateral at buyer discretion. The preeminence of the sovereign is broadly accepted. It is believed to be in the public interest, but it
should not be ignored by participants in the procurement
process.

The matter of accountability also distinguishes
federal and private procurement as shown in Chart 1-1.
Buyers and sellers in the private economy are expected to
comply with general legal and ethical restraints that
prohibit actions in restraint of trade and promote competitive behavior. When they participate in federal procurement, the system additionally imposes specific prohibitions respecting gratuities, entertainment and conflicts
of interest. Furthermore, oversight of the expenditure
of public funds is intensive and subject to challenge by
members of the Congress and to audit by the General

Accounting Office, the Offices of Inspectors General, and
to the examination of the public press. The standards of
right and wrong are subject to critical interpretation
with attendant publicity.

Complexity is present in all purchasing processes
because of the necessity for reflecting the interests and
concerns of each party in a contract. The relatively
simple and well known purchasing procedures of private
industry have been modified in detail in regulations
published for the guidance and direction of contracting
personnel of the government. Since procurement processes
involve innumerable variations depending on the nature of
the acquisition, of the industry, and of the particular
relationship to be established, the volume of specific
policy and procedure creates complexity. The need for
complexity is increased by use of cost and incentive
contracts and by the incorporation of special provisions
intended to advance, or substitute for, competitive procurement. It is also increased by incorporation of
social and economic objectives into the relationship.

The operational objectives of private and federal
procurement tend to differ. Most industrial purchasing
secures material for production, though it includes non-
product purchases, usually items with stable technologies. Federal procurement is more varied and generally
supports end use or consumption by the government as it
pursues diverse public purposes. Furthermore, federal
procurement includes a much higher proportion of research, research and development, and "major systems"
acquisitions.

In a sense, the greatest distinction between private
sector and federal procurement concerns end objectives.
The presence of the profit and loss standard against
which private management can measure success is absent in
public enterprise. Purchase decisions by industry respond directly to production cost and producibility factors with the purpose of competitive industrial effort,
but the motivating forces of profit and loss are not encountered by the public manager. The industrial buyer
can invariably assess achievements in terms of profitability or productivity by observing cost, price, and sales
relative to competitors. By contrast, federal procurement is afflicted with multiple objectives and lacks

objective standards of success such as profitability.
Objectives may include technical, schedule, or cost level
achievement, but they also include a multiplicity of
social/economic objectives or labor policies which de-
grade the usefulness of clear signals from objectively
measured costs or end results.

Integrated Materials Systems

In government there is a tendency to compartmen-
talize responsibilities in a way that isolates management
functions from each other. Examples include procurement,
audit, contract administration, pricing, program management, inventory management, property management, and so
forth. The subdivisions are endless and are in part
accounted for by the size, geographical distribution and
diversity of government operations. Part of the compart-
mentalization flows from the effort to create checks and
balances throughout the system; some may result from
empire building, some from tradition. The consequence is
that it appears to burden the system. Efficient systems
develop in organizations where management teams communicate fully and openly such that they fully integrate
their activities. The discussion which follows attempts
to address that need.

Materials Management and Procurement

Historically, materials management and procurement
have been producers of a giant volume of paperwork.
Effective performance of the functions has demanded
detailed and precise record generation and repetitive
entry of data in order to establish an adequate history
of actions. These clerical functions served for many
years to mask the substantial contributions to effective
management available through creative planning and careful analysis of inventory, purchase, traffic, production
control, distribution and related accounting operations.
In recent years this pattern has changed. The
buying and materials activities of governmental and
industrial organizations have assumed responsibility for

improved efficiency and more effective operations on a
system-wide scale. The advancement in computer technology and its application to the flow of material has made
feasible an increasingly influential role for a logistics
or materials manager because support of operations has
become only a part of his work. The increased availability of information allows materials and procurement personnel to plan and accurately project the consequences of
current decisions.

Materials management is a concept that integrates
the flow and control of materials and services beginning
with identification of the need and ending after delivery
to the ultimate user. In reality, the materials system
never completes its work since it is integrated with production and distribution functions. It cannot operate
without accounting functions; it is forever involved in
correction of variances, repetitive ordering, continuous
data generation and collection of information that drives
the flow of material. Currently, industry recognizes
materials management as vital to effective management.
In government much improvement in the integration of functional activities is achievable. The work of the materials (logistics) function may be summarized in the following manner:

1. Needs coordination and determination including
   analysis of project demands, design documentation,
   inventory status, pipeline status, and schedules
2. Requisition generation and status control
3. Solicitation preparation and status control
4. Proposal analysis and negotiation
5. Purchase order or contract issuance
6. Determination of order acceptance, production and
   delivery status including control of incoming
   traffic
7. Receiving, preparation of receiving report
8. Inspection and acceptance of delivered items
9. Warehousing and distribution operations
10. Document assembly, verification and payment
11. Generation of vendor, purchase and item history
    file
12. Shipping, export, insurance and related documenta-
    tion as required to maintain specified

levels of customer service
13. Documentation, training, and mobility arrangements that assure timely, reliable maintenance and operational readiness
14. Disposal action including review of inventory for excess or obsolescent items and redistribution or sale as required.

Materials Management Objectives

The objectives that govern the materials function are twofold. First, the materials manager must meet the schedule and qualitative demands of users. Secondly, he must secure material at the lowest feasible cost, considering long term maintenance of sources of supply and proper vender relations. The standard to be met is measurable in private sector operations in terms of profitability or competitiveness. In public sector operations the standards are more complex and may require subjective evaluations such as levels of service, equity, and public interest factors.

Design of the materials system requires greater specificity of objectives than the foregoing statement permits. As a consequence the following elements are suggested as operational standards for the system design.

1. <u>Price minimization</u>. Obtaining the lowest possible price for purchased materials is a valid procurement objective. It is limited by quality and production efficiency requirements, such that a measurement criterion of minimum net operating costs is a more viable objective for the materials manager. If met, this will advance productivity and competitiveness. Each of the following items will at times offset the price minimization objective.

2. <u>Continuity of long term supply</u>. When there are disruptions of supply, excess costs are inevitable. Production is jeopardized by supply interruptions as fully as by major strike actions. Highly programmed or automated processes are most sensitive to interruptions because rigid advance

commitments, critical supply schedules, and large investments are necessary for such operations. Some limitation of the frequency of competing purchases may result from analysis of this area of concern.

3. <u>Low inventory carrying cost</u>. When inventories are low in relation to sales, less capital is required. This enhances the efficiency of capital, improving return on investment. It also lowers storage and carrying costs such as warehousing, obsolescence, material handling, insurance and other costs associated with inventory. This concern affects purchase timing and quantity decisions.

4. <u>Low acquisition cost</u>. If materials are procured in larger quantities the efficiency of the acquisition process is improved, including purchase, expediting, receiving, inspection and other costs related to order size and frequency. This objective must be traded off against carrying costs. Acquisition and carrying costs are minimized not only by their formal trade-off relationship but also through efficient departmental operations.

5. <u>Low operation costs</u>. The objective of low operating costs is common to every organization. While emphasis on this objective may vary with economic conditions and corporate performance, the pressure for economy never ceases. The entire materials organization tends to be labor intensive and as a consequence, attempts to minimize payroll expenses. Nevertheless, achievement of system standards bars drastic cutting of these costs. A principal factor allowing reduction of traditional materials operating costs is effective use of the computer. Its speed in providing information, its accuracy, and its massive data storage capabilities are vital contributions to materials management.

6. <u>Control over quality</u>. End product quality standards depend upon the consistency and compatibilty of quality standards maintained by the materials organization. Just as the production manager is responsible for quality in production, the materi-

als department must maintain quality standards for procurement, simultaneously minimizing cost of acquisition.

7. Good supplier relations. Businesses rely on outside suppliers for more than material. They depend upon information, service and reliability. Furthermore, relations with suppliers may impact an organization's standing in the business community. One of the major problems of materials management is unexpected change in the demand for materials, requiring either rapid cancellation of existing commitments or extra output to prevent shortages. Cooperative suppliers frequently resolve problems of this kind.

8. Development of personnel. While all departments have an interest in developing the skills of their personnel, the materials area has a very special interest in its personnel. As with production-related activities in general, the materials area has traditionally lacked the glamor of other fields, and it cannot leave to chance the enhancement of the skills of personnel committed to its effective performance. Its leaders must agressively pursue improvement of recruitment standards and support for personnel training and upgrading.

9. Superior data and record retrieval system. Documentation, or in many cases electronic record keeping, is the lifeblood of a logistics system. Creating an effective system should be a principal objective of the materials manager. While records are not an end objective, they are vital to the flow of material and to effective relationships with suppliers. The record system should, however, be tailored to the types of material, services and sources of supply necessary to the particular materials activity. The major emphasis should be support of decisions such as necessity for changes from preplanned schedules, analyses of costs, verification of supplier capability, and consideration of design or delivery problems.

10. Standardization and simplification. The number of variations of design that enter into the materials system needs to be controlled. The

materials organization should support standardization work and facilitate negotiation of agreements
on standards governing materials entering the supply system. Effectively administered, the adopted
standard may increase reliability and aid in reduction of inventory items. The standardization and
simplification process achieves this result by
promoting:

a. specification identification and review
b. application of existing standards
c. classification and coding material for inventory and retrieval
d. cataloging
e. verification of qualification, testing and
acceptance standards
f. application of an authorization and allowance
system
g. verification of schedules
h. establishment of quantitative requirements for
each item considering all applications, users,
lead times and inventory status.

Inventory Policy Management and Control

Inventory policy management and control has close
ties with production, operational and financial concerns
and must be developed in close coordination with those
activities. It is central to the achievement of materials objectives. Inventories to meet seasonal and other
variations in demand, for transit requirements, for production continuity, work in process, and customer service
may be required. All types of inventories require data
to support decisions such as:

1. establishing or changing inventory levels, overall, and on an individual item basis
2. daily management of inventory
3. determining ordering strategy
4. initiating orders for specific quantities at the
time required to support demand
5. verification of inventory

6. screening inventory for disposal purposes
7. issuance and accounting for stock.

In many ways, the processes associated with procurement action are the most complex of the material functions. This assertion derives from the fact that buying requires satisfying both external and internal points of contact. Furthermore, the purchase constitutes a visible event that is critical to total program schedule. Additionally, the buying process varies in complexity, so that time required to place orders is difficult to predict, and sometimes difficult to manage. For standard items and repetitive purchases, firm schedules are established, but for unique items the solicitation and award process limits precise control. Variables include:

1. verification of requisitions as adequate and complete for procurement
2. identification of sources
3. qualification of sources
4. compliance with proper purchase order procedures and procurement policy
5. securing information from potential suppliers as required for specific actions
6. establishment of working relationships with potential suppliers, including, where indicated by needs, long-term contractual ordering arrangements
7. evaluation of bids and proposals for conformity with requirements and schedules
8. analysis of bids and proposals respecting price, elements of cost when pertinent, and value of item in relation to its application or alternatives
9. internal coordination of proposed sourcing decisions
10. adjustment of schedules in event of protest
11. completion of negotiations
12. award of contract.

Subsequent to award of contracts, expediting and/or contract administration begins. Ideally, these activities are routine and uneventful--the objective being very simple: delivery of the ordered items on time. The procurement organization cannot take that kind of perform

ance for granted, however. Actions to be supported
include:

1. clarifications of intended contractual requirements and quality assurance concerns
2. follow-up notifications and inquiries to ensure
   expeditious performance--expediting delivery
3. negotiating changes or modification to contracts
   as required
4. performing inspection during performance, if
   needed
5. administration to overcome deficiencies, delays,
   claims, and related problems arising during performance
6. verification of documents associated with payments, and authorization of payment.

The materials system fulfills its mandate with its
physical distribution activities. These activities are
vital to customer service regardless of the nature of the
customer, that is, internal organizations, external enterprises, governmental or private. The elements of the
system include:

1. establishing inventory points and warehousing
2. determining or negotiating shipping schedules and
   capacities and modes
3. adequacy of transportation documentation and
   follow-up
4. readiness of material handling facilities, equipment and labor
5. reliability of material flow through receiving,
   inspection, storage, issuance, and shipping
6. ensuring proper packing, packaging and preserving
7. providing a responsive ordering system
8. performing stock review for inventory management
   and disposal operations.

Statistical Summary of Federal Procurement

A wealth of new information has become available
concerning federal procurement, beginning with fiscal

year 1979. The Federal Procurement Data System, estab-
lished by Congress as a responsibility of the Office of
Federal Procurement Policy, collects, develops and dissem-
inates procurement data on a government-wide basis.
Quarterly and annual data are reported and special analyses are prepared by the Federal Procurement Data Center
(FPDC). Tables 1-1 and 1-2 were prepared by the author
from data generated by FPDC and data contained in the
Federal Budget of the United States Government, Fiscal
Year 1985. The charts are based on the latest complete
fiscal year, 1983.

Table 1-1 shows, for each major procuring agency,
the proportion of the total United States contract expenditures in FY 1983 expended by the agency's contract program. Headed by Defense with four-fifths of the expenditures, the table clearly shows which agencies account for
contracting volume.

Table 1-2 ranks the procuring agencies two ways, by
the number of contract actions and by the proportion of
the agency's budget spent by contract. The table gives
an indication of the agency's commitment to the contracting method. NASA expends a greater part of its regular
appropriations by contract than any other agency, 91.1
percent. The high proportions of GSA and DOE reflect
sales and other special factors. The Federal Emergency
Management Agency and Department of Defense both expend
more than 50 percent of their dollars by contract. The
table reveals in the aggregate that 19.4 percent of 1983
federal budget authority was expended by contract action.

Tables 1-1 and 1-2 (drawn from the latest full year
report of the Federal Procurement Data Center) give an
excellent view of the scope of the activity involved.
Some 21.2 million procurement actions valued at $168
billion were executed by the government in 1983. Of this
total (not shown on the tables) 20.7 million actions were
classified as small purchase orders. These orders
include those valued at less than $25,000 in the DOD and
less than $10,000 in the civilian agencies. In the
future all actions less than $25,000 are to be classified
as small purchases. The small purchases accounted for
$15.8 billion or 9.5 percent of the total. The balance
of the actions, 415,162 contract awards, totaled $152.3
billion, 91.5 percent. The statistic of interest is:

Table 1-1

U. S. GOVERNMENT PROCURING AGENCIES, FISCAL YEAR 1983
RANKED BY PROPORTION OF U.S. CONTRACT DOLLARS
AWARDED BY THE AGENCY (MILLIONS OF DOLLARS)

Department or Agency	Budget Authority[1]	Dollars Awarded By Contract[2]	Proportion of Total U.S. Contract Obligations
DOD	$242,910	$135,462	80.5
DOE	9,260	12,226	7.3
NASA	6,872	6,262	3.7
VA	25,234	2,634	1.6
Agriculture	56,409	1,785	1.1
Interior	4,955	1,673	1.0
GSA	697	1,652	1.0
HHS	280,152	1,243	0.7
DOT	26,264	1,100	0.7
FEMA	770	621	0.4
Treasury	117,074	447	0.3
Labor	36,413	406	0.2
EPA	3,688	404	0.2
Justice	3,046	374	0.2
TVA	762	370	0.2
Commerce	1,923	177	0.1
Subtotal:	$816,524	$166,838	99.1
Others:	50,221	1,536	0.9
Total	$866,745	$168,197	100.0

[1]Federal Budget of United States Government, Fiscal Year 1985, Congress, 2nd Session, House Document No. 98-138, February 1, 1984, Part 8, The Federal Program By Agency and By Account, pp. 8-1 to 8-197. (FY 1983 data)

[2]Federal Contract Actions, Federal Procurement Data System Standard Report, Fiscal Year 1983, Federal Procurement Data Center, Washington, D.C., p. 2.

Table 1-2
MAJOR U.S. GOVERNMENT PROCURING AGENCIES
RANK ORDER BY CONTRACT ACTIVITY
FISCAL YEAR 1983

Rank by Number of Contract Actions	Total Number of Contract Actions (thousands)[1]	Proportion of Contract $ to Agency Budget Authority	Percent[2]
DOD	14,763	GSA[3]	237.2
VA	1,934	DOE[3]	132.0
GSA	755	NASA	91.1
AGRICULTURE	739	FEMA	80.6
HHS	705	DOD	55.8
DOI	614	TVA	48.6
DOJ	472	DOI	33.8
TVA	341	DOJ	12.3
DOT	281	EPA	11.0
NASA	133	VA	10.4
TREASURY	121	DOC	9.2
DOE	58	DOT	4.2
DOC	41	TREASURY	3.8
EPA	40	AGRICULTURE	3.2
DOL	38	DOL	1.1
FEMA	4	HHS	.4
U. S. GOVT.	21,189	U. S. GOVT.	19.4

[1]Federal Contract Actions, Federal Procurement Data System Standard Report, Fiscal Year 1983, Federal Procurement Data Center, Washington, D.C., p. 2.

[2]Table 1-1 provides dollar values for this computation. Source: Federal Budget of United States Government, Fiscal Year 1985, Congress, 2nd Session, House Document No. 98-138, February 1, 1984, Part 8, Federal Program By Agency and By Account, pp. 8-1 to 8-197. (FY 1983 data)

[3]Contract dollars exceed agency budget. Intergovernmental transfers and other sales constitute sources of agency income over and above appropriated funds.

2.0 percent of government contract actions accounted for 90.5 percent of dollars awarded. The entire spectrum of materials and services obtainable from the worldwide economy is represented by this activity.

Planning Concepts and Strategy For Procurement Action

We shall reserve for Chapter 11 discussion of models of the acquisition and procurement processes. The term "acquisition" was adopted by the Department of Defense (DOD) during the 1970s as a descriptor of the total planning and management process necessary to fill mission needs of DOD. Since that time, the term acquisition has replaced procurement in many government documents, for example, in the title given to the regulation system. This has tended to confuse a previously widely accepted terminology, but it is debatable whether it has changed the processes.

Acquisition management is now well established in government as encompassing a set of management responsibilities broader than procurement. Chapter 11 discusses these ideas more fully and presents models of procurement and acquisition processes showing that both are initiated with "needs determination" and conclude with deployment, use, and disposal actions. However, the acquisition process encompasses several phases of activity. Each of these phases requires contract action, and the phases become a continuum, one leading to the next, with key decision points linking the activities from phase to phase. The procurement process uses many similar concepts but generally refers to the planning, execution, and administration of individual contract actions. This distinction fails to eliminate confusion and overlap, because many large dollar contracts continue throughout the acquisition process, some remaining active for longer than five years.

In Chapter 11 the concept of strategy will be discussed in relation to patterns employed in carrying out procurement actions. Procurement strategy forms a part of this and will be used to designate management actions that ensure source selection is effective in maximizing the likelihood of achieving acquisition objectives. In

government,   there   is   a   strong   tendency   to   invent
terminologies   that   relate   to   similar   activities   but
actually   address   very   different   perspectives   of   those
activities.   In the area of acquisition and procurement,
this tendency is pronounced and has resulted in a body of
terminology   related   to   five   distinct   cycles   which   are
commonly   referred   to   in   the   acquisition   and   procurement
communities.   They are the systems life cycle, the acquisition   cycle,   the   research   and   development   cycle,   the
procurement   cycle,   and   the   fiscal   cycle.   At   this   point
these concepts are merely identified.   In Chapter 11, we
shall attempt to interrelate them.

2 | Procurement Objectives and the Federal Environment

Chapter 2 discusses the role of procurement in the management of organizations, including government. It treats the peculiar setting and environment of procurement in the federal system, and the wide range and diversity of federal activities in the procurement area. The chapter also considers the varied objectives of government procurement activities and the complexity introduced into the system because of those objectives. In this context, the chapter takes up the design concepts set forth for the "New Federal Procurement System" (NFPS) which the Office of Federal Procurement Policy developed during 1981, proposed to the Congress in February, 1982, and which is now established--with modification--by implementation of the Federal Acquisition Regulation (FAR) and enactment of the Competition in Contracting Act of 1984 (CICA). The environment of federal procurement is further defined by addressing the source of authority, and its delegation, for contract action by agencies of the government. The specific delegation of authority to contracting officers and the limitations imposed upon their actions are discussed. This treatment extends into the special circumstances and conditions created by the Freedom of Information Act as it influences procurement information. The peculiar environmental circumstances of public procurement are further examined by discussion of individual and organizational conflicts of interest and the related ethical problems in public procurement. The chapter concludes with identification of the array of services and materials which are the subject of public acquisition programs.

Procurement: A Tool
and a Field of Management

The strategies, techniques and activities which make up the work of a buying community are appropriately studied under the aegis of procurement management, and in this book attention is focused on the federal system. While numerous texts have been written on the subject of purchasing, most of them are cast in the organizational setting of the industrial firm. A few of them have addressed public purchasing. The general thrust of most of these works has been to place purchasing activities within the context of materials management. In addition, most of them have emphasized the major contribution which effective purchasing can make to the containment of costs and improvement of the competitive position of the industrial firm.

It is a proposition of this work that while procurement is a tool of management, and often is oriented toward the containment of costs, its contributions to effective organizational performance have yet to be fully appreciated, and its principal purpose goes beyond enhancement of the profit and competitive positions of the firm. Rather, it is a more general function of management essential in all organizational life and critically important to achievement of organizational objectives.

In some organizational settings--particularly in government--procurement, coupled with supply support operations, is implicitly (if not explicitly) the objective of the organization. This is largely true of organizations such as the General Services Administration and the Defense Logistics Agency. The Commission on Government Procurement stated clearly the overall role of the procurement process in relation to federal objectives and missions in the following quote:

The procurement process is a support function--not an end in itself. However, its importance within the federal establishment cannot be minimized because the organizations and personnel engaged in performing the procurement process represent the means by which federal objectives and missions are accomplished. To the extent that these organizations and personnel operate at less than optimum level, the effectiveness of the process and the realization of national objectives suffer.[1]

While procurement would seldom be the stated objective of federal agencies, in many of them, procurement is the principal avenue by which their mission is accomplished and their resources are expended. For example, the National Aeronautics and Space Administration, whose mission has been largely research in aeronautical and space sciences, expends in excess of 91 percent of its appropriated funds through the procurement of services, materials and equipment from the private sector. Similarly, such entities as the Naval Air Systems Command are essentially in the business of procuring weapons systems for the military services. Relatively little actual research, development and production sponsored by agencies like these is conducted internally as a function of the agency. Much of the work is conducted by industrial or research organizations that supply the buying activity with its end product through long term contractual relationships. Thus we find that the vast technological and managerial capabilites assembled by such federal agencies are organized and directed through procurement management processes which we may refer to as the federal procurement system.

These activities must be managed effectively. However, let us place this topic in perspective. It is not adequate to speak of the federal buying system only in the context of the major acquisition agencies. Contracting is a minor part of the work of many agencies, and even those mentioned above do not perceive of themselves as procuring agencies, but rather as agencies responsible for achievement of some major national mission placed in their care by the Congress. This perception is reinforced because purchasing is a business function with wide geographical distribution, filling diverse demands, and

because many purchasing operations are essentially routine and require highly repetitive, preferably automated,
buying procedures.

The Proposed Uniform Federal Procurement System

In February, 1982, the Office of Federal Procurement
Policy (OFPP), in response to Public Law 96-83, completed
a report to the Congress which was titled "Proposal for a
Uniform Federal Procurement System." In the proposal particular features of the desired federal procurement system were listed and discussed. The features were aimed
at creating a system that would "effectively satisfy agency mission needs" and were to be formulated, in part, by
establishing an amended statutory foundation for procurement and by creating a "simple, understandable regulation." In summary form the stated system features were:

1. A streamlined management structure with clear lines
   of authority, responsibility and accountability.
2. Decentralized agency procurement operations that are
   responsive, efficient, and freed of cumbersome rules
   and regulations.
3. A professional work force with latitude for initiative and business judgment.
4. Understandable and measurable standards for management and operational performance.
5. A control system that identifies problems early.
6. Organized feedback of information on system performance.
7. A means to adjust the individual components of the
   system.

Subsequent to delivery of that proposal, on March
17, 1982, the President issued Executive Order 12352
entitled "Federal Procurement Reforms." The executive
order, the first such order to deal with procurement, was
aimed directly at "ensuring effective and efficient spending of public funds..." The order directed the heads of
executive agencies to take specific steps to improve management of procurement. It required completion and implementation of the new Federal Acquisition Regulation,

development of personnel policies that would generate a professional procurement work force, and confirmed the leadership role of the Office of Federal Procurement Policy in development of procurement policy and overall reform activities. The executive order is reproduced as Appendix 3 of this book.

No procurement could be more complete in the nature of the things it buys and in the types of buying processes it uses than federal procurement. Federal management processes are varied and range in complexity from the simplest tasks to those which are critical to major program decisions of the acquisition agency. In this treatment of the subject, we will attempt to address the system as a system and yet give recognition to each variation found within it and to show its unifying concepts, so that at the end of our study, we will have developed an integrated view of the entire acquisition process.

In addition to examining the management of procurement, this work provides to persons who are involved in marketing to the government a more complete understanding of their customer. Because of its size and the peculiarities associated with its methods of conducting business, the federal government may be an extremely difficult to understand and obtuse monolithic organization. It is difficult for many people to fully appreciate the mechanisms by which contracting with the government can be successfully sought. While there are great similarities in practices and procedures across the agencies, each exercises its own procuring authority and may adopt practices that are difficult for an outsider to correlate with the practices of sister agencies.

An illustrative problem is that of obtaining information from a federal agency by newcomers to the federal market. The critical factors are time, understanding of the system of procurement, and knowledge of needs. Government policy explicitly attempts to provide knowledge of public acquisition programs to all interested parties and to conduct its procurement processes on an objective and equally available basis. Unfortunately the processes vary, the needs are complex, and information flows imperfectly. This book examines the peculiar conditions associated with governmental processes and that are critical for successful marketing to the government.

Buying by the government is so large and varied in its scope that few persons, whether government employee, industrial marketer, policymaker, or interested member of the public, are fully cognizant of the range and dimension of the system being employed. The federal government is the largest single buyer of commercial products or modified commercial products. Its activity in the commercial product market, however, is not the principal procurement area. The larger acquisition programs include undertakings such as weapons development and production, atomic energy development and production, medical research, a great variety of physical and social science undertakings, space exploration, environmental improvement projects, and the procurement of services ranging from highly technical to routine.

The government spends its resources in two general modes. First, it undertakes many activities in-house, making those portions of its programs independent of the procurement system. Secondly, it buys commercial and industrial services, research, material from private firms, and varied services and research from nonprofit or educational institutions. Furthermore, its programs involving performance of work by nonfederal organizations include, in addition to acquisition by contract, assistance relationships in which a grant or cooperative agreement is established.[2] This text is principally concerned with the procurement-by-contract undertakings of the federal government rather than its assistance undertakings, but since the magnitude of either of these kinds of undertakings greatly exceeds one hundred billion dollars per year, recognition is given to the importance of each type of activity.

Federal procurement activities have never achieved a high level of esteem in the minds of the public. Its purchasing behavior has gained the perception that exorbitant sums of money are paid for relatively inefficient acquisition programs. Whenever examples of errors in this field are discovered, they are widely publicized, and they occur with sufficient regularity to present an image of inefficiency. This image particularly concerns practitioners and serious students of the process.

On one end of the spectrum, the public image of procurement is built by such undertakings as those sponsored

by Senator William Proxmire's "Golden Fleece Award." Generally the "Golden Fleece" is awarded each month to publicize the existence of some research undertaking by the
government that appears to be either inconsequential or
useless or downright undesirable, and it creates the general impression that the government wastes money through
its expenditures by contract with private enterprises. A
second area where the public impression of procurement is
regularly sullied is in its procurement of off-the-shelf
commercial products. Such products are easily recogniza-
ble to the public, and it is normally not difficult to
discover instances where the government has paid exorbitant amounts of money for items clearly available at
lower cost.

These two areas, research in unfamiliar topics and
procurement of standard items at exorbitant prices, are
destructive to a good image so far as federal procurement
management is concerned. However, it is the purpose of
this text to examine the broader range of government procurement activities. Most government expenditures are
not for esoteric research or commercial products but
rather for construction, production, development and systems acquisition programs ranging in complexity from
space exploration and construction of naval vessels to
manufacture of uniforms. Furthermore, the government
employs a substantial proportion of its total procurement
budget in the acquisition of special services, ranging
from facility maintenance to complex instructional,
design, equipment overhaul, and testing activities.

During the three years since the first edition of
this book was published, regular coverage in the media of
apparent waste, errors, or fraudulent behavior by government or contractor personnel occurred. The area of special focus during that period has been military procurement of spare parts. Highlights in the press have been
$450 hammers, $1300 plastic caps, and $7000 coffee pots.
These reports have stimulated a great deal of concern and
are unquestionably important factors in passage of the
Competition in Contracting Act of 1984 (discussed in some
detail in Chapter 6). The incidence of deficient procurement actions in relation to the total procurement program
summarized in Tables 1-1 and 1-2 probably does not warrant the attention given. The statistical improbability

of significant deficiencies is treated further in this chapter under Objectives for Acquisition and Assistance Programs.

One consequence of the range and diversity of federal activities is the complexity of its schemes for managing and controlling its procurement operations. The Congress has delegated the authority to procure to executive agencies, and each department or agency is semiautonomous in planning, organizing and controlling procuring as well as other activities. As a consequence, the organization and management of procurement gives rise to the need for innovative leadership and expertise. It also requires legislative oversight to attempt to ensure that a reasonable level of efficiency and effectiveness in performance is achieved, and to ensure that necessary coordination of supporting services, procuring activities and policymaking will enhance the overall system of acquisition.

Federal procurement management has yet to achieve full recognition by the public and other contemporary disciplines for its contributions to public objectives. However, with the emergence of strategic thinking among its practitioners and the growth of its significance in terms of dollar expenditures, its stature as a management discipline is strengthened.

Objectives for Acquisition and Assistance Programs

Industrial, governmental and commercial organizations all use procurement as a tool by which management obtains the materials, equipment, facilities or services necessary to performance of organizational missions. Thus the specific object of a procurement action may ordinarily be expressed as construction, research, or acquisition of an end item or service. Procurement is not commonly thought of as having its own set of end objectives. Instead, within the management planning of many organizations, it is viewed as a supporting function with a principal role in activities such as cost reduction or product improvement. It is recognized as the principal means of obtaining capabilities not held by the organization internally in a manner that promotes economy and efficiency. Additionally, and principally in federal procurement, policy objectives unrelated to the procurement action are imposed upon the contractual relationship. These objectives have gained such importance that procurement action in the federal government cannot be managed without consideration of its role as an instrument of social and economic policy. In short, federal contracts are multifaceted instruments. The objectives to be served are frequently conflicting and peripheral to the acquisition of services or material.

Besides its role in social and economic policy, the facet of the federal purchasing system that distinguishes it more than any other from that of the private organization is the mechanisms it has adopted to enhance and encourage, if at all possible, open and free competition through its formal solicitation and award processes. Significantly increased legislative pressures to required use of competitive procedures are established in the Competition in Contracting Act of 1984. Additionally, within the practice of federal procurement, adherence to procedures and practices required by regulation are a dominant theme which affect and channel managers' decisionmaking processes. These procedures and practices must be embraced by negotiators and contracting officers.

In addition to the contractual mechanism, the government extensively uses two types of assistance relationships, grants and cooperative agreements, which are designed to enable the transfer of funds to lower governmental levels or to nonprofit organizations (and under limited circumstances, to profit making ones) throughout the economy. The assistance relationship differs substantially from that established by a contract relationship. Contracts and grants are similar in that they both involve the disbursement of federal funds for specified public purposes. The two types of instruments are intended for different purposes.

Historically, the federal government never distinguished between a contract and a grant until February 3, 1978. At that time, the Congress enacted, and the President signed, the Federal Grant and Cooperative Agreement Act of 1977.[3] That enactment requires an executive agency that wishes to acquire property or services for its direct benefit or use to establish a procurement contract to define the relationship between the federal government and the other party. It also allows an agency to establish a relationship in which support or stimulation of activity is an authorized federal purpose but does not result in property or services for the direct benefit or use of the federal government. Under such a relationship, money or property may be transferred to the recipient by establishing either a public grant or a cooperative agreement. The public grant is pertinent only when there will be no substantial involvement by the federal agency in the performance of the undertaking. (In effect, the executive agency is involved primarily as a financing source.) By contrast, the cooperative agreement contemplates that there would be substantial involvement of the executive agency in performance of the undertaking. Like a grant, the cooperative agreement is aimed at achieving a public purpose other than direct benefit of the sponsoring agency. Both types of agreements create "assistance relationships."

The most recent contribution to defining objectives for federal procurement is the effort of OFPP pursuant to Public Law 96-83, "The Office of Federal Procurement Policy Act Amendments of 1979." Under that statute, an initial proposal for a "Uniform Procurement System" was provided to the Congress in October, 1980. The proposal was revised under direction of a new Administrator of Federal Procurement Policy (Mr. Donald Sowle), appointed by President Reagan in the Spring of 1981. Mr. Sowle undertook the revision of the report and completed it on February 26, 1982. His report has already been referred to in this chapter. It covers the following subjects.

1. Elements of a federal procurement system that included: a proposed management structure, ideas intended to simplify the government process, attention to increasing competition in federal procurement, and suggestions for professionalizing the work force.
2. An estimate of the costs and benefits to be expected through adoption of the proposed system. The estimate included qualitative assessments and some quantitative estimates of savings that would accrue from areas such as improved competition, simplification of

the process, and management improvements.

3. An approach to implementing the system, including a schedule of actions to be taken (significant parts of the schedule such as issuance of the procurement reform executive order were met, and some parts, including implementation of the Federal Acquisition Regulation were achieved ahead of schedule).

4. A proposed legislative action to amend the Armed Services Procurement Act, the Federal Property and Administrative Services Act, and the Office of Federal Procurement Policy Act. (The Competition in Contracting Act of 1984 amended those statutes, but in a manner significantly different from the OFPP proposal.)

Prior to beginning the proposal effort for the Federal Procurement System, Mr. Sowle issued a "System Scoping Paper" on May 14, 1981. Selected assumptions concerning the procurement system were set forth at that time and are included here because they constitute an excellent foundation on which better management of the public procurement process can be built.

1. Procurement is a function which supports an agency mission; it is not an end in itself.

2. As a support function, procurement does not encompass mission analysis or supply functions. However, the procurement system must be designed to clearly interface with those functions and influence the manner in which needs are expressed.

3. Procurement decisions will be made by properly authorized and designated procurement officials.

4. The system must be sufficiently flexible to serve federal needs for at least the next several decades.

5. Mechanisms and processes for developing and implementing individual substantive issues will be provided in the system, but solutions to such issues will not be offered.

6. Procurement operations in the executive branch will continue to be decentralized and conducted by the departments and agencies now performing them.

7. Consistency in procurement policy and regulation is essential for economy and effectiveness in federal procurement and reduced burdens on the private

sector.

8. Optimum performance of procurement responsibilities is contingent upon a well trained, experienced and motivated work force.

9. Fair and equitable dealings between the government and the private sector are essential to a productive relationship.

10. National goals of a nonprocurement nature will continue to be pursued, in part, through the federal procurement process.

In addition, Mr. Sowle's Scoping Paper set forth several objectives for the procurement system. They are summarized here because they are a concise and valid statement of system objectives. The system should:

1. Promote effective competition

2. Promote fair dealings and equitable relationships with the private sector

3. Provide clearly established authorities, responsibilities and accountabilities

4. Develop and maintain a professional, competent, ethical, and properly motivated procurement work force

5. Promote the responsiveness of procurement by simplifying, streamlining, and making procurement processes and programs more uniform

6. Accommodate emergency and wartime as well as normal and peacetime requirements

7. Promote procurement efficiency, effectiveness and economy within and outside the government

8. Promote greater reliance on the private sector and support the necessary industrial base to meet government needs

9. Eliminate fraud and waste

10. Provide adequate controls for centralized policymaking and decentralized and flexible operations

11. Provide for compatibility with other support (budget, logistics, etc.) processes and programs.[4]

While it was accurate to view the decade of the seventies as a period of reform for the procurement processes of the federal government, the early years of the eighties have seen concrete actions attempting to put reforms into effect. Nevertheless, federal procurement continues to encounter public criticism based on revelations of abuses. The system is susceptible to criticism because it is operated by a large and varied complement of personnel distributed throughout the nation and because it expends large sums of taxpayer dollars. Perhaps most importantly the number of procurement actions issued annually by the government has risen to twenty-one million. If one were to assume 99.999 percent of those actions to be free of fraud, waste, abuse, or error, the result would still leave .001 percent, or twenty-one thousand actions in which one of those problems may have occurred. Consequently, with 250 work days in a year, some 84 deficient or fraudulent actions per day could be occurring, even if the system were to be 99.999 percent perfect. Few human systems of any kind have even approached such a standard of excellence. Public acquisition is unlikely to meet such a standard, but normal oversight and audit activities have been so augmented that it appears to be the standard in effect. Specifically, an inspector general function has been added by statute at the top management level, in addition to existing audit activities. These offices focus on procurement. Additionally, establishment of hot lines has encouraged "whistle blowers" to highlight procurement blunders. As a result, for three years, public airing of procurement deficiencies has become a regular part of our media diet. Given the political appeal to legislators of revealing and acting to prevent such deficiencies, public awareness of procurement is likely to be enhanced further. Overall, the importance of the system warrants continuation of effort to strengthen and improve it. It is hoped that these efforts will not result in so great a level of checks and audits that procurement managers will be unable to make the judgment-based decisions required for effective action.

Federal Authority for Procurement Action

Procurement authority for the federal government has been derived under the Constitution as a power incident to the general powers of the Sovereign granted by the

Constitution.   This basic authority has been affirmed
through action of the Supreme Court in the case of U.S.
vs. Allegheny County, 322 U.S. 174 (1944).   While the
Constitution does not address the subject of procurement
directly, Article 1, Section 9, does provide that "no
money shall be drawn from the Treasury but in consequence
of appropriation made by law."   Under this provision, the
Congress makes appropriations and regulates their use.
It has done this through numerous statutes governing the
use of appropriations and in statutes specifically relating to procurement.   The Constitution also granted the
Office of the Chief Executive, the President, with power
to carry out government functions.   However, the authority to prescribe, to standardize and to control the procurement process has been exercised primarily by the Congress under its general authority to control the expenditure of appropriated funds.

Delegation of Authority

The secretary or administrator of most federal
departments and agencies is authorized to make purchases
and contracts for property and services and to perform
other actions related to procurement.   The agency head
normally delegates contracting authority to the directors
of offices which carry out procuring activities.   These
officers are authorized to enter into, modify, administer
and terminate contracts for property and services.   They
are also empowered to settle termination claims, to
appoint contracting officers, and to issue procurement
directives which are in conformity with the policy of the
department.   These powers of delegation and redelegation
are specified in legislation pertinent to each agency.
Contracting officers are designated in two ways.
First, they are empowered as an authority incident to the
holding of a given office, as with the agency head.   By
appointment to office, the incumbent in such positions
has the authority to act as a contracting officer.   However, most contracting officers are appointed through
issuance of a certificate of appointment by the heads of
procuring activities.   The appointments are made in writing and specify the individual's name and any limitations

on the scope of the authority to be exercised by the particular contracting officer.   The certificate should be
readily available for inspection by individuals who may
question the authority granted.

The contracting officer operates as an agent of the
government but not as a general agent.   Rather, s/he is
an agent for particular purposes.   S/he is authorized to
execute two-party agreements wherein the government contracts to have work done and agrees to make a payment of
appropriated funds for that work.   This type of authority
is recognized as that of contracting officers under the
system of procurement as it has been defined by the
Congress.

The federal government is a government of delegated
powers under which the power delegated to a contracting
officer is limited and specific.   S/he is not authorized
to obligate the government in any manner in excess of, or
different from, the authority which has specifically been
granted.   This is also true of government officers in
general.   This limitation on exercise of authority is
extremely important in establishing an understanding of
the relationship between the government and its suppliers.   The contracting officer can operate only in a manner that is in accordance with expressed authority and
cannot bind the government to an agreement for which he
did not have properly delegated authority.

By comparison, private individuals or corporations
acting as principals are bound to the extent of the power
they have apparently given to their agent.   The United
States is bound only to the extent of the power it has
actually given to its agents, and the unauthorized acts
of such agents do not stop the government from asserting
their invalidity.

Limitations on Actions
of a Contracting Officer

While the scope of the contracting officer's authority is commonly limited by the document conferring it,
the authority delegated is also limited by regulations.
Regulatory restrictions on an agent's authority, when published in the Federal Register, are binding in transac-

tions even though the other party had no actual knowledge of the regulations. As a result, the Federal Acquisition Regulation and agency supplements constitute a set of limitations on the authority of a contracting officer to take action. The regulatory constraints expand the prescriptions of the basic procurement statutes, the appropriations statutes pertinent to a procurement, and the authorizations for programs and other enactments of the Congress. It is incumbent upon the contracting officer and upon the potential contractor to be aware of all limitations placed on the authority of the contracting officer by these various statutes and regulations.

With respect to limitations on the authority of the contracting officer to obligate funds, the appropriations statutes are extremely important. There are a number of these statutes, but of particular importance is 31 U.S. Code 665, which prohibits expenditures or contract obligations in excess of funds appropriated. This act is popularly known as the Anti-Deficiency Act. It contains several other provisions. It does not, however, prohibit a conditional contract where the government's liability is contingent upon future availability of appropriations. The contracting officer may be authorized, where necessary, to initiate a procurement which will be charged to funds of the new fiscal year, prior to their availability. But such contracts are entered into only when conditioned upon the availability of the funds. Legal liability for payment is delayed until funds are available. This type of action is limited to operating, maintenance, and continuing services. All required reviews, clearances, or approvals must have been obtained, and all applicable regulations and requirements of law must have been met.

Of the requirements, funding limits are perhaps most critical. Certification is required by the responsible fiscal officer that funds are availabile prior to their obligation. Furthermore, the contracting officer must have made any necessary determinations and findings, such as the authority to negotiate a contract or to employ certain types of contracts. Additionally, s/he is obligated to obtain competition among sources whenever feasible; to determine positively that s/he has selected a responsible contractor; to obtain from the contractor, in negotiated procurement, any required certification of current cost and pricing data; to perform price and cost analysis (in negotiated procurement); and to obtain any administrative approval required by the management of his agency.

It should also be recognized that each agency has various management instruction or directive systems and, within their context, substantial restraints are placed upon the decisionmaking authority of officers of the government, including contracting officers. For example, in negotiated procurement, the authority to select a source from several competitors will often be determined by agency officials at a level higher than the contracting officer, and under the CICA, competition advocates will review and approve all noncompetitive source decisions.

Thus, one can see that there are substantial limitations placed upon the contracting officer through statutory, regulatory, financial, and policy constraints which are built into the federal system for controlling the actions of its agencies and officers.

As the government's agent, the contracting officer's responsibility, prior to executing a contract document, is to satisfy himself that the document he is signing and the processes leading up to the preparation of that document reflect a business relationship that will achieve the procurement objectives, is in the public interest, and is in accordance with the statutes, regulations, and management instructions under which he operates.

Freedom of Information Act

Under Public Law 90-23, known as the Public Information Act, the Congress has established an open-door public information policy. The policy describes what records are to be made available to the public and mandates procedures for obtaining these records. The objectives of the act are to inform and educate the public, to increase its confidence in government, and to safeguard against ill-conceived government action.

The act (5 U.S.C. 552) provides for making information available to the public by three mechanisms: by publishing information in the <u>Federal Register</u>, by allowing individuals to read and copy records, and by furnishing a copy of properly described records on request. The act sets time standards (10 days) for release of information in response to requests and exempts specified records from disclosure. Agencies are required to limit charges to individuals for the service to the recovery of duplication costs. The openness of this policy has generated a large demand for agency records. In 1983, the agencies reported administrative costs of $48.5 million in response to 262.3 thousand requests for information. This does not count any cost for diversion of agency effort from its regular responsibilities. Fees collected totaled $2.2 million, or 4.5 percent of agencies' reported costs.[5] Proposals for modifying the act to better manage the burden of responding have been introduced to the Congress and hearings, conferences, and other activities related to it, were much in evidence during sessions of the 98th Congress. The matter is unresolved at this time.

This disclosure of information under the Freedom of Information Act (FOIA) is extremely important for its specific effects on the procurement process. The procurement management problem is to establish a system and a fully acceptable agency policy governing those records pertinent to procurement actions which can and should be made public information. Much of the information acquired for procurement has commercial, financial, and professional value and is provided by a person with a proprietary interest. The question arises, should it be disclosed if the information was conveyed to the government in confidence?

Decisions whether to release procurement information in response to FOIA requests are extremely difficult and have led agencies into litigation when objections have been raised by contractors. Conflicting objectives arise in this matter. On one hand, the public interest calls for public disclosure of information on how public money is expended, yet on the other hand, substantial injury or harm to a firm's competitive position may be caused by disclosure.

Numerous significant contractual documents are listed among the records which are available to the public. These records include correspondence between the department and individuals or organizations outside of the executive branch of the government which relate to official business of the department. Contract instruments are public information; so also are portions of offers reflecting final prices submitted in negotiated procurement. Furthermore, final reports of audits, surveys, reviews or evaluations for the department become public information after a lapse of a specified period of time. On the other hand, trade secrets, commercial or financial information, personnel files, or medical files provided to the government are not available to the public; but each request for information may require some review to determine the status of that information. Any denial of information under the act must be coordinated with the appropriate FOIA officer.

The foregoing points should be recognized as illustrative only. A full understanding of the Freedom of Information requirements can be obtained only through study and review of the full scope of the applicable statutes, regulations and cases.

Ethical Problems in Procurement

Two general areas exist that give rise to ethical problems in decisionmaking involving procurement expenditures. The first of these areas concerns the improper business practices and personal conduct of individuals. The second area concerns the creation of organizational conflicts of interest which may arise through award of contracts to individuals or organizations. These may occur as a result of decisions under the contract which influence designs or systems in such a manner that an advantage in the award of subsequent competitive procurement contracts is conferred upon the holder of the earlier contract.

The possibility of improper business practices or unethical personal conduct fall into the following categories:

1. conduct of federal employees and the problem of gratuities
2. public policy that officials (such as congressmen)

should not benefit from public contracts

3. certification and evaluation of certifications of independent price determination
4. offering of gratuities by a contractor to an employee of the government
5. violation of antitrust law and evidence thereof
6. prevention of improper contingent fee payments for securing public contracts.

Since procurement decisions involve expenditure of large sums of public money and of necessity require exercise of discretion by numerous individuals, great concern exists over the impartiality of decisionmakers. This concern is periodically inflamed as public disclosures of impropriety arise. Attempts to reduce or eliminate opportunities for impropriety are the source of numerous types of statutory and regulatory restraints on exercise of discretion by public employees. Efforts by professional associations, such as National Contract Management Association (NCMA), National Association of Purchasing Management (NAPM), and National Institute of Governmental Purchasing (NIG), to develop codes of ethics constitute one approach to the problem. The codes are of value in clarifying what types of behavior the profession expects of its members.

In public procurement, reliance on the ethical codes of the profession is not believed to be a sufficient protection of the public interest, and as a result, legal standards have been developed. With respect to standards of ethical conduct, the President issued Executive Order 11222 on May 8, 1965. The order authorized agency heads, in coordination with the Civil Service Commission, to issue regulations covering standards of conduct. Also, the executive order sets forth standards and procedures and reporting requirements. In particular, it declares the intent that employees should avoid any action that might result in or create the appearance of:

1. using public office for private gain
2. giving preferential treatment to any organization or person
3. impeding government efficiency or economy
4. losing complete independence or impartiality of

action
5. making a government decision outside official channels
6. adversely affecting the confidence of the public in the integrity of the government.[6]

The general rule governing the conduct of federal employees requires the employee to avoid any conflict of interest, or the appearance of a conflict of interest, when involved in government contractor relationships. An additional standard requires an employee to conduct official business in such a manner that s/he would have no reluctance to publicly disclose the nature of actions taken.

Government employees may not solicit or accept, directly or indirectly, gratuities, gifts, favors, entertainment, loans, or anything of monetary value from any person who has business or is seeking to obtain business with the employee's agency. Nor may they hold financial interests which might be affected in any substantial way by the performance or nonperformance of the employee's duties.

In addition, individual agencies are required to issue standards of conduct under which individual agencies may provide exceptions to the general rules and may provide disciplinary measures for persons who violate the standards of conduct. Each of the other five areas in which improper business practices or unethical personal contact may arise are subject to extensive definitions and procedures which should be studied thoroughly by persons involved in the public contracting business, regardless of their status as government employees or as contractor employees. Currently, regulatory coverage of these matters is contained in Part 3 of the Federal Acquisition Regulation.

Organizational conflicts of interest raise a different set of ethical problems from those identified as standards of conduct, although the basic issues of preferential treatment--private gain, impartiality and public confidence--are the same. Organizational conflicts arise from the fact that the government must often use procurement contracts to obtain the expertise necessary to develop and evaluate systems specifications and to direct performance of systems contractors. As a consequence, an agency may issue contracts to a corporation for systems engineering or technical direction work. The recipient corporation may, however, be a potential source for pro-curement of the system in subsequent, presumably competi-tive, contracting actions. The potential for inappropri-ate preferential design or selection decisions by the systems engineering or technical direction contractor is quite evident.

This type of situation may be preventable, and is an objective of policy. However, it may be difficult. Clearly, one approach to prevention is not to place systems engineering or technical direction (SE/TD) con-tracts with potential systems suppliers. Unfortunately, in some cases, that approach eliminates the most highly qualified source for the SE/TD effort. Another approach, essentially with the same impact, is to include a "hard-ware exclusion clause" in the SE/TD contract that bars the contractor from competing for the systems procure-ment. A third approach is to use a Federally Funded Research Center for SE/TD effort. Possibly a more viable approach is employment of alternative systems contractors each performing the conceptual and SE/TD efforts for a systems alternative. Under this approach, the competitor whose alternative systems concept is successful should continue his work to completion as the original systems concept developer. This approach is being examined as part of the implementation of major systems acquisition policy enunciated in OMB Circular A-109.[7] That policy is discussed more fully in Chapter 15.

Public Acquisitions Categories

Federal procurement touches nearly all industrial and commercial groupings in our economy. A good indica-tion of the range and diversity of its acquisition pro-grams is gained by reviewing the Commerce Business Daily (CBD). Appendix 1 lists all categories of servi-ces for which synopses were published over the sampling period. Appendix 2 is a similar list for supplies, equip-ment and material actions with value greater than ten thousand dollars. The listings present a rather complete summary of the categories of services and supplies normally acquired by the government. Nearly all categories of products and services contained in the federal cataloging program are represented.

Notes

[1] *Report of the Commission on Government Procurement*, Volume 1, G.P.O., p. 43.

[2] *Federal Grant and Cooperative Agreement Act of 1977*. Public Law 95-224, February 3, 1978, distinguished grant and cooperative agreement relationships from procurement relationships.

[3] Ibid.

[4] "Development of a New Federal Procurement System, System Scoping Paper," (Draft), Office of Federal Procurement Policy, May 14, 1981.

[5] "Access Reports, Freedom of Information," *The Washington Monitor*, Volume 10, Number 17, August 29, 1984.

[6] Executive Order 11222, May 8, 1965.

[7] Office of Management and Budget Circular A-109, issued April 5, 1976.

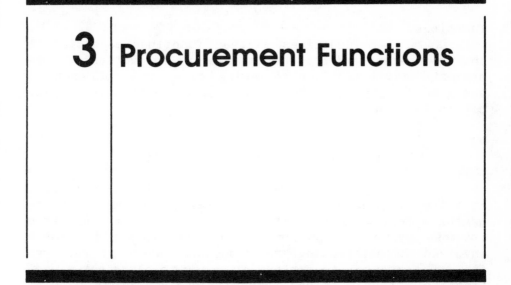

3 | Procurement Functions

The subject of this chapter is work performed by government procurement personnel. Several functions are discussed including ones performed primarily within central procurement directorates. Others are discussed that are performed in field offices under the direction of a contracting officer, as is the case with many functions associated with contract administration. This chapter identifies these functions and forms a basis for more complete discussion of procurement organization found in Chapter 4.

An appreciation of procurement functions must include the broader range of work identified in Chart 3-1, but at this point, only procurement and contract management functions are discussed. It is through the objectives determination and resource mobilization functions that procurement action is initiated. An overview of those functions is provided in Chapter 1 and further discussion is included in Chapter 10.

The functions treated here are associated with carrying out the action. They account for much of the lead time (often referred to as Procurement Administrative Lead Time or PALT) for large procurements. Numerous personnel, in addition to the buyer or negotiator, are required to successfully fulfill each of the necessary functions.

Chart 3-1 identifies sixteen functions essential to the procurement and contract management activities of government agencies. The following discussion of each is designed to highlight the nature of the activities implicit in the function.

Policy and Procedure Development

Policy and procedure development is a principal activity of procurement directorates at the agency headquarters level. Each of the major agencies has initiated its own system of procurement regulation and is deeply involved in determining the procedures which it requires its own personnel to perform in order to carry out a contracting action. In one sense, this function is no different from any corporate activity in which a policy and procedures manual is developed and/or interpreted, but it differs in scope because a government-developed procurement policy often has a direct impact on the private sector. Government procurement policies not only determine how the government conducts the public's business, but often attempt to outline how private sector organizations must conduct business. As a consequence, the policies are of vital interest to contractor organizations. Furthermore, since the procurement policy process results in the formulation of mandatory rules and procedures on both the government work force, and on the contractor and the contractor's work force, they are published as procurement regulations.

With implementation of the new Federal Acquisition Regulation (FAR) on April 1, 1984, agency level regulations are made subordinate to the broader policy. The expectation of OFPP is that the total volume of procurement regulations should decrease, since agency issuances are not to duplicate the FAR. Nevertheless, each agency is expected to continue to produce supplementary regulations.

Furthermore, at the individual command and buying activity level, implementing policy and procedure is written. In addition to regulation writing activities, procurement policy offices at each level must interpret

CHART 3-1

PROCUREMENT RELATED FUNCTIONS
IN GOVERNMENT

Objectives Determination and
Resource Mobilization Functions

Mission Definition
Analysis of Needs
Requirements Generation and Definition
Program/Project Definition and Approval
Acquisition Planning and Strategy
        Subdivision of Work
        Sourcing Outlines
        Scheduling
        Cost Projection
Budget Presentation and Authorization
Appropriation and Funding Processes

Procurement and Contract
Management Functions

Policy and Procedure Development
Personnel Training and Development
Procurement Action Review
Legal Review
Buyer and Negotiator Units
Technical and Price Analysis
Procurement Operations and Control
Advocacy Offices
Source Identification and Qualification
Source Selection Planning and Control
Procurement and Contract
  Management Review
Contractor Procurement Systems Review
Contract Administration and Quality
  Assurance
Contract Audit
Contract Adjustment
Contract Appeals

and apply existing policy as needed for each contractual action.

In conclusion, responsibility for policy and procedure development, implementation and/or interpretation is assumed, to some degree, to be the responsibility of each purchasing activity. Consequently, staff policy offices support procurement officers at all levels.

Personnel Training and Development

The development of procurement personnel is a continuing responsibility of all federal agencies but one not consistently fulfilled. Most new personnel enter into the procurement field with little understanding of the process. While a number of in-house schools have been developed by the military services, and to a lesser extent by other agencies of the government, the contracting officer is confronted with a continuing need for personnel replacement and training programs for the improvement of skills. Individual agencies have attacked this problem in varied ways: on-the-job-training, employing consulting firms to develop and present training courses, detailing personnel to available military courses, and introducing procurement training into the agency's training institutes. Most agencies plan and arrange their training programs through personnel offices but draw upon the functional offices, such as procurement, for guidance and expertise. Senior procurement officers are continuously involved in providing that guidance.

Help in expanding training programs for procurement personnel is anticipated by the Office of Federal Procurement Policy through the introduction of procurement executives into each procuring agency. Under the leadership of procurement executives, agency-wide master plans for training of procurement personnel are to be developed and sufficient resources are to be provided for implementation. Also, President Reagan's Executive Order 12352 directs agency heads to establish career management programs to include the full range of personnel management functions which will result in a highly qualified, well managed professional procurement work force.

Academic institutions have not traditionally addressed a great deal of effort to the training of people involved in procurement. Although a number of schools have provided courses in purchasing and materials management, only a few have developed programs which deal with the special complexities of the procurement programs of the government. In its proposal for a uniform federal procurement system, the Office of Federal Procurement Policy has stated that there is remarkable growth in the number of colleges and universities offering procurement related courses. This growth began in 1968 at the George Washington University with the introduction of its procurement and contracting program. Under the OFPP, the Federal Acquisition Institute has, since 1976, stimulated many new collegiate offerings and has also encouraged development of internal training initiatives within the agencies. There is considerable resistance to expanding the collegiate offerings in government procurement and contracting, in large measure, as a result of the fact that the federal government, under its personnel policies and practices, is unable to effectively recruit new personnel from among the graduates of the collegiate institution. OFPP made this statement in its proposal for a federal procurement system.

The prevailing qualification standards and selection procedures have encouraged the promotion of clerical and technical employees into professional level procurement positions, while inhibiting the recruitment of college graduates. In recent years two-thirds of the government's entry level procurement positions were filled from the clerical and technician ranks.

Procurement Action Review

The principal method through which procuring agencies control the quality of the procurement product is the establishment of procurement review offices. The function of these offices is to examine each procurement action to determine compliance with regulatory requirements and adherence to the overall management, direction and guidance of the individual procuring activity. They also ensure that business relationships and financial considerations adopted by the buyer or negotiator are appropriate. There are numerous types of procurement actions which must be reviewed by such an office prior to execution.

The review of procurement actions by a policy and review office varies with each procuring activity. Some of the principal types of review actions are indicated below. Perhaps most important is the procurement plan. It is a preliminary device, one which is prepared well in advance of actual solicitation and award of contracts. Depending on the agency's management approach, the procurement plan may be critical to the coordination of agency activities and resources to ensure timely award of contracts. More importantly, it improves the likelihood that a contract will achieve the objectives for which it is intended. A fully developed procurement plan involves all elements of a procuring agency: technical, financial, schedule, contractual, quality assurance, reliability, and logistics activities. It provides a mechanism by which each interested office within an agency is able to determine that a proposed procurement action will meet the needs of that office. While the content of a procurement plan varies with each agency, it should establish the schedule of actions for the procurement process, delineate the nature of a competitive process to be followed, identify interrelationships between individual procurement actions, and provide an insight into the magnitude of resources being committed by the proposed procurement action. Overall, the procurement planning document is critical to effective purchasing actions, since it sets forth, in advance, the sequence of actions to follow. The inclusion of a requirement for advanced procurement plans in the CICA should bring about increased attention to this tool by executive agencies.

Closely associated with the procurement plan is a source selection plan which may be prepared as a formal document for large procurements, a less formal document, or even simply a section of the procurement plan. Regardless of its form, the source selection plan sets forth, in advance of issuing the solicitation document, principal considerations which will influence the evaluation of competitors. The degree of formality in a government source selection plan varies with the magnitude of the procurement action, but the plan may become more formalized when a procurement is highly visible and critical to the agency, regardless of the financial commitment being made. In any case, a source selection plan must comply with the agency's procurement policy governing how it should be prepared. Most procuring agencies have developed a formal policy regarding the evaluation and selection process for major procurement actions including a method of designating the source selection official. Depending on agency policy and the magnitude of the proposed contract, the source selection authority may be vested in the contracting officer in a local contract review board or at higher management levels up to the agency head.

To date, source planning by government agencies has been largely limited to the development of the source selection plans. However, under the CICA some extension of sourcing activity into market search and development of sources may occur because the CICA has directed the agencies to perform market research activity. This area, however, will be a new development within the federal bureaucracy and will require a considerable degree of initiative on the part of the procurement manager.

Procurement action review is also concerned with proper legal justifications for contract actions. In the government's scheme of procurement, the process of negotiation of contracts has been differentiated from that of formally advertised contract actions. Until the effective date of CICA, April 1, 1985, negotiated procurements must be authorized as individual actions or, in some cases, as a class of procurement actions based on a request for authority to negotiate. Each request provides reasons for using negotiation procedure instead of formally advertised procedure and has been prepared by the negotiator assigned to the procurement, routed through the procurement action review office, and ultimately to the agency head for approval.

Although the request for authority to negotiate will now disappear, the justification for noncompetitive procurement will become a critical and pacing document for many procurement actions. It is critical because any noncompetitive process is a fundamental departure from public policy. Both public policy and good business practice dictate that more than one competitor be given the opportunity to prepare an offer and to compete for the award of most procurement actions. Nevertheless, a drastic change will be required to meet the objectives expressed in CICA. The current level of procurement dollars awarded on a noncompetitive basis is 65 percent. This high percentage is a result of the large amounts of government procurement which are highly specialized, technical, or of a follow-on nature, when technology transfer to new producers is impractical. Numerous other factors also intervene in the competitive process such as the existence of substantial capital investment possessed by a particular producer, or technology that is proprietary to a particular source. Much of the complexity of the administrative processes associated with government procurement is related to the problem of noncompetitive procurement. A substantial administrative effort is required to find a mechanism in which either a competitive procurement process can be used or an adequate justification for noncompetitive procurement prepared. This is a principal responsibility of the procuring activities of the government. The procurement review function monitors and effectuates policy in this area. Under the CICA a new review and approval authority, the competition advocate, will likely become a part of the policy and review office.

One central role of procurement action review offices is the review of prenegotiation plans. These plans summarize the government position prepared for the direct interaction, discussions, and negotiations involved in reaching an agreement with prospective sources of supply.

In organizations such as the Department of the Navy, prenegotiation plans are known as contract clearances. The clearance document is submitted for review and approval by the contract review office prior to the initiation of negotiations with the proposed sources of supply. As a result of the review process, an approval or a disapproval is made with respect to the negotiator's plan to proceed with negotiations. Through its procurement action review process, the agency is in a position to determine whether its personnel are properly preparing for and conducting their procurement responsibility. The prenegotiation clearance is followed (subsequent to negotiations) by a post-negotiation review. During the post-negotiation review, agreement reached with the source of supply is examined with respect to the prenegotiation position which was approved earlier.

From the foregoing, it can be seen that the process of reviewing procurement actions can effectively control the quality of procurement. Some issues of principal concern in the review of negotiation plans involve whether the negotiator: has met all legal and regulatory requirements for the proposed contract, has obtained appropriate audit review of the contractor's proposal, has prepared an adequate analysis of the contractor's cost and price proposals, has gained the input of appropriate technical personnel in review of the contractor's technical plans for carrying out the contract, and has developed a viable position and set of objectives for negotiation. The negotiation plan should set both quantitative and qualitative objectives for contract negotiation and disclose the principal reasons for positions the negotiator is planning to take during the negotiation. Approval of prenegotiation clearance is essential for the negotiator to proceed with the negotiations, and approval of the post-negotiation clearance is essential for the contracting officer to proceed with the execution of the contract.

Legal Review

Closely related to the procurement action review process is the legal review of government contract actions. Legal review is a function of offices of general counsel, and in the case of large government agencies, such offices may have units devoted principally to the review of contract documents. The purpose of legal review is to assure compliance with statutory, regulatory, and general management requirements for entering into contracts. The procedural aspects of government procurement are complicated and rooted not only in statutory and regulatory issuances but in numerous, pertinent board and court decisions, making the legal review of proposed actions a critical step in the successful solicitation and award process. To some degree, legal review overlaps and may be redundant to procurement action review.

Buyer and Negotiator Units

The organizational units of buyers and negotiators are central to the action of the procurement office. These units are staffed with personnel who carry out planning, coordination and documentation prerequisite to the issuance of solicitation documents. They are responsible for the evaluation of proposals, the preparation of positions for negotiations, and the conduct of negotiations with suppliers. The negotiation units prepare contract documents and make the award of contracts. The role of the negotiator in these organizations is to take a procurement request or requisition through the internal justification and preparation stages necessary for solicitation and for execution of all of the responsibilities associated with the solicitation and award process. These organizational units may hold responsibility for the administration of awarded contracts. However, depending on the policy and manning of each agency, all or part of the contract administration functions may be assigned to field activities.

Since administrative action associated with contracts involves interaction with contractors during the performance period, competition is inevitable between the negotiator's responsibilities for carrying on procurement actions and his responsibilities for administering existing contracts. The government agency may have substantial capability for field administration of contracts, making this an important alternative to having the procurement negotiator assume those responsibilities.

Many administrative functions are assigned to field organizations. However, some critical administrative actions are such an integral part of the performance of the project that procurement managers are unwilling to transfer this authority to independent field organizations. Critical contract administration actions include the issuance of change orders, and the allocation or negotiation of additional increments of work, particularly ones involving substantial funds or schedule adjustments. Many federal agencies do not have significant field contract administration offices and as a result, the buyer or negotiation organizational units in the procuring office may, of necessity, carry out most contract adminis-

tration functions. Regardless of the organizational
arrangements for the administration of contracts, the
principal role of buyer units includes negotiation,
award, and significant administrative contract actions.

Technical and Price Analysis

Four types of analysis are used in support of the
source selection and negotiation processes associated
with each contract award. They are audit, technical,
cost and price analyses, and evaluation for source selection purposes. The analyses may be handled in several
ways depending upon the organization of individual government agencies and the type of solicitation used. When
proposals are received from contractors in a competitive
procurement, they will normally be analyzed from technical, audit, and cost or price point of view. One purpose
for this analysis is to determine which of several competitive proposals should be selected for award. Technical
assessments designed to support the source selection
decision compare the quality of each proposal relative to
the evaluation criteria specified in the solicitation.

The second purpose is to establish a government position regarding the amount of effort and cost that should
be recognized in determining the price of the contract.
When a proposal has been submitted on a noncompetitive
basis, the predominant objective of analysis is to determine the content of work, to validate in detail the costs
of performing it, and to assess its worth or value in
relation to the price.

In most government organizations, technical analysis
is performed by the technical or program offices that
sponsor the procurement action. Additionally, audit,
technical, and price analyses may be prepared in field
offices located at or near the proposing contractor's
plant or offices.

The technical analysis used to develop a position
for negotiation provides quantitative and qualitative
assessments of the direct resources estimated by a contractor for performance of the proposed contract. These
direct resources include direct labor (hours and classifi-
cations), material (types, quantities and qualities),

travel (quantity and purposes), special tooling (types, quantity), and computer effort (hours, capacities). The resource implications of the proposer's conceptual approach to the undertaking are assessed and compared with estimates made by the agency's technical staff.

The price analysis function can be organized as a separate and independent step in the preparation of nego- tiation positions. In agencies that operate in this man- ner, the assignment of responsibility for negotiation to a procurement office does not include the responsibility for price analysis work. Instead, a separate price analy- sis organization hires analysts that use audit and techni- cal information, together with proposal and other data, to prepare pricing reports which are then incorporated into prenegotiation positions. Other agencies assign responsibility directly to the negotiation unit which employs technical analyses, audit and field pricing reports, and proposal data to develop and build a negotia- tion position.

Price analysis in support of noncompetitive propos- als is based largely on the contractor's proposed costs evaluated against requirements of the specification and on any historical and organizational peculiarities associ- ated with the proposed contract. With a competitive nego- tiation, price analysis may not depend on the contrac- tor's cost of performance. Instead, it may be based on comparative price information found in the agency's rec- ords and/or in the price proposals. One of these ap- proaches to technical and price analysis will have appli- cability to each procurement action.

Procurement Operations and Control

One critical function performed in every buying office is control of procurement operations. The procure- ment operations section records the transactions of the procurement office. These offices record procurement requests, assign the requests to negotiators, maintain records of the progress of each action, and in general, maintain a current status report for all activities of the procurement office. In addition, they will generate procurement action reports for use of higher levels of management and for input to the Federal Procurement Data Center.

Advocacy Offices

The function of an advocacy office is to promote and guard the interests of small or minority-owned busines- ses. Under CICA, the advocacy function will be expanded to include the new competition advocate.

The advocacy employee is chartered to intervene in the procurement process by reviewing planned procurement actions with the objective of causing the contracting officer to restrict the competition to a protected group. Now, under CICA, the reverse objective, prevention of restricted sourcing, other than in favor of protected groups, will become an advocacy responsibility. There- fore, advocacy personnel must be certain they obtain cur- rent knowledge of incoming procurement requests. This requires them to work closely with procurement operations personnel. For many years, one principal function of the small business advocacy office has been to obtain a set- aside of procurement for competition by small and/or minority business organizations.

Source Identification and Qualification

Identification and qualification of sources of sup- ply is critical to effective operation of a procurement organization. One of the products of this function is the bidders lists which should be properly organized, sub- divided, and indexed so that, as each new procurement request is received, appropriate sources of supply can be identified for competitive solicitation. This is a diffi- cult function to carry out successfully. While adding names of supply sources to the bidders list is straight- forward, it is difficult to properly qualify and classify sources for specific solicitations. This procedure is particularly difficult for small or minority business organizations because they are not as well known. Pro- curement actions in excess of $10 thousand are published in the Commerce Business Daily, thereby enhancing the competitive process. However, the preparation of bidders lists and the direct solicitation of potential sources of supply are a central part of the effort to open contract bidding to competing businesses. The key government procedure for this purpose is submission by interested parties of Standard Form 129, "Solicitation Mailing List Application."

Source Selection, Planning and Control

Regardless of dollar magnitude, the source selection decision is critical to effective, efficient and economical performance of contracted work. Consequently, source selection planning and control processes assume great importance to the procurement office and to the entire agency. Since the selection of winners in competition involves evaluation of technical, management, financial, schedule, and risk factors, all elements of an agency are involved. For large contracts, control is often held by top level management. To date, the government has done little pro-active market research aimed at increased competitive activity. However, under CICA, Congress has directed that market research be done. Therefore, increased action toward source development should begin to emerge.

Source selection, planning and control are viewed as a key to successful procurement, and while many agencies organize and staff the function as part of the procurement office, several alternative procedures are devised with varying degrees of formality depending on the dollar magnitude of the procurement.

Procurement and Contract Management Review

The procurement directorate is responsible for the quality of work performed by subordinate procuring offices and for the proper functioning of the contract administration organization. To effectively control these areas, the directorate may have an organized procurement and contract management review process. The objective of staffing these review capabilities is to bring about

better prime contractor selection, negotiation and administration procedures. The staff must be expert in defining the objectives, policies, procedures, practices,
areas of judgment, and mandatory elements of effective
procuring or contract management offices. Their work
includes field audits and examination of procedures and
decisions made by subordinate organizations. The product
of this effort should include the documentation of agency
practices in the procurement area and input of information to the procurement training and personnel development program. Its objective is to achieve broad systems-
wide improvement. The likely process by which such a
review office will achieve its goals is through scheduled, periodic examinations of each major subordinate
office and examination, on a sampling basis, of the work
of minor subordinate offices.

Contractor Procurement Systems Review

Analogous to procurement and contract management
review is contractor procurement systems review. One of
the principal responsibilities of agency management is to
make certain that public funds are expended in a proper
fashion regardless of the level at which the expenditures
are made. An important facet of procurement is that a
very substantial proportion of public funds expended
through the process is actually expended by subcontractor
organizations. Subcontract dollar amounts can approach
60 and 70 percent of prime contract awards. As a consequence, it is important that the agency have insight into
the procurement systems of prime contractors. An agency's interest in its prime contractor's procurement process introduces complexity to contracting because some
challenge of contractor decisions by agency managers
occurs. Challenges may arise over decisions such as
selection of subcontractors, pricing of subcontract work,
and enforcement of public policies. The complexity is
heightened, in the case of large prime contractors,
because their procurement process may involve hundreds of
personnel and millions of dollars annually in subcontract
awards.

While it is well established in law and regulation

that the government agency has a right to review and con-
cur in principal subcontract awards of its prime contractors, the process of individually reviewing each subcontract award is extraordinarily cumbersome and virtually
impossible to carry out effectively on a case-by-case
basis. As a consequence, the idea of government review
of contractor procurement systems has strong appeal. One
problem with this concept, however, is the substantial
number of personnel and the time required. Consequently,
all federal agencies are not able to mount such an
effort.

In the DOD, a major portion of contractor procurement systems review is assigned to the Defense Contract
Administration Services (DCAS). This assignment of work
does not relieve agency management from considering effective performance of this function. Although DCAS performs the work, the responsibility for results remains
with each agency head and director of procurement.

Contract Administration and Quality Assurance

Contract management review and contractor procurement systems review are a small part of the agency's
responsibilities for contract administration. Devising
an appropriate method for carrying out the broad range of
contract administration responsibilities is an even more
difficult challenge.

Contract administration is a function that is analogous to expediting the execution of purchase orders. The
objective is to ensure that contracts are performed on
time and in accordance with their provisions. For long
term contracts and for programs with multimillion dollar
budgets, the contract administration process can become
complex. Its complexity is increased by the responsibility, during the administration of a contract, to ensure
not only that the contractor makes appropriate progress
during his performance period, but also that he carries
out general public policy matters which may be incorporated into his contract.

The contract administrator's work also requires
management of the business relationship between the
agency and its sources of supply. The work is challeng-

ing because it includes a mixture of many administrative processes, some routine and repetitive, others, not only nonroutine but critical to the effective prosecution of the government's program. For example, the administrator is responsible for payments made to the contractor as work progresses--a routine process. However, when schedule and design changes, or test and qualification issues arise, the solution to the problem may involve substantial financial or schedule impacts. The burden of these complex problems can fall upon the contractor, or depending on circumstances, upon the agency. Effective administration is vital to proper allocation of responsibilities.

Related to this are the staffing and organizational problems in distributing responsibility for contract administration decisions between central buying and field contract administration locations. The approach an agency takes toward staffing its contract administration function has significant impact on its total manpower profile. Inherent in this problem is that many facets of the administration of a contract require direct interaction with contractors at plant sites remote from the procuring agency's purchasing office. Some facets must be performed centrally.

Regardless of organizational assignment, contract administration involves financial management (including audit and cost verification responsibilities), payments, and approval of appropriate reimbursement rates. It includes administration of government property held by the contractor, surveillance of production processes, and determination of the status of production, especially progress against schedule commitments. Additionally, it includes verification and surveillance of quality assurance activities of the contractor, consideration of logistics issues (such as selection and/or pricing of spares and replacement parts necessary during the deployment of products delivered), administration of change orders, and negotiation of adjustments in the terms of the contract. The largest manpower groups within contract administration are quality assurance and audit. Both of these areas are highly specialized and labor-intensive.

These activities are essential elements of the project that aid in the gathering of data, the completion of the contract, and preparation for contract closeout and final payment. In a small but significant number of cases, the contract administration process leads to the administration of claims and support of litigation that arise when disputes cannot be resolved through negotiation processes.

Contract Audit

The principal audit agency for government contracts is the Defense Contract Audit Agency (DCAA). This organization is responsible for detailed examination and review of contractor records and books of account. Although it is an independent agency, DCAA functions as advisor to contracting officers. Furthermore, it is the only arm of the contracting office that has access to the contractor's internal accounting records. While nondefense government agencies have limited contract audit capabilities, most audit work is assigned to the Defense Contract Audit Agency. Responsibility for obtaining and coordinating audit support rests with the agency's procurement managers.

Audit reviews are needed in the administration of government contracts in several situations. During the initial pricing process, if a contract is negotiated on the basis of cost and price data, the agency examines the contractor's proposal to verify the accuracy, currency, and completeness of cost data on the basis of which the proposal has been prepared. It also verifies the contractor's consistency and propriety in preparing the proposal. These reports are used in the agency's development of a negotiation position for pricing the contract. The audit agency also performs reimbursement cost verifications for administration of cost contracts and for incentive and redeterminable fixed-price contracts. The audit organization provides input for the final payment of cost contracts.

Contract Adjustment

Under Public Law 85-804, 50 U.S. Code 1431, Congress

has authorized extraordinary contractual adjustments to be made by procuring agencies (those authorized by the President to use the act) under limited circumstances. Several categories of extraordinary adjustments exist which a contractor may request. In general, these adjustments involve formation, or amendment of contractual relationships under circumstances where fairness requires an adjustment, provided the agency head deems that the action will "faciltate the national defense." Adjustments are made to achieve a prompt and fair result even though there may be no judicially actionable basis.

To carry out this responsibility, internal procedures for review and decision of contractor requests for such adjustments must be established. Normally, for actions of $50 thousand or more, an agency contract adjustment board considers requests. For actions of less than $50 thousand, authority may be delegated to the heads of procuring activities. Actions taken are reported to Congress annually, are matters for public record, and are based on facts and sound judgment. These decisions are administrative.

Contract Appeals

When contracting officers and contractors are unable to negotiate differences, litigation is initiated by issuance of a contracting officer's "final decision" and appeal of that decision by the contractor. Under the traditional system of disputes, the agency head provided a system for making decisions on contract appeals. The Contract Disputes Act of 1978 has now provided a government-wide, congressionally authorized system for dispute resolution. It significantly modified, but largely retained the traditional system. Under it, agency heads appoint boards of contract appeals to decide issues. At the present time, there are fourteen boards of contract appeals established by the various agencies. Where agencies do not establish their own board of contract appeals, the agency head delegates the responsibility for hearing appeals to one of the existing boards. The appeals process is somewhat complex and discussion of it is not an objective of this book. It is, however, an administrative procedure for which agencies must make provision.

4 | Organization of Government Procurement

Congress has approached organization of procurement in government by authorizing nearly all agencies and independent offices to issue contracts. In 1983 the number of agencies reporting significant contract activity had risen to sixty-one, and examination of agency organization reveals wide diversity in organizational patterns. Guided by manpower authorizations, mission assignments, and appropriations, an agency head has discretion to determine not only his organization's structure but also the extent to which his procurement responsibilities will be carried out.

Our examination of organization in this chapter is oriented toward understanding the concepts employed rather than attempting to set forth in detail the resulting structures that exist. While examples of organizations are included, the reader should recognize that change occurs frequently and, therefore, the examples should be viewed as illustrations, not as authoritative, current cases.

While it allows a great deal of discretion in organizational matters, the Congress imposes limitations on organizational factors such as authority to delegate or redelegate decisionmaking power. For example, under CICA, an agency head cannot redelegate authority to use noncompetitive procurement procedures in the public interest. Similarly, Congress often vests administrative responsibility for policy development in specific areas in agencies external to the procurement agency. As a consequence, several special policy agencies hold specific authority to prescribe policies that must be carried out by the procuring agencies. An example of this is Department of Labor policy control over labor-related questions. Similarly, small business policy questions have been assigned to the Small Business Administration.

Other examples of organizational guidance imposed by Congress include the determination that small business officers should report to the agency director, and the mandate that offices of inspector general be established within the top structure of agency management. Similarly, organizational preferences of Congress are reflected in formation of agencies such as the Defense Logistics Agency, the General Services Administration, and the Defense Contract Audit Agency, each of which consolidates a segment of procurement or procurement related activity.

Congressional Actions Affecting Organization

Congress is situated at the apex of procurement hierarchy. It is Congress--not the executive branch--that holds the power directly pertinent to procurement activity: the ability to draw funds upon the Treasury. In exercising its power over the contractual method of using funds, Congress takes several actions that are prerequisite to the exercise of procurement authority. Congress acts to:

1. establish missions to be executed
2. create executive agencies
3. authorize specific programs
4. assign program responsibility to agencies
5. authorize funds for programs annually
6. appropriate funds for programs annually
7. authorize agency manpower levels
8. delineate the broad outlines of a standardized procurement system
9. establish oversight procedures for agencies and pro-

grams
10. assign responsibility for "special policy" concerns
    to existing or newly created agencies.

These actions are shown in Chart 4-1 which also illustrates some key organizational effects. Chart 4-1 does
not identify many of the nuances of federal procurement
superstructure; it does show the top level policy generating groups and their relationship to Congress and the
community of contractors. It does not show the role of
presidential executive orders or policy statements.

Of the special policy agencies, the most recently
created is the Office of Federal Procurement Policy
(OFPP). It was established in 1974[1] for the purpose of
bringing into existence a single central policy office
within the executive branch with the authority to interact with the Congress and the responsibility for coordination and development of the procurement regulation system. The OFPP was established as a part of the Office of
Management and Budget (OMB). Its assigned role is to
function as a policy office, not as a procurement activity. OFPP's purpose is to exercise influence over the
procuring agencies and to coordinate among the agencies
those issues and proposals pertinent to the procurement
process. In carrying out these functions, it has extensively used the device of the interagency working group
to develop and coordinate positions on issues.

Within the jurisdiction of OFPP, there are two offices designed to carry out parts of its mission--the Federal Acquisition Institute (FAI), and the Federal Procurement Data Center (FPDC). (Both have been established
under administrative jurisdiction of the General Services
Administration.) FAI's job is to improve the professional standing of the federal procurement work force.
The FPDC is charged with developing and implementing a
government-wide procurement data system capable of generating consistent and accurate statistical reports of government-wide procurement activity.

The Congress has assigned a number of responsibilities to the Department of Labor (DOL) which affect procurement by the other agencies. These responsibilities
deal with labor policy and are protective features for
particular groups in the labor force that may be ad-

CHART 4-1

CONGRESSIONAL ACTIONS/ORGANIZATIONS FOR DIRECTION
CONTROL AND OVERSIGHT OF FEDERAL PROCUREMENT

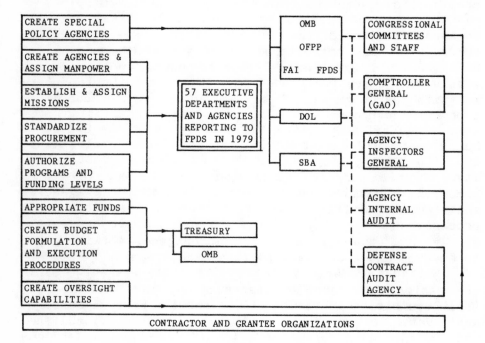

| PROCUREMENT-
RELATED ACTIONS
OF THE CONGRESS | ORGANIZATIONAL STRUCTURE RELATED
TO FEDERAL CONTRACTING
POLICY AND OVERSIGHT |

versely affected by procurement practices, particularly competitive practices, that tend to reduce pay levels and other benefits. Examples include administration of the Davis-Bacon Act under which construction labor is given certain protections, most importantly, wage protection. Under the act the Secretary of Labor is empowered to specify prevailing wages pertinent to construction trades. The DOL administers the Service Contract Act which has an analogous set of provisions designed to protect service contract labor. Additionally, it administers the Walsh-Healey Act and is responsible for the administration of labor standards. The DOL implements Executive Order 11246 which mandates that contractors exercise equal employment practices and establish affirmative action programs. In these various capacities, the Department of Labor is a nonprocuring agency charged with policy development and implementation.

The Small Business Administration (SBA) is comparable to the DOL in that it influences procurement but is not principally a procuring agency. Its responsibilities are to advance and protect the interests of small business organizations in the United States, and in recent years, has been assigned responsibilities for allocating contracts to minority-owned enterprises. The SBA role in procurement is:

1. to define, for purposes of SBA programs, the small business firm for each industry group in the country
2. to determine the competence and, more broadly, the responsibility of small business firms to be awarded government contracts
3. to secure the set-aside of government procurement actions for participation by small and minority-owned business firms and
4. to provide advisory services and support of small or minority business firms.

The SBA also has general responsibilities for the promotion and financing of small business in the economy whether in relationship to government procurement action or otherwise.

Regardless of the importance of the special policy agencies discussed above, the principal action in procurement is not performed by them. Rather it is carried out by the numerous procuring agencies, each of which has been established by the Congress to perform a particular function or mission. As shown in Chart 4-1, sixty-one agencies reported procurement actions to the FPDS in 1983. Each department and most independent offices of the government are given a charter through the legislative process; however, some, such as the Environmental Protection Agency, are organized under executive order. Under their charter, agencies may be specifically granted the authority to use procurement action or alternatively, the authority to use such action is implicit in the charter of the agency. The general principle with respect to this was established by the Supreme Court in United States vs. Tingey.² While the Tingey case does not examine all of the limitations and exceptions which may arise based upon the distribution of powers in the United States government, the general principle is clearly expressed in the following extract from the case.

> Upon full consideration of this subject, we are of opinion, that the United States have such a capacity to enter into contracts. It is, in our opinion, an incident to the general right of sovereignty; and the United States being a body politic, may, within the sphere of the constitutional powers confided to it, and through the instrumentality of the proper department to which those powers are confided, enter into contracts not prohibited by law, and appropriate to the just exercise of those powers.

From this quote, it would appear that an agency of the government would hold the power to contract as one means of carrying out its work, unless there is incorporated into its grant of powers, a limitation with respect to the exercise of power to contract.

It is also within the powers of the Congress to establish the mission of the various agencies and instrumentalities of the government. Furthermore, it is within the discretion of the Congress to determine which agency or instrumentality should be authorized to pursue each of the various and sundry missions and/or programs. Thus, in some cases, agencies are created to pursue a mission which the Congress feels should be undertaken by the government, and in other cases, an existing agency may be assigned a new mission by the Congress simply by the enactment of a statute directing the agency to pursue the particular effort.

Chart 4-1 also reflects that, in addition to the creation of agencies and the establishment of mission, the Congress has provided procedures by which the procurement process is carried out within the various agencies. Numerous statutes contain procedural guidelines imposed on the procurement processes of agencies. However, the two statutes which, as of today, are the most comprehensive with respect to procurement procedures are the Armed Services Procurement Act (ASPA) of 1947, as amended, and the Federal Property and Administrative Services Act (FPASA) of 1949, as amended. These two statutes have standardized the procurement process of the federal government for the defense and the civilian sectors, respectively.

In addition to establishing a procurement process, the Congress has established procedures for the purpose of formulating the budget of the United States and for executing the budget, once the funds have been appropriated. The basic statute now pertinent to the process is the Budget and Accounting Act of 1921, as amended. Within this process, the Office of Management and Budget is the principal executive agency in charge. It operates as an arm of the President and negotiates with or directs the procuring agencies regarding their budget requests for inclusion in the President's budget. The OMB (following the apportionment process guidelines established by the Budget and Accounting Act), provides the appropriated funds to the agencies incrementally through the budget year.

Recognizing the importance and centrality of each of the foregoing congressional actions, the Congress takes three specific actions with respect to each program. First, an authorizing statute is enacted to establish the program. Secondly, on an annual basis, it sets forth the funding level authorized for each program (both the program and its funding level are defined by an authorization statute). Authorization of program funding in order to provide the needed capital must be followed by an appropriation statute specifically allocating funds for expenditure in pursuit of the program's objectives.

This superstructure of congressional action essential to carrying out the procurement process is made complete because Congress also has reserved the ability to oversee operations of the agencies. There are several institutions which ensure that oversight is effective. Most important of these is the committee structure of the Congress. The area of responsibility of each committee includes oversight of those programs and activities for which the committee has been the principal legislative sponsor. While the jurisdictions of various committees of the Congress overlap, it is through the work of the committees and their staffs that the Congress is made aware of the effectiveness, efficiency and general economy of government operations. Oversight is pertinent in each of the areas where the Congress has authorized procurement to take place.

A major supporting arm of the Congress is established in the General Accounting Office (GAO) which operates under powers delegated to the Comptroller General of the United States. The GAO is an extention of the Congress, not of the executive branch, and is charged with carrying out audit and investigation into the operations of nearly all of the government agencies. Reports by the Comptroller General to the Congress have been influential in development of policy toward procurement activities.

The Inspector General offices, established in several procuring agencies at the direction of Congress, also conduct investigation to oversee the appropriateness of the agencies' operations throughout all levels of activity. These independent audit and investigative capabilities help to ensure that the expenditure of appropriations is carried out in accordance with Congress's dictates and with the general legal, accounting, and ethical guidelines pertinent to operations.

Audit is the final area in which the procurement-related superstructure is operative. The agencies of the government have internal audit capabilities designed to oversee the general effectiveness and efficiency of their operations. More directly pertinent to the procurement process, the agencies also may have contract audit capabilities designed to support the negotiation, award, and administration process associated with contracting. Many employ the Defense Contract Audit Agency, the principal U.S. government agency for contract audit. It includes an extensive field audit organization, with manpower to visit contractor plants and to examine and review the books and records of contractors, which are pertinent to their systems, for estimating and recording the costs of government contract activities. The agency also has capability for general review of contractor accounting systems and practices, and for preparing reports to contracting officers for their use in the negotiation and administration of government contracts.

By referring to Chart 4-1, the foregoing discussion of the procurement-related superstructure may be better perceived. It should be noted that the channels for information flow and the channels by which procurement action is controlled have overlaps and crossovers.

Procurement-Related Functions in Government

At this point, it should be evident that a substantial institutional structure has been created with the intent of having the executive branch carry out its procurement work in accordance with the intentions of Congress. The objective of this section is to suggest the importance of the functions of procuring agencies when considering the potential subdivisions of work. Chapter 3 discusses the functions internal to the contracting offices. In Chapters 10 and 11, objectives and resource decisions, as well as the broader functions critical to adequate planning and strategy development for acquisition, are discussed. Together, these considerations make up one element of the organizational concepts and choices considered by executive or legislative leaders or agency managers. Reference to Chart 3-2 facilitates the discussion at this point by summarizing both groups of functions. Recognizing the role of functional analysis, our discussion now focuses on several concepts and factors which have served as the bases for subdivision and departmentation of procurement.

Organizational Concepts and Choices
in Federal Procurement

The subdivision and departmentation of work in federal procurement has been approached in a number of different fashions.   Chart 4-2 provides a summary of concepts that are important for the organization of procurement responsibilities and lists a number of factors that are used. These factors are not entirely independent. Some of them clearly overlap and/or complement each other. Nevertheless, each one could independently govern organizational decisions made by an agency.

Method of Procurement

Method of procurement is one basis for organizing procurement activities. It is derived largely from the procurement statutes. Four methods are recognized that involve distinguishable types of activity. They are sealed bidding, competitive proposals, small purchases, and assistance. Sealed bidding procurement uses a highly structured set of procedures that lead to formal bid openings. The opening is followed by responsiveness and price evaluation techniques entirely different from the techniques and procedures pertinent to the other methods. Personnel specialization leads to subdividing work by sealed bidding, competitive proposals, and small purchases though many exceptions apply.

Competitive proposal solicitation procedure is pertinent for requirements that are less well defined than those for which sealed bidding is applicable. As a result, central procurement organizations establish offices that deal exclusively with competitive proposal (better known as negotiated) procurements.[3] This occurs when the mission of the agency involves work that is not well defined, such as research or research and development. Similarly, small purchase actions are seldom mixed with major negotiated procurement actions. This division of work occurs naturally because small purchase actions are not only small in magnitude but highly repetitive in character. Furthermore, most have a short reaction time. A group of buyers dealing with small purchases cannot di-

CHART 4-2
ORGANIZATIONAL CONCEPTS IN PROCUREMENT

I. Method of Procurement
      Formal Advertising
      Negotiations
      Small-Purchase Procurement
      Assistance Agreements
II. Category of Acquisition or Commodity
      Construction, A&E Services
      Automatic Data Processing Equipment and Software
      Research, Research and Development
      Supply and Logistics Support
         Construction, Electronic Equipment
         Fuel, General Supply
      Production, Commodity Assignment Program
      Major systems
III. Organization Level and Type
      Centralized at Headquarters
      Field Organization, Government Operated
      Government Owned, Contractor Operated
IV. Industry
      Construction, Aerospace
      Research and Development
      Computer, Petroleum
V. Function
      Purchases, Price Analyses
      Policy, Operations
      Procurement Action Review
      Advocacy Offices
VI. Role Performed in the Procurement Process
      Procurement
      Contract Administration
      Verification of Quality Assurance
      Audit, Financial Planning & Management
      Development of Requirements
VII. Geography, Installation and/or Magnitude
      Base Procurement
      Central Procurement
      Cost, Economy and/or Communications Advantages
VIII. End Result
      Product or Project
      Matrix

vert time needed to process small orders to the lengthy
and more complex deliberations associated with major
negotiated contracts.

The fourth subcategory under method of procurement
is assistance. Most government procurement offices are
not involved in the award of grants and cooperative agreements; however, those which are have explored (but not
all have adopted) the alternative of establishing separate organizational units to handle the assistance type of
actions. Part of the reason for an organizational subdivision is the Federal Grant and Cooperative Agreement Act
of 1977 (Public Law 95-224) which established statutory
distinctions between assistance and procurement. Assistance refers to federal financing for public purposes
through transfer of funds to state or local governments
or to other recipients.

The principal distinction between an assistance
arrangement and procurement is found in the purpose of
the funding. If the purpose is to sponsor property or
support services not for the government's express use or
benefit, assistance arrangements are used. Within the
category of assistance, there are two principal types of
instruments. One is the grant, the other is the cooperative agreement. The distinction between the grant and
the cooperative agreement relates to management. Under a
grant arrangement, there is little or no federal involvement in the management of the work being funded. Substantial funding of nonfederal, governmental undertakings is
financed by the grant process. In addition, research
grants are awarded in substantial number by some government agencies. The cooperative agreement is different
because the government agency is involved in management
of the undertaking. Furthermore, cooperative agreements
are often established with private enterprise organizations. Such agreements may provide for sharing the cost
as well as the management of the undertaking. Agencies
such as the Department of Energy (DOE) have engaged in
extensive cooperative agreement types of actions.

Commodity or Service Category

The second group under Chart 4-2 is the commodity or

service category. This group evolves from analysis of the work to be performed and is similar to the fourth group--industry. An excellent example is construction contracting. Major construction is normally procured by a government-buying activity established specifically to manage construction and architectural and engineering work. An example is the Federal Building Service, a part of the General Services Administration which is responsible for the construction, purchase and/or lease of public buildings. Similarly, in the Department of the Navy, the Naval Facilities Engineering Command is responsible for naval construction. The major activity of the Department of the Army Corps of Engineers is the construction of facilities, either in-house or through contracting. Furthermore, the Corps of Engineers is the agency the Congress uses for construction of large public works projects such as dams and navigation facilities. Construction of major facilities by other agencies of the government is limited, although minor construction and repair is procured by numerous local purchasing offices throughout government.

Automatic data processing equipment (ADPE) and software purchases, as a category, are differentiated not only by the character of the material or services being acquired, but by statutory allocation of responsibility for such purchases. The Congress vested the General Services Administration with the responsibility for procurement of automatic data processing for all agencies of the government. This allocation of responsibility applies to general purpose equipment, such as weapons and space systems equipment, not to special purpose computer equipment and software. The General Services Administration is not chartered to develop or plan requirements for ADPE; therefore, each agency must plan and develop its own set of ADPE requirements. Nevertheless, in the procurement process for equipment, the agencies must assign the procurement action to the General Services Administration. In many cases, GSA reassigns the procurement to the agency originating the requirement (via a delegation of procurement authority) to carry out the contracting process.

Research activity is undertaken extensively by both military and civilian agencies. In some of these agen-

cies, research organizations are established to execute
basic and advanced research that enhances the scientific
and technological bases of the agencies. Thus, major
research organizations such as the Office of Naval
Research and the National Bureau of Standards conduct
extensive in-house as well as contracted research work.

Some of the largest procuring activities in government are those devoted to research and development. In
addition to basic and advanced research, these agencies
conduct programs in applied research, development and
testing of prototype hardware, and in conversion of prototypes into operational systems. Examples include the
Naval Sea Systems Command, the Naval Air Systems Command,
NASA research and development centers, and the Air Force
Space and Missile Systems Organization of the Air Force
Systems Command. Military R&D leads to procurement of
military hardware production and results in the largest
individual contracts awarded. The production awards are
often a follow-on procurement action to the successful
research and development of a military system.

Several large supply and logistic support subdivisions are identified in Chart 4-2. Each is assigned to
organizations responsible for acquiring adequate stocks
of defined material items and services needed to support
agency operations. Organizations involved in this type
of business are well established in the federal procurement system. The General Services Administration, as an
example, operates the Office of Federal Supply and Services which negotiates large numbers of contracts that support the Federal Supply Catalog. Under the FSS contracts, federal agencies acquire standard items directly
from suppliers through a simple requisitioning process.
Somewhat analogous to the Federal Supply Service operations is the Defense Logistics Agency (DLA), established
as a procuring activity of the Department of Defense.
The Defense Logistics Agency has generally subdivided its
responsibilities by commodity or service categories. The
Defense General Supply Center, the Construction Equipment
Supply Center, the Defense Fuel Supply Center, and the
Defense Electronics Supply Center are examples.

An additional subdivision of acquisitions along the
commodity line is illustrated by the Defense Commodity
Assignment Program. Responsibility for the acquisition

of groups of commodities is delegated, through regulation, to one of the defense procurement agencies. These commodity assignments enable agencies to employ an adequate complement of specialists so that negotiation and purchase of commodities is accomplished efficiently.

Organizational Level and Type

The third approach indicated in Chart 4-2 is subdivision by organizational level and type of activity. Under this concept, an agency may centralize procurement operations either at the headquarters level or it may delegate authority to field organizations. In some cases, the responsibility is delegated to government installations operated by contractors.

Each of these approaches has been employed extensively. For example, the Department of the Navy has centralized procurement work in the Navy Material Command (NMC). Under NMC, five major systems commands operate as headquarters functions at the Navy Department Headquarters in Washington, D.C. One of these commands, the Naval Supply Systems Command, is responsible for and oversees a system under which navy supply activity, including the procurement of supplies, is handled by field organizations. Major acquisitions are contracted by the headquarters level systems commands.

Under the Department of the Army, major procurement activities are conducted by central procurement organizations located at several major army installations in the United States. Thus, under the Department of the Army, centralization of procurement is within field organizations. The National Aeronautics and Space Administration has followed a similar concept in that it has allocated major procurement responsibilities to NASA centers located in several parts of the country. Each center is responsible for an assigned area of space or aeronautical research and development work.

A third technique is employed extensively by the Department of Energy particularly with respect to its atomic energy program. Under that program, the agency (at the time, the Atomic Energy Commission) established major government installations throughout the country.

Those installations, however, are not operated by government employees. Instead, each is operated by a management contractor with a long-term contract. Some contracts have existed as long as the Atomic Energy Commission and its successor organizations combined.

A somewhat analogous approach is the NASA Jet Propulsion Laboratory (JPL). JPL is owned by NASA but is operated under contract by the California Institute of Technology. Organizational arrangements such as these arise because of technological and expertise needs, cost effectiveness considerations, policy favoring private sector performance of work, and the availability of management capacity. The organizations are known as federally-funded research and development centers (FFRDCs). The FFRDCs possess facilities and expertise that meet specific agency mission segments and are continued for that reason. As an example, NASA assigns responsibility for deep space research and development to JPL. This assignment is similar to the assignment of responsibility to the Ames Research Center for aeronautical research activity (in-house management), and to the manned space program, including the Space Transportation System (Shuttle). Over time, these assignments of responsibility for categories of acquisition activity become well established. Nevertheless, opportunity for revision of work assignments is one of the areas where management discretion is vital and where agency politics may be of considerable importance.

Industry

Organization based on the performing industry group is clearly evident in procurement. It is reflected in the commodity or service categories already discussed but is often a factor in itself. For example, governance of NASA procuring activities was placed under the Armed Services Procurement Act because NASA deals primarily with aerospace and electronic industries, similar to many defense acquisition efforts. Establishment of the Defense Fuel Supply Agency, in part, was based on the need for expertise in dealing with the petroleum industry and its system of distribution of petroleum worldwide.

Function

Within government agencies, procurement is generally organized as a functional directorate with its top offi-cial at the second to the fourth level of the agency. Work under the procurement directorate is subdivided by function, a subject analysed in Chapter 3. The functions may be set up as divisions or other organizational units for purchases, policy, operations control, price analy-sis, advocacy, procurement review and others, depending on the needs and perceptions of the procurement director and agency management. Within the purchase units, work is subdivided by commodity or project and often is a part of a matrix structure. One example of matrix organiza-tion is the GSFC co-location concept illustrated later in this chapter.

Role Performed in the Procurement Process

This is one of the principal ways in which the gov-ernment has subdivided its work force in the field of acquisitions and procurement. Five subdivisions of pro-curement-related activity are indicated under this head-ing. The first of them, procurement, represents the buy-ing organizations set up by government agencies. These organizations are staffed with negotiators, contract specialists, and contracting officers who are delegated the authority to negotiate and award new procurement actions. In central procurement these functions are carried out in an organization which includes a full com-plement of organizational functions such as engineering, scientific, financial, schedule, personnel, and many other functional specialties. The contracting office in such an organization is principally responsible for the award of contracts and is seldom staffed with contract administration personnel to any significant extent.

Under the government's scheme of organization, con-tract administration is largely organized as a separate entity, and the personnel within it are primarily located in field activities spread across the country and over-seas. The contract administration group is responsible for contracts after they have been established and is

concerned with securing timely performance in accordance
with the requirements of the contract. Numerous specific
responsibilities are carried out by this group. The
largest single contract administration organization is
the Defense Contract Administration Services organized as
a part of the Defense Logistics Agency.

The verification of quality assurance is also a part
of the contract administration function in government.
However, it is operated in a semi-independent fashion as
part of the Defense Contract Administration Services. It
involves a large number of quality assurance personnel
assigned at field locations throughout the country who
supervise and oversee the quality assurance systems used
by contractors in performing work for the government.

The government's contract audit organizations are
chartered to perform a particular aspect of contract
administration. With particular reference to the Defense
Contract Audit Agency, the Congress has played a role in
establishing that the contract audit function should be
independent of other contract administration or procurement organizations. As a result, Defense Contract Audit
Agency reports to its own director who, in turn, reports
to the Secretary of Defense, and the structure is relatively independent of the procurement organization at all
levels of the Defense Department. The DCAA also conducts
audit work for other agencies and is the principal arm of
the contracting officer for audit services. The financial planning and management function indicated under
this section of Chart 4-2 is an activity that will be
staffed within each of the types of organizational entities discussed. Its principal responsibilities are the
formulation of budget estimates and execution of allotted
funds.

The last area indicated under part VI of Chart 4-2
is the development of requirements. This activity is
largely a technical effort and is organized within the
central procuring activities of the government or within
numerous specialized organizations that hold the specific
scientific, engineering, or other technical expertise
that analyzes needs and develops requirements into actionable statements of requirements. These groups are responsible for the initiation of action leading toward solicitation and award of contracts.

Geography, Installation and/or Magnitude

Government procurement is also organized by geographical consideration or on the basis of support requirements for particular installations. A good example is the establishment (at dispersed government locations) of a procurement and supply office with authority to conduct small purchases and minor construction modification activities in support of the installation. Base and local purchasing activities usually are not given authority to make major procurements of material, equipment or services. In general, local purchases in the federal government are centralized in a purchase and supply office at the base or installation being supported.

Procurement involving large sums of money or requiring immediate and intricate communications with technical, scientific, or program management offices, is assigned to central procuring activities. For complex procurements, physical proximity of buyer, technical and user personnel is vital to smooth and accurate information exchange. Centralization of major procurement promotes specialization and technical communication. Even with a high degree of centralization, it is not likely that the procurement process will be carried out at the headquarters offices of the agency. Of the three illustrations of centralized procurement at the end of this chapter, one (Navy) performs most of its procurement as a headquarters function, one (NASA) procures primarily out of field centers, and one (EPA) has both headquarters and field activities procuring major items.

End Result

The last subdivision of these organizational concepts is organization of procurement activity by end result. This involves project and program management or matrix organizations. They are discussed more fully in Chapter 8. The manager is a results-producer who must approach his work in a single-minded fashion. When a project-managed undertaking is established, the project manager secures personnel from each of the functional areas that support the project's planning and administration processes. Extensive examples of this kind of organizational concept are found in government procurement activities. Research and development work is normally organized by project, and the project manager is responsible for the successful achievement of the project objectives. Although a project manager is not primarily a procurement manager, many federal projects are performed almost entirely through use of contracting. Facilities, expertise, management structure, and manpower are obtained by contract.

In some cases, an acquisition project is granted status as fully projectized. The project manager is allocated an adequate number of personnel to perform all the essential central governing and planning activities necessary for the project. Major projects have technical, financial, business management, and procurement personnel to support the project.

Full projectization is impracticable for most undertakings. A more prevalent method of management is the matrix structure in which the project manager is able to call upon the functional divisions of the agency to support the project where necessary. Under the matrix organizational concept, a procurement officer or a negotiator may be assigned to carry out all of the project's contracting requirements, but is available for assignment to other projects when full-time attention to the original project is not necessary. A similar concept applies to each functional support area of a project.

Illustrative Government
Procurement Organizations

This discussion illustrates the organizational features of three government procurment programs. These three organizations were selected because they differ in mission, size, and organizational level. They are the Naval Material Command (NMC), the Environmental Protection Agency (EPA), and Goddard Space Flight Center (GSFC).

The Naval Material Command, the central organizational unit responsible for the entire Navy acquisitions and contract management program, is a headquarters organization responsible for management of a vast system of procurement and for Navy logistics support. The magnitude of this operation is much greater than either the EPA or the GSFC. The procurement division of the EPA is a headquarters-level office of a medium size civilian agency. EPA's mission is to protect and improve the nation's physical environment. In contrast, the GSFC organization accounts for only a portion of the National Aeronautics and Space Administration (NASA) procurement program. Thus, it is an example of an individual government procuring activity. NASA's mission is space and aeronautical research and development.

Navy Organization for Acquisitions and Contracting

The Naval Material Command (NMC) manages the world's largest procurement organization. It is responsible for the entire acquisition program of the U.S. Navy Department and employs in excess of 214,000 people. The command is managed by a headquarters staff of 700. Its five systems commands employ 189,000 personnel and are organized as headquarters activities of the Navy, centralized in Washington, D.C. The systems commands include extensive field activities within their aggregate personnel complement. NMC headquarters is best distinguished by its role as a "corporate" level office. It does not buy; it reviews, analyzes and controls its buying activities, primarily the five systems commands.

In addition to acquisition, NMC is responsible for the Navy's programs in logistics and in reliability, maintainability and quality assurance. One of its five systems commands, the Supply Systems Command is responsible for 176 major field activities and approximately 600 minor field activities involved in the buying process. These field procurement offices are known as the Navy Contracting System which is organized under nine regional centers and provides procurement support to the organizations known collectively as the Naval Shore Establishment. Functional procurement management of this system is exercised by the Supply Systems Command.

The contracting program of the Navy is carried out

under the Armed Services Procurement Act of 1947, as amended. Line authority to contract for Navy purposes is vested in the Secretary of the Navy, who delegates authority to issue contracts through three assistant secretaries, the Commandant of the Marine Corps and the Chief of Naval Operations (CNO).

Chart 4-3 shows in simplified fashion the organization of the Navy Department. The chart emphasizes the position of the Naval Material Command in relation to the Secretary of the Navy. Delegation of authority to contract follows the line of command indicated by the chart, but the secretary directly delegates to the Naval Material Command authority to set policy and regulations, specifically to issue the Navy Contracting Directives (NCD), and to monitor and control the Navy's acquisition processes. While Chart 4-3 does not show the functional authority relationships, it depicts, in skeletal form, the flow of command authority--that the Commander of the Naval Material Command reports to the Secretary of the Navy through the Chief of Naval Operations. The positions of the assistant secretaries of the Navy, in relation to the Secretary are shown. However, the chart does not identify the roles of the three assistant secretaries, the CNO, or the Commandant of the Marine Corps in relation to procurement. All of these officials are designated acquisition executives, vested with legal authority to issue contracts in their respective areas of jurisdiction, including contracts issued by the systems commands under NMC.

Legal authority is important because it vests the acquisition executive with power to sign key authorizations and approvals necessary to award major contracts. A dual flow of authority results from this arrangement. For example, under the Assistant Secretary for Research, Engineering and Systems, is the Office of Naval Research (ONR), an important contracting arm of the Navy. Line authority for ONR flows through the Assistant Secretary, but functional procurement management authority is exercised by NMC. This dual flow of authority for contracting reflects separation of line and functional authority, a concept widely practiced by Navy. It exists with respect to ADPE acquisition (under the Assistant Secretary for Financial Management) and with respect to pro-

CHART 4-3

RELATIONSHIP OF NAVAL MATERIAL COMMAND
TO THE NAVY DEPARTMENT

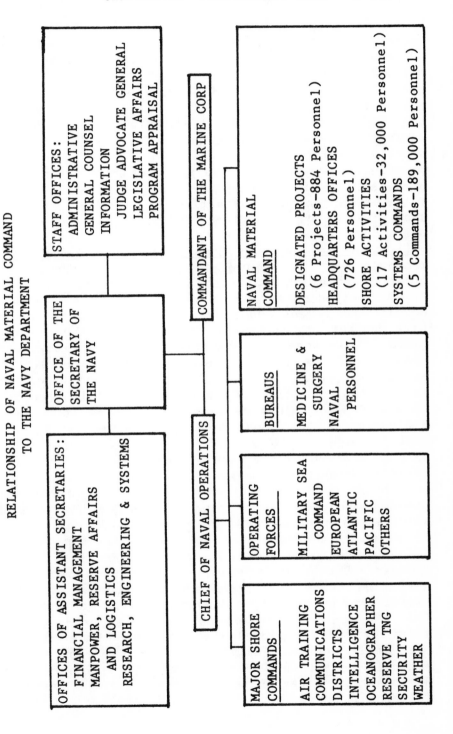

curement by the Marine Corps. While the systems commands differ in being organized as line responsibilities of NMC, the dual flow is still in evidence, since contracting authority is delegated through the acquisition executives. In all cases, NMC exercises policy and review authority over contractual actions. For this purpose, the Deputy Chief of Naval Material for Contracts and Business Management, as shown on Chart 4-4, acts for the Secretary and for CNM.

Chart 4-4 shows a simplified diagram of the internal organization of NMC Headquarters giving emphasis to the acquisition management functions. Chart 4-4 is an expansion of the "Headquarters Offices" portion of NMC as shown on Chart 4-3.

Chart 4-3 provides some perspective in terms of the manpower level of each of the major categories of offices in NMC. It also identifies the two fundamental organizational philosophies for organization of projects, full project management and matrix management. The concept of full projectization is carried out in the designated projects. There are six programs in this category, and the project offices employ approximately 880 people. These particular projects have a degree of priority and significance such that the Navy has determined to provide each of the project managers with a dedicated staff to cover the essential functional support areas, including procurement. However, the largest portion of Navy procurement work is handled by the five systems commands.

These systems commands are staffed to execute all facets of the acquisition process. The procurement of one or more of 47 major projects and 495 less-than-major acquisition programs is assigned to the five commands. In general, the commands employ a matrix management concept. Under that concept, each project has a project manager with overall responsibility for success. However, the project managers are dependent upon the functional groups within their respective system commands. Thus the support work essential to most projects is provided by the functional organization. Under the matrix management scheme, individual support personnel such as contract negotiators are assigned to specific projects. Nevertheless, they remain administratively under their functional supervisor. Also, for smaller undertakings,

CHART 4-4

HEADQUARTERS, NAVAL MATERIAL COMMAND

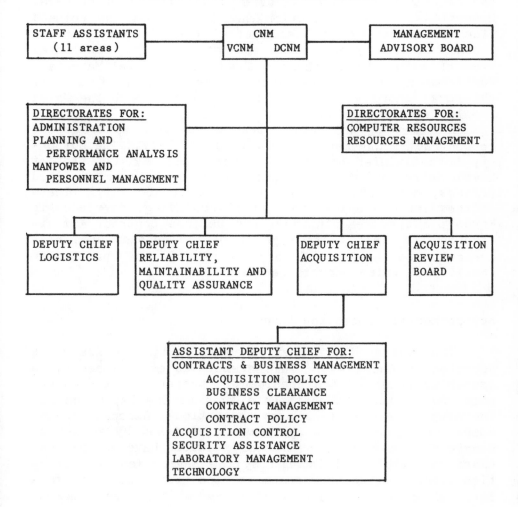

support personnel may be assigned to more than one project at a time.

Chart 4-3 identifies the 17 Naval shore activities
which employ some 32,000 people and shows that these
activities report directly to the Chief of Naval Material. The chart also shows these same shore activities
(shore commands) reporting directly to the Chief of Naval
Operations. The distinction, again, is that the command
line of authority is through the Chief of Naval Operations but the procurement and acquisitions functional
line of authority is through the Chief of Naval Material.
Furthermore, as has been stated, the procurement work of
the naval shore activities is controlled though the Naval
Supply Systems Command.

A somewhat analogous structure exists with respect
to contract management authority in the Navy. The authority to administer contracts is controlled by the Chief of
Naval Material but is assigned to several types of field
offices, some of which are not part of the Navy. These
offices include supervisors of shipbuilding, Navy and Air
Force plant representatives, and Defense Contract Administration services. The type of office depends upon historical assignments of cognizance of the particular
facility at which work is performed.

Environmental Protection Agency

The United States Environmental Protection Agency is
depicted in Chart 4-5. This agency was established by an
executive order of the President; therefore, it does not
hold the status of departments such as the Department of
the Navy or agencies such as the National Aeronautics and
Space Administration which were established by an act of
Congress. However, a number of statutes have established
missions to be administered by the Environmental Protection Agency. Thus, the status of the agency as an organizational entity is less solidly rooted than the numerous
environmental policies for which it is responsible. A
perusal of Chart 4-5 shows no indication of the location
of the procurement function. However, by referring to
Chart 4-6, one can see that the procurement and contracts management division reports to the Office of Admin-

CHART 4-5

UNITED STATES ENVIRONMENTAL PROTECTION AGENCY

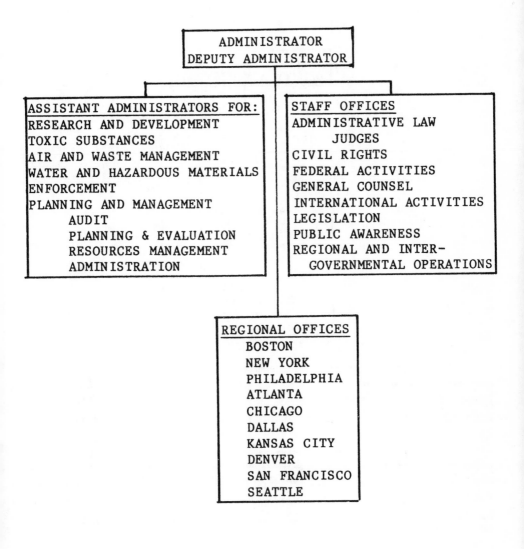

ADMINISTRATOR
DEPUTY ADMINISTRATOR

ASSISTANT ADMINISTRATORS FOR:
RESEARCH AND DEVELOPMENT
TOXIC SUBSTANCES
AIR AND WASTE MANAGEMENT
WATER AND HAZARDOUS MATERIALS
ENFORCEMENT
PLANNING AND MANAGEMENT
     AUDIT
     PLANNING & EVALUATION
     RESOURCES MANAGEMENT
     ADMINISTRATION

STAFF OFFICES
ADMINISTRATIVE LAW
     JUDGES
CIVIL RIGHTS
FEDERAL ACTIVITIES
GENERAL COUNSEL
INTERNATIONAL ACTIVITIES
LEGISLATION
PUBLIC AWARENESS
REGIONAL AND INTER-
     GOVERNMENTAL OPERATIONS

REGIONAL OFFICES
     BOSTON
     NEW YORK
     PHILADELPHIA
     ATLANTA
     CHICAGO
     DALLAS
     KANSAS CITY
     DENVER
     SAN FRANCISCO
     SEATTLE

CHART 4-6

UNITED STATES ENVIRONMENTAL PROTECTION AGENCY

PROCUREMENT ORGANIZATION

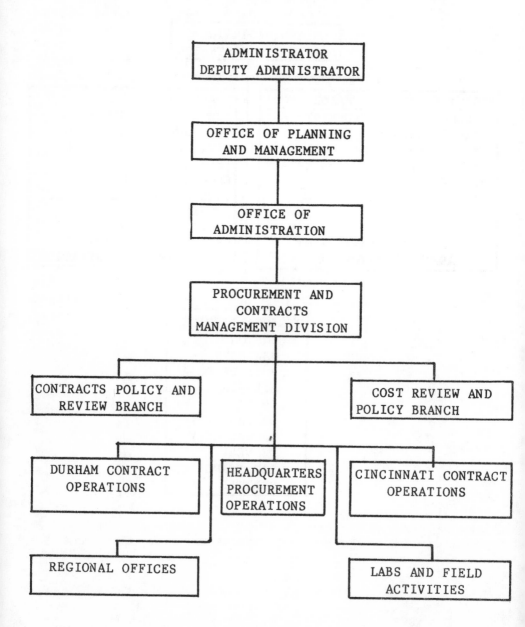

istration which, in turn, reports to the Assistant Administrator for Planning and Management, who, in turn, reports directly to the administrator of the agency. This
places the Director of the Office of Procurement and
Contracts Management at the fourth level in the agency's
structure.

The Director of Procurement and Contracts Management
is responsible for the procurement program of the entire
agency. Under the director, there are three major procurement offices. One is located at the headquarters
organization and referred to as the Headquarters Procurement Operations branch. Approximately one-half of the
agency's total procurement volume is contracted for by
the Headquarters Operations Office. The other two principal offices, Cincinnati Operations, and Durham Operations, represent one-third and two-thirds of the balance
of the total procurement volume of the agency ($450 mil-
lion per year). EPA's annual volume can be compared, for
the purposes of this discussion, to the volume of Goddard
Space Flight Center which exceeds $700 million per year
and to the Naval Material Command, with annual volume in
excess of $23 billion. To carry out its workload, the
EPA procurement organization at headquarters employs 118
people. Thirty of these are contracting officers. At
the Durham contract operations office, there are eight
contracting officers, and in Cincinnati, there are three.
One of the principal operating procurement control systems at EPA is the annual procurement plan. This plan is
a time-phased budget plan for the procurement work of the
agency. It amounts to a schedule for the initiation of
procurement requests and is useful as a check against
receipt of commitments for procurement action. It should
be noted that the procurement and contracts management
division of this agency does not handle assistance types
of agreements because these are organized as an independent activity of the agency.

For major procurement actions, the EPA has established a source selection board procedure which applies
to contracts awarded at a value in excess of one million
dollars. The agency delegates source selection authority
to the laboratory directors when the contract is in the
one to five million dollar range. For actions in excess
of five million dollars, the director of procurement and

contract management is the source selection authority.

The agency's procurement organization is a functional support system. The procurement personnel are part of the procurement operations branches and are used to support the programs of the technical directorates that have programmatic missions. The headquarters procurement operations branch is organized into units designed to support the work of an assistant administrator for each of four programmatic areas. The areas are Water and Hazardous Materials, Air and Waste Management, Toxic Substances, and Research and Development. The organizational level of the procurement director is perhaps reflective of the proportion of agency resources-- 11.3 percent--expended through the contracting process. The agency's organizational concepts and its program are in a state of change at the time of this writing.

Goddard Space Flight Center

Since 1974, the Goddard Space Flight Center (GSFC) has employed a unique concept in procurement organization: co-location. Chart 4-7 is a simplified presentation of the GSFC co-location system. The Center is organized into eight directorates which, as indicated in Chart 4-7, report directly to the director of the center. A partial breakout is illustrated for three of the eight directorates--Management Operations, Flight Projects, and Engineering. The breakouts are representative of the co-location organizational pattern employed by the center for the support of flight projects and technical directorates. The Management Operations Directorate, Code 200, contains several of the functional support organizations necessary to the operation of the center including the Procurement Management Division, the Financial Management Division, the Functional Support Division and the Project Support Division. Of these divisions, Procurement Management and Financial Management constitute home base for functional expertise and direction of personnel that are co-located in support of the center's technical research and development program.

An important aspect of the GSFC organization is the position and role of the procurement officer. This offi-

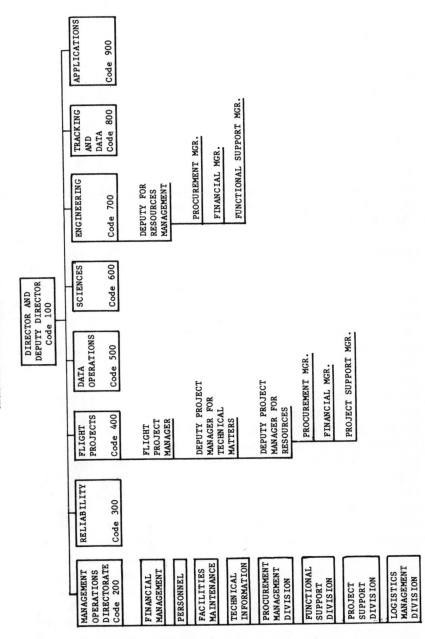

CHART 4-7

GSFC CO-LOCATION CONCEPT
ORGANIZATIONAL OUTLINE (PARTIAL)

cer directs the Center's procurement process but is a member of the Management Operations Directorate staff. The assignment of functional procurement personnel is divided. Half are assigned to the Procurement Management Division and half to the project support or functional support divisions and are co-located at offices around the center. A distinctive feature of Goddard's management system is the manner in which the functional personnel provide support to the flight projects and to the technical codes of the center.

Goddard's flight projects are assigned to Code 400, the Flight Projects Directorate. Under that directorate are several independent flight projects sponsored by the center. The organizational concept employed is the appointment of a project manager for each flight project. Reporting to each project manager are two deputy project managers: one for technical matters, one a deputy project manager for resources. The deputy for resources is co-located from Code 200 and secures procurement, financial, and project support personnel from the Project Support Division, Code 280. Under this organization, the procurement manager is not part of the procurement division, although a strong functional tie is maintained through biweekly meetings with the procurement officer.

Directly analogous to the support of flight projects, the technical directorates (such as the Engineering Directorate, Code 700) have, within their organizational structure, a deputy director for resources management, a procurement manager, a financial manager, and a functional support manager. Again, these managers are co-located with the technical directorate which they support, but they are administratively assigned to the Functional Support Division, Code 260. Additionally, within each co-located support office, there may be several support personnel co-located with the functional managers. For example, the procurement manager supporting the Tiros Flight project may have several negotiators working under him. The actual number of personnel assigned to each flight project and to each technical code is dependent upon the work load requirements of the particular organization being supported.

The co-location concept makes the procurement, financial, and operations support personnel project-oriented individuals. It enhances both communications within and across the project as well as the responsiveness of support personnel to the needs of the project manager. This organizational concept enhances the ability of the functional support personnel to become involved in and to influence the planning and execution of project operations. The project and functional managers find they are able to rely more fully on the co-located members of their staffs, and the functional expert feels much more closely aligned with the project as a team member.

On the other hand, the advantages of this organizational concept are not without their costs. In the case of Goddard, there are about eighty procurement negotiation personnel distributed throughout the center. Their identity with the procurement office and their degree of commitment to the basic objectives of centralized procurement is unclear. One of the factors that complicates this organizational structure is that it tends to be somewhat rigid in the reassignment of manpower. The problem potentially encountered here is that project needs may vary more rapidly than personnel can be moved from one project to another or from one office to another. The effect is that this form of projectization tends to be a resource-consuming method of organization. Thus, in terms of control of the procurement process, and of total manning requirements, the co-location system may be somewhat undesirable. Nevertheless, it provides a high level of support and service for each project and for the technical codes of the center.

Under the co-location concept, the Procurement Management Division retains a functional staff responsible for certain centralized functions that are critical to the establishment and maintenance of appropriate controls over the procurement process. Under the division head is found ADP, construction, institutional procurement, operation of the bid room, and small-minority business offices. Additionally, five other functions are performed centrally. These are: procurement review, procurement policy, operations control, technical responsibility for training of procurement personnel, and administration of the center's source evaluation board and performance evaluation board activities. As part of this set of responsibilities, the procurement officer is responsible for advocacy of small and minority business programs. The system has given rise to special effort by the procurement officer to develop and maintain strong functional ties with the co-located personnel. Legal review of Goddard Space Flight Center contracts is conducted by the General Counsel's office. It is through these centralized functional activities of the procurement officer and the center management, that GSFC seeks to preserve its control over the procurement process as well as to carry foward its program responsibilities. Overall, the center believes this system provides better functional service to its programs, and that it enhances the programmatic involvement of its functional personnel.

Notes

[1]Public Law 93-400.

[2]United States v. Tingey, 30 U.S. (5 Pet.) 114 (1831).

[3]Prior to passage of the Competition in Contracting Act the term "negotiated procurement" included the procedure now referred to as competitive proposal procurement. Both terms are used interchangeably throughout this book.

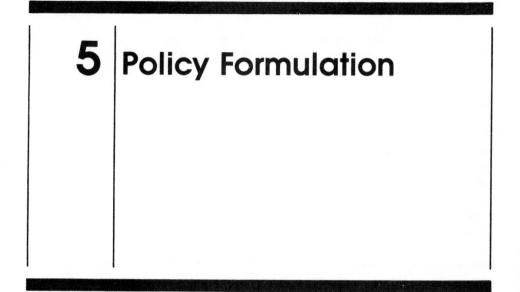

5 Policy Formulation

Policy formulation is a complex aspect of government procurement because there are divergent objectives of multiple competing interest groups in the expenditure of public appropriations. If procurement policies were concerned primarily with internal operations of the government, their formulation would be simpler. The reality is that contractors and many segments of the public in general are affected. Furthermore, the interests of government employees and other groups in the bureacracy must be considered as policies are generated.

Completion of the work of the Commission on Government Procurement and establishment of the Office of Federal Procurement Policy were principal products of the policy formulation process during the past decade. Implementation of the Federal Acquisition Regulation (FAR) in April, 1984, is a recent example. This chapter summarizes these developments and describes the principal contributors to the formulation of policy. An effort is made to explain the roles of the Congress, the Office of Federal Procurement Policy, the Comptroller General, and the procuring agencies of the government.

The Report of the Commission
on Government Procurement

December, 1972, marked the completion of the work of the Commission on Government Procurement. The Commission was created by Congress in November, 1969,[1] to conduct a comprehensive investigation of the government procurement process. This action resulted from growing concern as to whether procurement processes were being conducted effectively. The product of the commission was a four-volume report[2] that defines and describes policies, practices, and management of the federal procurement system.

The commission's report is a notable contribution to management thought. It addresses the many dimensions of a federal business operation, which at the time of the study (1972), had expended $57.5 billion by procurement and $39.1 billion by means of public grants.[3] As disclosed in Table 1-1, by FY 1983 the dollar volume of procurement alone had risen to $168.2 billion. The commission proposed the creation of "an integrated system for effective management, control, and operation of the federal procurement process." The report included 149 recommendations, but its "integrated system" concept proposed a way to help federal executive agencies conduct procurement operations in a business-like, orderly and efficient manner. The elements of the system, as proposed, are:

1. The creation of an Office of Federal Procurement Policy in the executive branch to ensure fulfillment of government-wide statutory and executive branch requirements in performing procurement responsibilities
2. An integrated statutory base for procurement, implemented by a government-wide regulatory system, to establish sound policies and simplified agency procedures to direct and control the procurement process
3. Latitude for federal agencies to carry out their responsibilities within the framework of government-wide statutes, policies and controls
4. Availability of funds in time to permit improved

planning and continuity of needed federal and contractor operations
5. Government-wide recruitment, training, education and
   career development programs to ensure professionalism in procurement and the availability of competent, trained personnel
6. Carefully planned agency organizations staffed with
   qualified people and delegated adequate authority to
   carry out their responsibilities
7. A coordinated government-wide contract administration and audit system to avoid duplication and deal
   uniformly, when practical, with the private sector
   in the administration of contracts at supplier locations
8. Legal and administrative remedies to provide fair
   treatment of all parties involved in the procurement
   process
9. An adequate management reporting system to reflect
   current progress and status so that necessary
   changes and improvements can be made when the need
   appears
10. A continuing government-wide program to develop bet-
    ter statistical information and improved means of
    procuring goods and services.[4]

The commission stressed the importance of management
in the procurement process, apparently because their findings suggested that government executives had ignored a
businesslike process and because in government, as in the
private sector organizational success depends largely on
effective contracting.[5]

The core proposal, creation of a policy office with
government-wide influence and authority, was completed by
Congress on August 30, 1974.[6] On that date, the Office
of Federal Procurement Policy (OFPP), within the Office
of Management and Budget (OMB), was established. The
authorizing legislation provided a five-year initial
period for the new office.

In October, 1979, Public Law 96-83 was passed which
extended the life of the OFPP for an additional four
years. The law required the Administrator for Federal
Procurement Policy to review the recommendations of the
Commission on Government Procurement and to report their

status to the Congress with further recommendations for completing, amending, or rejecting ones which had not yet been adopted. This requirement was in addition to Congress' requirement that a uniform procurement system proposal be developed (as discussed in Chapter 2).

The Congress

The first and final authority for procurement rule-making in the United States is the Congress. Congress writes its policy into law, exercising the authority of the sovereign. Laws are written to protect and promote the public interest and to promote fair play among contractors. Congress establishes the framework for procurement but until enactment of the Competition In Contracting Act of 1984, left most administrative detail to lesser bodies--the administrative agencies of the government. CICA differs in laying down detailed administrative procedures. It raises a difficult question. Has Congress breached the level of detail at which the rigidity of statutory policy should be imposed upon the procurement process? An administrator can easily change an unsuccessful policy, but the process of statute modification directly involving the political process and positions of elected legislators is much more cumbersome.

There is more prestige and potential for enforcement in a measure passed by elected representatives and signed by the President than in administrative regulation. But statutes have rigidity that administrative regulation may avoid. The questions raised by CICA will be answered over time, but at this writing the Congress has spoken through CICA directing in the strongest possible terms that U. S. government procurement should be awarded using competitive procedures.

Authorization and funding statutes, for better or for worse, represent the congressional power of the purse and the legislative means for controlling the government. The Congress does not buy and manage; these are executive functions. But the Congress can approve or deny authority or funds requested for these purposes.

Even without the formal enactment of law, Congress intervenes in the procurement process in many ways. It seeks information to legislate more effectively, and it investigates and holds hearings to expose administrative excesses or deficiencies. The chairmen of congressional committees may request a given course of action, such as withholding a regulation or contract award pending the outcome of an investigation. Committee reports contain frequent cautions and admonitions, requests for information, restrictive language on expenditures and other directives or instructions which are ignored at the risk of reprisal in future authorization and funding legislation.

Office of Federal Procurement Policy

The role of the Office of Procurement Policy is to provide central policy direction for procurement. Since its establishment in 1974, the office has developed OMB circulars, OFPP policy letters, and numerous other policy documents. In the area of procurement policy, the office functions as the only entity with executive branch-wide authority. As a result, the OFPP has an opportunity to make strategic and far reaching improvements in the efficiency, effectiveness, and economy of government procurement.

Of the various projects sponsored by the OFPP to date, the most ambitious is probably the writing of the Federal Acquisition Regulation (FAR). The FAR project began in January 1978 and was completed with its implementation in April 1984. It is a single federal acquisition regulation replacing the Federal Procurement Regulations and major portions of the Defense Acquisition Regulations as well as portions of the regulations issued by other agencies. Since the General Services Administration, the Department of Defense, and the National Aeronautics and Space Administration have procurement policy issuance authority, these three agencies have been directly involved in developing and jointly issuing the new FAR. Although the FAR was implemented in April, 1984, passage of the CICA three months later initiated a substantial rewriting of the regulation. The leadership and coordination team for the new regulation is staffed by DOD and GSA but is a responsibility of OFPP, which holds statutory authority to issue regulations in the event DOD, NASA, and GSA are unable to agree on needed policy change.

In the management of federal procurement, the OFPP represents an important step. Prior to its creation, no single or central organization existed within the executive branch of the government whose purpose was to consider the effects of procurement practices or to evaluate the personnel capabilities of those who actually perform the federal purchasing operations.

OFPP is an organizational innovation. It holds no operating responsibilities and has neither the staff nor authorization to function in an acquisition role. Acquisition functions and personnel remain within the jurisdiction of the procuring agencies. Furthermore, the OFPP was not given exclusive policymaking authority. The basic structure still exists where the numerous executive agencies all promulgate policies that govern agency-unique aspects of procurement. OFPP, although established within the OMB as a part of the executive branch and subject to the direction of the President, is also directly granted specific powers. The Administrator must report annually (and at other times) to the Congress. To facilitate his work, Congress directed executive agencies to make their services, personnel, and facilities available and to provide information and records to him as requested. This unique status gives OFPP great potential influence over improvement of the procurement system. However, at the time of this writing, the effectiveness of the Administrator and the longevity of the office are not yet fully established.

During its short life, the OFPP has not been without controversy. It is believed that the first two administrators resigned their positions under pressure because certain projects were associated with controversial issues. Illustrative of the controversy associated with its actions are:

1. Criticism of OFPP's regulatory authority as giving the OFPP powers of review and approval which other agencies, particularly the Department of Defense (DOL) and the Department of Labor (DOL), felt to be

beyond the intent of Congress. Some agencies, such
as DOD, have even objected to the existence of OFPP.

2. Continuance of the use of the Walsh-Healy Act,
   rather than the Service Contract Act, for engine
   overhaul, maintenance and repair contracts. This
   issue resulted from a contrary action of the (DOL)
   and raised the fundamental question of whether procurement policy of the OFPP or labor policy interpretations by DOL should govern.

3. Government make-or-buy policy covering cost comparison guidelines. Policy in this area is discussed in
   Chapter 7, but it is an area under OFPP cognizance.
   It remains hotly controversial whether commercial/in-
   dustrial types of activities should be performed
   in-house or under contract and whether economic
   criteria like cost comparisons should be the basis
   for decisions.

Substantial controversy over cost comparison practices arose because they could affect existing institutional matters such as employment levels. A revised
supplement for application of OMB circular A-76, entitled
"Performance of Commercial Activities," dated August,
1983, was issued to guide and control the process by
which agencies are to prepare and carry out cost comparisons. Chapter 7 is an examination of this matter.

The foregoing items are examples of issues that
arise at the policymaking level. There are many others.
The role of the OFPP in these matters is new, but it has
caused questions to surface which have remained unresolved for protracted periods of time. It is hoped that
the work of OFPP will encourage more effective procurement planning and strategy development.

Some of the controversies associated with early
actions of the OFPP were less of a problem during the
administration of Mr. Donald E. Sowle. Mr. Sowle's experience included work as Director of Studies for the Commission on Government Procurement. His philosophy is shown
in the following statement:

. . . we must be wary, I believe, of providing
quick solutions to longstanding issues of substance.

Instead, we must move methodically to describe and establish a structure by which solutions to substantive issues can be identified, studied and resolved in a thoughtful systematic fashion. It is that fundamental structure that we are attempting to define in our current proposals. While we will not be dealing immediately with "burning" issues affecting one policy or another, we will be treating with issues of structure. For example, I don't believe that our proposals would recommend specific increases in absolute dollar thresholds for various socio-economic programs (an issue of substance). I do believe, however, that we should propose establishing mechanisms for the continuing review and establishment of increases in such thresholds (an issue of structure). To take the other approach would, I am convinced, result in our becoming bogged down in a morass of highly controversial and complex matters which are not necessary to resolve in order to develop the system and the draft statute.

Mr. Sowle's approach seems to have worked. Under his tenure the OFPP was again reauthorized, the first presidential executive order on procurement was issued, the FAR was issued, several statutes influenced by his office were enacted, and a revised productivity management orientation was given to OMB Circular A-76. All this with no clamor for his removal.

Rulemaking and
Policy Development

Rulemaking in federal procurement receives almost more attention than the acquisition of goods and services. Since the power to buy involves immediate application of public monies at organizational locations too numerous and incidental to be individually visible, extraordinary measures in the form of detailed statutory, regulatory and management issuances have developed to define, prescribe, standardize and control the whole system. Thus we see many statutes, regulations, management issuances, and as many sources of such rules as there are federal agencies. Additionally, since large segments of the industrial community are directly affected by the rules, participation of industry representatives and associations in the rulemaking process is extensive.

The primary rulemakers, however, are members of Congress, the OFPP, the procuring agencies themselves, the Comptroller General, and agencies with a particular clientele, such as the Department of Labor and the Small Business Administration (SBA). Of these, the most prolific rulemaker has also been the largest buyer--the Department of Defense. The DOD has proven to be a leader in procurement policy development, perhaps, if for no other reason, because of its extensive experience and expertise in procurement situations. The General Services Administration (GSA), in its role as developer of the Federal Procurement Regulations, has also been a major contributor to policy development.

The future development of federal procurement regulations will be led by two councils, the Civilian Agency Acquisition Council (CAAC) and the Defense Acquisition Review Council (DARC). DOD and NASA will staff the DARC and the major civilian agencies will staff the CAAC. The FAR is a significant step in procurement policy development.

The Federal Acquisition Regulation (FAR)

A new book was published on April 1, 1984, which is very important to the people of the United States, but it will not be reviewed by any of the literary journals. This book is entitled "The Federal Acquisition Regulation" or, the "FAR." Produced over a period of six years by a team of several dozen writers, it affects the efficiency and effectiveness with which a large portion of our productive economy will operate in the coming decades. The lack of popular reporting on the FAR results from the fact that it is a regulation designed to prescribe, structure and control the methods and procedures by which business is conducted in a defined segment of our economy--government procurement. Appendix 4 outlines the FAR in detail.

Becoming familiar with the government's method of doing business is essential to government workers in the field, and to those who market goods or services to the government. For private business it leads to profitable business opportunities and avoidance of pitfalls, an unpleasant and frequent occurrence for unwary government contractors.

Many have found the government buying process to be arcane and difficult to master, complex for many reasons, such as its magnitude and diversity. The FAR should reduce these difficulties. It contains eight subchapters that are meaningful in terms of the subjects covered, a refreshing change from predecessor regulations. Further subdivisions include 53 parts and 231 subparts dealing with specific subjects.

The FAR should be carefully reviewed by those affected by it including all who have become used to the other numerous government procurement regulations. One objective of the team of FAR writers was to avoid changing policy inadvertantly, yet to logically reorganize and simplify it to improve readability. The product, a single procurement regulation with government-wide applicability, seems to have achieved those objectives.

For several months, commentators who are expert in government procurement have questioned numerous aspects of the new regulation. Most severely criticised are the unknown possibilities for conflict and litigation which may be incorporated by means of language changes from pre-existing regulatory systems developed over a period of about thirty-five years which dealt with the same federal procurement process. The predecessor regulations included the Defense Acquisition Regulation, previously known as the Armed Services Procurement Regulation, which was developed under the authority of the Armed Services Procurement Act (ASPA) of 1947 and the Federal Procurement Regulations which were based on the Federal Property and Administrative Services Act (FPASA) of 1949. In addition, the new regulation supercedes significant portions of the National Aeronautics and Space Administration Regulation (based on the National Aeronautics and Space Act of 1958). Each of the other government agencies that issue significant numbers of contracts also has developed a set of regulations pertinent to its internal contrac-

ting and procurement operations. These too are super-
seded, at least in part, by the Federal Acquisition Regulation. (Their trimmed down versions have become
"supplements" to the FAR.) The preexistence of these
substantial documents, and the long period of time over
which each has been applied and interpreted by practitioners, lawyers, courts, and boards, raises concern over
potential hidden impacts that may be derived from the new
issuance.

This discussion is oriented somewhat differently
from that of most of the commentators who have published
articles on the FAR. Niceties of language and pitfalls
which may arise because of changes in language are really
secondary questions. The important question regarding
use of the Federal Acquisition Regulation is, will it
facilitate effective management of government contracting
operations, or will it simply continue the practices in
existence for many years, which have tended to discourage
innovative and creative managerial action? The stated
purpose of the FAR system is to codify uniform policies
and procedures for acquisition by all executive agencies.
The system is actually made up of the FAR and agency
supplements to it. Issuance of agency supplements is
authorized to implement or supplement the FAR when necessary in establishing and controlling the relationship
between the agency and the contractor. Agency supplements should not be issued when they repeat material
already contained in the FAR, or revise FAR materials,
unless a deviation has been processed through the appropriate government-wide review council.

Questions regarding the effectiveness of management
under the regulation might begin with consideration of
the management process set up for the administration of
the regulation itself. The FAR is not issued by a single
authority but by agreement between the Secretary of Defense, the Administrator of NASA, and the Administrator
of the General Services Administration. This arrangement
was keynoted by congressional action. Congress refused
to consolidate the ASPA and the FPASA into one procurement statute. However, Congress supported the idea of a
single government-wide regulation. As a consequence the
executive branch has formulated and will maintain the FAR
working under the preexisting statutory foundation, even

though recent legislation, including CICA, has changed the government procurement system in other ways. Under this arrangement the FAR, although it is a single government-wide regulation, will be the product of negotiation beween the three respective agencies. The maintenance of the regulation is a responsibility of the CAAC and the DARC as discussed earlier.

These two councils are supported by a FAR secretariat which is established as a responsibility of the General Services Administration. The agency level secretariat and councils develop revisions or modifications, and interpret the rules which have been promulgated. The Administrator of Federal Procurement Policy is vested with authority to resolve controversies between the respective agencies or between the councils over the issuance of a Federal Acquisition Regulation modification. Although OFPP has power to intervene, it is likely that the agencies would be reluctant to pass the responsibility for decision to that office.

There is a legitimate question whether the United States government needs the extensive regulatory structure that it has in order to accomplish its procurement. An objective analysis of what is required to buy materials for the government requires the conclusion that a significant part of government buying is no different from purchasing by companies and lower levels of government. Even when the object of procurement differs in substance, the actual process—solicitation, proposal, agreement, award and performance—is not fundamentally different from that carried on by all organizations in the country. Regardless, the history of the United States government seems to totally reject any thought that less regulation of procurement might be profitable or possible. The FAR has not reduced regulation—it has reorganized it. For several years to come it will result in expansion and increased complexity because existing contracts will continue to be guided by predecessor regulations. The issue of actual reduction in regulation has not been seriously considered. The trend toward increased regulation is keynoted by the Competition in Contracting Act of 1984, passed into law three months after implementation of the FAR and requiring major revision and expansion of regulatory prescription. The need for a comprehensive regulation system is a function of the nature of government--particularly the U.S. government--with its open political processes and the extraordinarily efficient means by which its actions are made public. Public airing of perceived deficiencies in the process generates quick fixes in legislation, often with consequent increases in procedural steps that may cost more than the correction saves.

To gain perspective, the reader should recognize that most well organized corporate entities develop a set of procurement policies and procedures for the guidance of its personnel. These policy and procedure materials are ordinarily published in a manual which is readily available to employees. However, a comparison of the government's procurement regulations with the policies and procedures of other buying organizations is a gross oversimplification. The average policy manual published by corporate America is intended to direct the internal relationships and actions of the personnel employed by its publisher. Very little information directly impacts the mode of operation of the suppliers of those buying organizations. By contrast, the Federal Acquisition Regulation is principally concerned with the behavior, actions and procedures of the supplier. To illustrate, the part of the FAR devoted to solicitation provisions, contract clauses, and contract forms, is equal in volume to the entire first fifty-one sections of the regulation which contain the instructions for carrying out the procurement policies of the government. One does not have to examine the solicitation provisions, clauses, and forms for very long to discover that most of the material is directed toward controlling the policies and practices of the supplier rather than the government employee. Furthermore, many of the first fifty-one parts of FAR prescribe rules affecting supplier practices--not government practices. The need for these comprehensive regulations is partly justified by public interest concerns, such as control of cost when competition is not effective, pursuit of social or economic objectives, and acquiring service or products not of use except in government (such as many defense products). Much of the regulatory complexity is created in an effort to respond to profiteering and excessive prices that are periodically discovered. Regardless of these proper concerns, the comprehensive regulatory scheme represented by FAR and its agency supplements has become an objective in itself. Government procurement personnel must first become expert in the regulation. They may then become expert in the matters pertinent to what they buy. Unfortunately, the processes of change in the regulation system are so active, little time is left for creating expertise in the object of the purchase.

The Comptroller General (CG)

One agency stands out as the key element in legislative oversight of federal procurement. That agency is the General Accounting Office (GAO), organized as an arm of the Congress and headed by the Comptroller General. The audit and reporting activities of the GAO have greatly impacted (in fact, have led to) many of the policies, systems, procedures, attitudes, and philosophies which today are the federal processes of procurement. Both Congress and writers of procurement regulation are attentive to the work of the GAO.

The U.S. General Accounting Office is an independent, nonpolitical agency in the legislative branch of the government. It provides the Congress, its committees and members with information, analyses and recommendations concerning operations of the government, with primary reference to the executive branch. GAO concerns itself with how the federal departments and agencies, through their programs and activities, carry out the mandate or intent of legislation enacted by the Congress. Therefore, it plays an important part in the legislative oversight role of the Congress.

The office was established by the Budget and Accounting Act of 1921. Since then, GAO's responsibility and authority have been considerably broadened by various acts of the Congress and by interpretations of its powers by the Comptroller.

The Comptroller General plays an influential, often dominant role in the government's contracting activities. This position is one of the most powerful offices in government. The CG has unusual independence because a single appointment is made for a period of fifteen years, during which time the appointee cannot be removed from office except for just cause by joint resolution of Congress. The office is able to exercise great influence through audit and investigative activities, even though its statutory base has in some respects been vague as to its delegation of authority and power. The GAO has been at or near the center of almost every major controversy involving contracts of the federal government.

Nor has GAO's impact on the procurement process been confined to matters within the government. Exposures and criticism of waste, inefficiency, and poor negotiation practices have led to the adoption of numerous statutes and regulations which shape and control many activities of government contractors. For example, GAO audit reports and testimony before Congress were principal factors leading to passage of the Truth in Negotiations Act and later, the Cost Accounting Standards Act. The GAO has become the forum for resolution of competing offeror's protests, and CG decisions are the primary source of guidance relating to permissible uses of appropriated funds. The GAO is considered by many to be the final word on the propriety of questionable payments.

Until passage of the CICA the CG had not been expressly granted powers with respect to contract protests. GAO activity in the field has resulted in an extremely important decisionmaking process. Under the Budget and Accounting Act of 1921, the CG holds the power to settle and adjust government accounts. Since procurement involves the expenditure of federally appropriated funds under specific statutory and regulatory guidelines, the CG asserted an extensive role in the field of bid protests under which GAO has reviewed in detail the administrative procedures of federal agencies. These reviews are aimed at determining whether the agency (in its procurement process) has complied with the statutes, policies and regulations which govern federal procurement procedures. As a result, past decisions on protest cases are used as a guide in the development of government practice during the bidding and awarding of government contracts.

Quite independently of his role in protests, the CG answers questions asked by federal agencies that are uncertain of the appropriate procedure to follow under contractual circumstances. The CG's rulings in these cases are generally final with respect to the federal administrative agency.

Through legislation, Congress has given the GAO authority to initiate reviews and audits pertaining to government operations. These reviews are directed toward areas of direct interest to the Congress and to areas which, in the CG's judgment, show the greatest apparent need or potential benefit to the government. Specific factors that influence the decision to make an audit or review include:

1. Statutory requirements
2. Congressional requests and indications of congressional interest
3. Potential areas of improvement in government operations
4. Areas which have been identified as involving weaknesses in management controls and operations
5. Deviation of agency policies from congressional intent
6. Programs with large expenditures, assets or revenues.

The duties of the GAO in auditing the operations of executive agencies include examination of contract activities. To facilitate this, the Congress has required inclusion of a clause in negotiated contracts that allows the GAO access to pertinent records of government contractors.

Audits of negotiated contracts may include:

1. Type of contract selected--it may be any of several fixed price or cost reimbursable types
2. Review of the contractor's cost representations and pricing proposals
3. Comparison of the contractor's cost estimates with his cost experience
4. Costs incurred in those cases in which reimbursement is based on or affected by actual costs
5. Review of the contractor's negotiation and administration of subcontracts.

Audits of contractors are coordinated with reviews of administrative agency actions during negotiation and administration of contracts. Underlying causes of poor or costly procurement practices are sought, and recommendations are made for improving contracting practices and administration.

Since the GAO is an agent of the Congress, its primary reporting responsibility is to the Congress. A report to the Congress is made for specific contract audits if, in the GAO's judgment, the information is significant, or if the conclusions reached and the knowledge gained is of interest to the Congress and its committees. Those reports given to Congress provide a significant source of information which is utilized by the Congress in exercising legislative oversight and considering authorization and appropriation requests by the executive branch. If the findings, conclusions and recommendations in GAO reports do not require action by the Congress or are not of interest to the Congress or its committees, the reports are then issued directly to the agency or department officials concerned.

Major weapons procurements have regularly dominated other procurement programs in terms of dollar magnitude. As a result, Congress (and the public) expresses deep concern when, as often occurs, actual costs exceed by significant amounts the initial estimates of costs for system development and production. Also, when time schedules and deliveries are extended, and when deployment of the system is deferred, studies and investigations of the reasons are to be expected. (Often actual performance characteristics of the systems fall substantially short of those expected from the original plan.)

The GAO has responded to these concerns by designating a special staff to make continuous reviews of major weapons systems which are in the various stages of the acquisition cycle. The primary objective of the system acquisition review is the determination of the basic causes of weapon system cost growth, schedule slippage, and deterioration of the originally expected performance characteristics. A secondary objective is identification of the options available for the remainder of a program and development of recommendations for improving the acquisition process. Reports resulting from these continuing reviews provide a means for keeping the Congress and interested committees informed on the progress and status of the major programs. The reports are valuable tools used in formulating decisions affecting authorization and appropriation of funds for the programs.

The impact of the GAO on the procurement process becomes readily apparent when one considers the scope of its audit and reporting duties. It is involved indirectly but strongly influences formulation of procurement policies and procedures.

The Procuring Agencies

In many respects, policy formulation at the agency level is more pertinent to the management of procurement than those of the GAO, the OFPP, and congressional levels. The agencies have developed procurement regulations (FAR Supplements), and each has also established management issuance systems as guidelines for operating executives to manage and control their resources. Much of the material included in management issuance systems (such as DOD directives and instructions) is concerned with internal management, staffing, organization, control and reporting processes. However, these systems include directives and instructions that vitally affect procurement management. (Examples include project organization and management instructions, major systems acquisition directives, source selection procedures, configuration management directives and instructions, and a multitude of others.)

One of the issues raised by the DOD in connection with the OFPP's regulatory authority was concern that OFPP would interject itself in the issuance of agency management documents whenever a procurement policy matter might be involved. Total resolution of this issue is difficult, because management and procurement policies are not independent elements of agency business. There is general agreement that procurement regulations are an identifiable subset of overall management policy issuances.

Notes

[1]Public Law 91-129.

[2]Report of the Commission on Government Procurement, Volumes 1, 2, 3 and 4, U.S. Government Printing Office, December 31, 1972.

[3]Ibid. Volume 1, Appendix D, p. 155.

[4]Report of the Commission on Government Procurement, Volume 1, p. 6.

[5]Ibid., p. 7.

[6]Public Law 93-400.

[7]The decisions of the Comptroller General are published in Comptroller General's Procurement Decisions, Federal Publications, Inc., Washington, D.C.

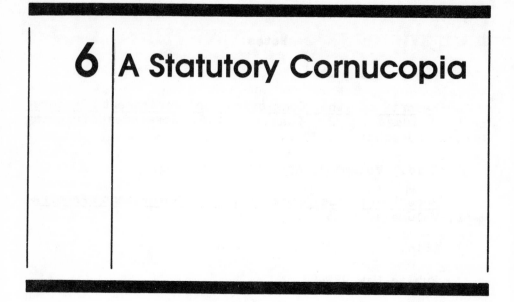

6 | A Statutory Cornucopia

It is not an overstatement to say that the 98th Congress of the United States generated a horn of plenty with its activities in the procurement area. Congress-watchers enumerated at least one hundred-fifty separate procurement-related bills introduced during its sessions. Many of those bills were the subject of hearings and prolonged discussions generated by constant media reports of deficiencies in the government procurement system, particularly the DOD procurement system. This plentiful supply of legislative proposals contained many duplicate and contradictory initiatives. One theme seemed to emerge from this activity: Congress believed that more effort was required to obtain competition in procurement.

A Keynote for Government Procurement: Competition

In terms of completed legislation, one statute may stand out as being the keynote for government procurment processes during the next decade and perhaps for much longer. The Congress enacted, and the President signed, the Competition in Contracting Act of 1984. The act was passed as Title VII of the Spending Reduction Act and Deficit Reduction Act of 1984. While each portion of the overall enactment has ramifications for different aspects of government operations, it is the competition in contracting portion that is likely to have the greatest long term impact on the contracting operations of the government. Additionally, it may have significant impact on the operations of the private sector especially that part of it which deals with the government on a contract basis.

It seems appropriate to examine this new statute, Public Law 98-369, in some detail. It has reversed long-standing public policy concerning the administrative procedures associated with the solicitation and award of public contracts by the United States government. Furthermore, the statute addresses numerous specific details and issues which have accumulated over the years as matters of concern with respect to the operation of the public contracting system. In fact, the detail to which the Congress has gone in prescribing rules and procedures for the procurement of goods and services has generated the allegation that Congress has descended from its role as a legislature and entered into the daily routine of decisionmaking and processing of contract actions, previously the sole domain of the executive branch. In effect, it has been alleged that the Congress has micromanaged, or perhaps microlegislated, how the government should spend its money through this mechanism. While such allegations are debatable, there is no question but that a significant amount of new statutory prescription has been introduced into the world of government purchasing.

The new statute is an amalgamation of bills which have been considered in the 98th Congress bringing together parts of several Senate and House resolutions. Much of the new statute amends the Federal Property and Administrative Services Act, the Armed Services Procurement Act, and the Office of Federal Procurement Policy Act. It has made substantive changes regarding the essential nature of the government contracting system. Probably the most significant traditional practice of the government altered by this statute was its historic preference for formal advertising; the preference has been abandoned. This decision by Congress follows the 1972 Report of the Commission on Government Procurement (chartered by Congress in 1969) which included a recommendation that the two principal modes in which the government issues solitations and receives bids or proposals--that is, formal advertising and negotiated procurement--should have equal standing under the law. The decision reverses nearly two centuries of tradition.

Although the elimination of the preference for formal advertising is a drastic change in terms of the traditional position of the government, the practical impact of the decision is probably not very great. It has been evident for many years that formal advertising was not the predominant mode of operation for government contracting. For practical purposes, the statutory mandate for formal advertising has been set aside during wartime, and has been ineffective since enactment of the Armed Services Procurement Act of 1947. That act set forth seventeen exceptions under which the requirement for formal advertising could be waived by the executive agency. Since that time, relatively little procurement has been awarded under the formal advertising scheme. In a statistical sense, approximately 90 percent of all government contract dollars is spent via the negotiated procurement technique, and it is likely that the 10 percent or so of government contracting which has been formally advertised through the current time frame will continue to be handled in that manner.

The Paperwork Impacts

There is one practical impact of dropping the preference for formal advertising; it should reduce procurement administrative lead time (PALT). Traditionally, much effort has been devoted to writing formal determinations and findings and processing requests for authority to negotiate through all echelons of the government agency. That reduction of the administrative process is significant, because it frees administrative time for other duties which may be more important than processing the required papers.

It would be a mistake to leave this subject without immediately addressing the additions to the administrative process which this new statute imposes on the executive branch. There are several new innovations requiring substantial internal administrative processing to enable the government to issue a contract. Whether the new administrative processes will take more or less time than those which have been abandoned may be debatable. Nevertheless, review of the new requirements by this author has resulted in the conclusion that substantial net increases will occur in the administrative processing time, and in the amount of effort required of government procurement people to issue a contract.

Those aspects of the new legislation which will require significant administrative effort include: (1) preparation and processing of justifications for noncompetitive procurement; (2) carrying out enhanced public notification requirements in the Commerce Business Daily with time delay imposed prior to the release of solicitations and additional time between CBD publication and award of contracts; (3) fulfilling statutory requirements for advanced procurement planning and market research; (4) requiring, reviewing, and analyzing cost and pricing data at the reduced threshold level of $100 thousand; (5) accommodating procurement operations to reviews by a new, statutory, advocate for competition appointed for each procurement activity within each awarding agency; (6) accommodating executive agency actions to GAO regulations (yet to be issued) which are required by Congress' creation of a statutory basis for the General Accounting Office to perform its traditional function as the resolver of bid protest actions; (7) formulating administrative practices necessary to support the new authority of the General Services Administration Board of Contract Appeals to review (and, if necessary, suspend action on) ADP procurements against which a bid protest has been lodged.

Much of the language and many of the provisions of this new legislation are items that have been recommended to the Congress by the Office of Federal Procurement Policy (for example, in its "Proposal for a Uniform Federal Procurement System") and by the other expert organizations in the field of government contracting. The total mix of new statutory requirements, some of which were not requested by the executive branch may have unpredicted results.

Congressional Direction and Policy Statements

The Congress' new statute, which the bureaucracy has now dubbed the CICA (pronounced seeka), contains a number of policy statements that are directives, but when carefully analyzed, really amount to congressional urging for the bureaucracy to do certain good things. One of these is that the government procurement organization develop an advanced procurement plan associated with its contracting activity, buttressed by market research. Although the advanced procurement plan is a term which has existed within the government for at least twenty-five years, this new legislative mandate clearly calls for better planning on the part of the government buying community. The evident thought behind this requirement is that the Congress does not believe the executive branch procuring work force is doing the kind of advanced thinking and planning necessary to achieve an effective and efficient procurement process, and specifically, one conducted on a competitive basis.

The legislation does not define an advanced procurement plan. However, there are several places in existing procurement regulations, policies, and in government management instructions where the required kind of thinking and the documentation process involved is spelled out. Several elements of the advanced procurement planning philosophy are incorporated in this book in Chapter 10.

The new legislation has imposed a requirement for agencies to engage in market research associated with their solicitation and award procedures. Again, the legislation does not define what a market research process involves. Furthermore, in the case of market research, it is not clear that the procurement work force is sophisticated in the research techniques necessary to tap the marketplace for information in a way that will carry out such a mandate. While government procurement people have for many years given at least some attention to the subject of advanced procurement planning, there are no historical precedents for presuming that those currently employed in the process are familiar with the concept of market research as a viable tool for assessing where to secure their needs.

In the academic world, market research generally has

been developed as a study within the marketing field of business administration. Substantial background and experience has been developed and recorded in this field, so that the concept of market research is well understood in certain circles. However, significant effort will be required to bring the government's procurement personnel up to an effective level of competence in applying the techniques of market research to their source finding, qualification, and selection responsibilities. Nevertheless, this is a challenging and attractive indication of the willingness of the Congress to introduce new kinds of thinking into the public bureaucracy. There is no question in the mind of this author that a thorough market research capability developed within the government's procurement hierarchy would substantially strengthen the ability of the government to effectively use and enhance competitive procedures.

In reading the new statutory injunctions, an objective observer may be concerned whether the demand for a competitive procurement posture overstates that objective. Will the bureaucracy seek competition for the sake of competition? Will the move toward greater competition drive executive action to the point that programmatic success, schedule, or cost issues will be lost or overwhelmed? Numerous government contracting and procurement activities involve work and missions which do not lend themselves to clearly competitive procedures. This is a very real concern on the part of objective analysts of the procurement process. If the nature of a project does not allow competitive procedures to operate effectively, the creation of competitive conditions (as compared with noncompetitive procedures) may require an investment cost and time delay, impacting total costs and schedules adversely. This possibility reinforces the need for procurement personnel to develop a thorough understanding of the market environment in which they are seeking goods and services. With that increased knowledge, they should be able to make a far better judgment as to the most effective method of achieving their needs. The implied coupling of market research with moves to increase competitive procurement could prove to be a significant step toward improved government contracting.

A third injunction of the Congress is for the government procurement expert to find a way to simplify and to streamline the procurement process. This objective is not new, but the clear statutory statement in favor of a simpler process is a welcome perspective. Unfortunately, in reviewing and analyzing the government's contracting environment, it appears almost impossible that simplification could take place. Congress has indicated it wants a simpler procurement process--that's helpful--but it regularly imposes upon the government bureaucracy an increasing array of socioeconomic or procedural requirements and oversight or review checkpoints. These must be carried out in performing the procurment function and detract from the desire for simplification. As an example, the very statute that we are now talking about, CICA, includes a significant increase in the administrative requirements. It is not likely that true simplification or clarification of the contracting work of the government is going to occur regardless of the words which exist in the statute.

The simplification objective itself will demand that substantial effort be addressed to studying and attempting to find ways to make the procurement process simpler and more understandable to the average person. Legislators should note that it is far easier for the government official to fulfill specific congressional policies (such as writing justifications for a noncompetitive process, preparing a document such as an advance procurement plan, or responding to a bid protest filed with the Comptroller General) than it is to devise ways to explain and/or restructure the procurement process in a simpler, more clearly stated, fashion.

A fourth area in which the Congress has provided strong advice to the federal bureaucracy is in the use of more commercial products to fulfill government needs. The legislation states that the government should purchase commercial products wherever and whenever such items will meet its needs. This clear statutory policy is a helpful indication of intent. Nevertheless, achieving a significant increase in the number of commercial products which the government buys, vis-a-vis products which the government narrowly defines through writing its own specifications, is extremely difficult. A large bureaucratic organizational commitment in terms of

people, facilities and processes is devoted to the development and use of specifications requiring nonstandard
products. Furthermore, the government's historical preference for formal advertising has been interpreted for
years as requiring it to develop detailed specifications
for the products it wants to buy, so that formal advertising may be employed. The new legislative thrust to
abandon the mandatory use of formal advertising and to
express government preference for commercial products
over those uniquely designed for the government, could
introduce significant savings in the procurement process
and broaden competition.

A fifth area (but one that is related to the commercial product preference) in which the Congress has directed the bureaucracy to improve is in the use of functional specifications, a type of specification not defined in
the new legislation. However, it is well known among
procurement experts that a functional specification
states the manner in which the government intends to use
its product and permits selection of any product that
will meet that use. This type of specification is quite
different from the detailed design specification which
has traditionally been developed through the government's
standardization processes. The perceived advantage of
functional specifications is in the area of purchasing
commercial products. When a functional specification is
used, it should be feasible for competitive commercial
products having distinctive or unique design details to
meet its requirements. As a result, its use will permit
greater infusion of proven commercial products into the
government's system.

It should be noted that CICA also encourages the use
of performance specifications. When read carefully, CICA
gives no particular preference to either functional or
performance specifications, but calls for their development in such a manner that full and open competition will
be obtained. The performance specification differs from
the functional specification because it delineates specific measurable capabilities or parameters for which a
product can be tested as part of the acceptance procedure. Performance specifications have normally been used
in research and development procurement and it is probable they will continue in that use. It is unlikely that

they will be used extensively in the commericial product arena.

Each of the foregoing five congressional initiatives is incorporated into the CICA. While they set forth specific policies, they seem to be more like statements of objectives and do not establish clear standards by which one might state definitively that the bureaucracy is or is not complying.

CICA Innovations

Upon examination of the CICA, the government bureaucracy is discovering that several entirely new statutory injunctions have been established. The most significant of these innovations is the mandatory use of a competitive procedure. Having dropped its historic distinction between formal advertising and negotiated procurement, Congress has installed a new distinction between competitive and noncompetitive procurement procedures. This simple restatement of congressional policy should enhance its effectiveness because it addresses a real issue. For many years the formal advertising and negotiation distinction has been misinterpreted to imply that formal advertising is a competitive procedure and that negotiation is a noncompetitive procedure. Actually, competitive negotiation has been practiced for years, at least since 1962 when the Truth in Negotiations Act was passed. Nevertheless, Congress has replaced the old rule and established the concepts of sealed bidding and competitive proposals as distinctive, but generally equivalent, methods of buying materials and services.

Sealed Bidding

Of much greater importance than the change from the traditional distinction to a new one is the set of rules, and exceptions to the rules, now operative for all government procurement. The statute specifies that executive agencies shall obtain full and open competition through the use of competitive procedures. It then defines competitive procedures.

One form of competitive procedure is solicitation using sealed bids. When time permits its use, the sealed bidding procedure is to be used. The award will be based on price and other price-related factors after considering the solicitation, submission of bids, and evaluation processes necessary to make the award. When using the procedure, the agency should reasonably expect to receive more than one sealed bid in response to its solicitation and should not consider it necessary to conduct discussions with the sources submitting bids. These rules are similar to the traditional ones which governed formal advertising except for one major omission and one significant addition. The statutory statement includes no reference to the adequacy of the technical specification for use of a sealed bidding procedure. This omission is notable because traditionally the principal reason for not using formal advertising was the inadequacy of specifications for the highly structured procedural steps involved. However, the statute adds the concept that if it is not necessary to conduct discussions with the responding sources, then the sealed bid procedure is to be used. By implication, inadequate technical description of the job to be performed would remain a principal reason for having to conduct discussions. Reasonably interpreted, this rule may cover the question of the specification's adequacy.

Competitive Proposals

The second major competitive procedure identified by the statute is the competitive proposal procedure. It is considered appropriate when sealed bids are not pertinent to the requirement. With competitive proposals it is an expectation of the agency that it would hold discussions with each of the offerors, after receipt of their proposals, in the process of arriving at an agreement prior to the award of a contract. However, under competitive proposal procedure, the agency is required to reserve the right to award its contract without discussions. Such an award requires a determination by the agency that acceptance of the initial proposal would result in the lowest overall cost to the government.

Noncompetitive Procedure

The CICA enumerates seven circumstances under which the executive agency is allowed to conduct procedures other than competitive procedures. The enumeration includes a wide range of circumstances that presumably cover all of the situations in which a noncompetitive contract award should be made. The seven circumstances are precisely stated and quite detailed. They are summarized below; however, the reader should refer to the statute for an exact interpretation.

Agencies are allowed to use procedures other than competitive ones:

1. when only one responsible source is available and no alternative type of property or services will satisfy its needs.
2. under unusual and compelling urgency, when the government would be seriously injured unless the agency limited the number of solicited sources.
3. when restriction of an award to a particular source is required because of:
   (a) the necessity to maintain a particular source to ensure its availability in the event of national emergency or to achieve industrial mobilization or
   (b) the award is required in order to establish or maintain an essential engineering research or development capability provided by an educational or other nonprofit institution or a federally funded research and development center.
4. when the source is restricted under the terms of an international agreement or treaty or by direction of a foreign government that is reimbursing the executive agency for the cost of the procurement.
5. when the item is a brand name commercial item for authorized resale, or a statute expressly authorizes or requires that the source be restricted.
6. when national security requires that disclosure of the executive agency's requirement be limited to the particular source(s) from which it solicits the bid or proposal.
7. when the head of the executive agency determines it to be necessary in the public interest to use proce-

dures other than competitive procedures. This exception must be the subject of a written notification
to the Congress, thirty days in advance of the award
of the contract.

It is quite clear from the foregoing that the authority for noncompetitive procurement procedures is severely
restricted by the new statute. When one considers that
in excess of 60 percent of all government procurement
dollars is currently awarded on a noncompetitive basis,
the impact of the statute may be substantial. On the
other hand, the exceptions probably cover all or most of
the circumstances on the basis of which restricted source
procurements are currently being awarded. Nevertheless,
the explicit statutory requirements and the restricted
basis for exceptions, plus the notification and procedural requirements, coupled with the high level of agency
approval for noncompetitive procurement, create a strong
preference for using one of the two authorized competitive procedures.

Exclusion of Sources

The CICA has incorporated a new authority for agency
heads which may be significant in enhancing competition
but may also stimulate protests. The statute expressly
allows agency heads to exclude particular sources from a
competitive procurement, if such exclusion is necessary
to enhance competition in a particular service or supply
area. Authorization of this ambit for discretion is
extraordinary in government procedure. However, it
should be recognized that in normal commercial practice,
the key officials of private firms have always exercised
such discretion in connection with their basic management
prerogative and responsibility for effective performance
of their competitive business. The ability to exclude a
particular source, such as the existing one or a dominant
one, may be essential in order to protect or increase the
number of effective competitors. However, the government's open invitation (reinforced by CICA) to unsatis-
fied competitors to challenge (protest) the decisionmaking process could delay action.

CICA has introduced a new concept in authorizing agencies to restrict procurement to competition by small business firms. Agency heads are given this authority with the proviso that such a restriction is authorized only when all small business firms are allowed to compete for the procurement. This authority is separate from and does not supercede other small business policies which may permit award of a contract to small business without competition at all, such as under the SBA's Section 8(a).

Synopses

For many years, government contracting officers have been required to write synopses of their proposed procurement actions and to publish those synopses in the Department of Commerce's <u>Commerce Business Daily</u> (CBD). Congress has significantly expanded the mandatory use of the <u>Commerce Business Daily</u> for all government agencies subject to the act. The new rules mandate that (in part) virtually all solicitations involving $10 thousand or more be synopsized by the CBD at least fifteen days prior to release of the solicitation, and that deadlines for receipt of bids or proposals be not less than thirty days after publication of the synopsis. Notice of award also must be published for procurement actions of $25 thousand and over if subcontracting opportunities are likely to occur. The time frames undoubtedly are valid requirements with respect to the opening of procurement to greater competitive action, but they have a cost in the form of extension of the overall procurement administrative lead time (PALT) associated with all government procurement. The requirement decreases the administrative flexibility of the government's contracting processes.

In addition to specifying time requirements for synopses, the CICA also has delineated specific content for each synopsis as well as several exceptions to the requirement. These decisions to raise the status and improve the content of procurement synopses by statute have brought about a substantial expansion of the <u>Commerce Business Daily</u>. (In part, the requirements were enacted in earlier legislation by the 98th Congress in P.L. 98-72.)

In sampling the <u>Commerce Business Daily</u> in 1981 prior to the publication of the first edition of this book (see Chapter 2 and Appendix A), the author found that the maximum length of each issue of the CBD approximated thirty-two pages. Currently some issues run sixty-four pages. Each synopsis is somewhat more detailed and there are more of them in the publication. The requirements for an acceptable synopsis are, first, that it accurately describe the government's requirement without unnecessarily restricting the competition. Secondly, it must clearly state where a copy of the solicitation may be obtained and must provide the name, business address, and telephone number of the contracting officer responsible for the procurement. Third, it must contain a statement that all responsible sources may submit offers which shall be considered by the executive agency. In the event that the synopsis covers a procurement for which a restricted number of sources is established, that fact must be stated in the synopsis and include the basis or reason for the restriction, as well as the identity of the intended source of supply. It is clear from these requirements that the intent of Congress is for government procurement work to be fully disclosed and available to the general public.

The new requirements for publication provide an excellent basis for any dissatified potential competitor to challenge or protest the government's decisions regarding the specification it is using or the decision to use sole source, whenever the potential competitor finds such decisions to be unreasonable, restrictive, unfair, or not in accordance with congressional policy. At this early stage in the implementation of the new statute, it is not clear what impact this may have on the government's procurement process. A substantial amount of protest activity may be stimulated, in which case, a severe strain will be placed on the ability of the government to resolve them and to meet its procurement needs in a timely manner.

Synopses are not required in all situations. First, the possibility that disclosure of the agency's need would compromise national security is recognized as a valid basis for not publicizing. Secondly, any procurement resulting from the acceptance of an unsolicited pro-

posal may be awarded without synopsis. However, the
exception in unsolicited proposal cases would apply only
where information contained in the proposal is unique and
innovative and where its disclosure would compromise the
proprietary position of the originator. Third, procurement of perishable subsistence supplies need not be synop-
sized, nor must orders placed under a requirements contract. These exceptions to the requirement for publication may be sufficient to allow the government to carry
out its intended course of action and to protect the
interests of the parties. But again, some experience
with the statutory implementation of these policies will
be necessary prior to reaching final conclusions.

The Advocate for Competition

Perhaps a most significant innovation of this new
statute is the creation of a new position--the advocate
for competition. The advocate for competition is chartered by the Congress to be appointed by each executive
agency and for each procuring activity of the executive
agency. The advocate must be a senior official and must
not be burdened with other responsibilities which might
conflict with the advocacy role, such as duties involving
the procurement process. In addition, the advocate is to
be furnished with a staff and resources necessary to perform assigned work in a significant fashion. The statute
gives the competition advocate considerable power and
leverage with respect to the procurement officer of the
agency, since s/he will review and approve all noncompetitive sourcing procedures for contracts exceeding $100
thousand. Although the contracting officer originates
and prepares the justification for noncompetitive procurement, it is the advocate for competition who will now
decide whether the procurement can go forward on a sole
source basis. (For high-dollar procurements, the review
and approval authority rises to the procurement executive
or agency head.) An interesting sidelight to this statute is the decision of the Congress that the contracting
officer should originate the justification for noncompetitive procurement. Traditionally this responsibility has
been placed on the technical groups within an agency that

are knowledgeable of the technical requirements of the procurement, and who presumably have some knowledge of the capabilities of the private sector organizations which might carry out the required work. Approval of the justification was given by the contracting officer or higher authority, depending on the amount of the procurement. Another interesting sidelight is that the advocate for competition in OFPP's proposal for a Uniform Federal Procurement System was to be the procurement executive—a person fully responsible for procurement activity. Under the statute the advocate will be someone other than the procurement executive and thus independent of the procurement process. Again, it is not entirely clear at the time of this writing, how important or significant the advocate for competition may be in terms of the efficient and effecive prosecution of government contracting work. It is clear, however, that his role is not structured to expedite the agency's internal decisionmaking processes for issuing noncompetitive solicitations.

An additional administrative hurdle respecting noncompetitive procurement is the new requirement for each agency to periodically submit a report to Congress outlining its method for increasing competition in procurement. This reporting process will place the agency head, and all personnel under him, in the position of constantly searching out new ways to meet the requirement for competition. Coupled with this reporting requirement, the Congress has also imposed upon the agencies mandatory creation of a computerized record of all of its procurement transactions. Each record is to be maintained for a period of five years. The record must be categorized by whether or not the procurement was awarded on a competitive basis.

The sections of CICA establishing the synopsis, the advocate for competition, the reporting, and the computerized record requirements, (and, in fact, the entire statute) are strongly oriented toward increasing competition. References to the economic, programmatic, or social objectives of creating competition are almost entirely omitted. It is the omission of any treatment of these objectives (beyond the creation of competition) that is most questionable in respect to the long run effectiveness and success of the act. Although the portion of the statute that amends the Armed Services Procurement Act (Subtitle B amends Title 10, U.S. Code) sets forth a statement of defense procurement policy that speaks of timeliness, economy and efficiency, there is no place where seeking competition is coupled with objectives of cost savings, innovation, schedule benefits, or economy and efficiency. One must, therefore, be concerned that the statute will encourage competition for competition's sake, regardless of other effects.

Protest Procedure - Comptroller General

CICA's imposition of increased synopsis and documentation requirements associated with procurement procedures is coupled with the creation of a statutory foundation for the protest hearing activities of the Comptroller General of the United States. The Comptroller's procedures have developed over a period of approximately forty years beginning with the Budget and Accounting Act of 1921. The Comptroller General, through interpretation of that statute, has asserted the authority to make a review and to decide on the validity of contract awards made by government procuring agencies. CICA, for the first time, gives the work a statutory foundation. This appears to add significantly to the leverage and influence that the Comptroller General may exercise over government procurement actions and expenditures. Under the statute, the Comptroller General is called to issue new protest regulations that implement his new authority. However, the statute itself contains the most significant points because, within the statute, agencies are almost barred from proceeding with procurement actions if the Comptroller General is reviewing a bid protest which has been filed on time and in accordance with his procedures. Once a protest has been filed, and the Comptroller General has notified the agency that he is considering the protest, the agency cannot award a contract unless the head of the agency's procuring activity makes a written finding that urgent and compelling circumstances require the award of a contract and notifies the Comptroller General of that finding. Even in the case of a contract which has been awarded at the time that the notice of protest is supplied to the agency, the statute requires that the agency immediately direct the contractor to stop his performance effort. The contract performance may not be resumed while the protest is pending unless the head of the procuring activity has made a finding that performance of the contract is in the best interest of the United States or that urgent and compelling circumstances require continuation without delay. The Comptroller General must be notified of this finding.

The Comptroller General is directed by the statute to establish an inexpensive and expeditious method of resolving any protests which may be filed. His procedure must provide for final decisions on protests to be made within ninety working days after the date the protest is submitted to him. Adjustment of that time restraint is possible if the Comptroller General determines, and states in writing, the reasons for extending the time period. The Comptroller General also has authority to dismiss a protest if he determines that it is frivolous or on its face, does not state a valid basis for protest.

When the Comptroller General, in his decision on a case, finds a valid basis exists for the protest, the statute directs him to recommend any of several potential actions: (1) the agency should refrain from exercising any of its options under the contract;   (2) it should issue a new solicitation;   (3) it should recompete the contract immediately;   (4) it should terminate the contract;   (5) an award should be made which is consistent with the requirements of the statute or regulation which has been violated. In addition, the Comptroller General may recommend any combination of these actions or may make an entirely different recommendation. Furthermore, the Comptroller General is required to make his recommendations without regard to any cost or disruption which might occur because of the determination, recompeting, or reawarding process which may follow. The Comptroller General is also empowered to make a monetary award to a protestant covering costs of filing and pursuing the protest (including reasonable attorneys' fees) and bid and proposal preparation, if it is determined that the award or proposed award did not comply with a statute or regulation. These awards shall be paid out of funds of the agency available for the procurement of property and services. The Justice Department has ordered agencies to ignore these provisions for protest as unconstitutional. An early court test is highly likely.

Special Protest Procedure for ADP

The CICA introduces a new test procedure for hearing and decision concerning bid protests over automated data processing procurements. It establishes the General Services Administration Board of Contract Appeals (GSA-BCA) as the review authority for all such procurements. This review authority applies to all ADP procurements which are conducted under the procurement authority of the administrator of GSA or a delegation of his procurement authority for automated data processing procurements. This review authority could affect all agencies of the government, since, under the Brooks Act of 1965, all general purpose automated data processing equipment must be procured by the Administrator of General Services or pursuant to a delegation issued by him. CICA now gives the GSA-BCA authority to suspend the administrator's procurement authority or his delegations of procurement authority during the processing of protests filed with the board. The full procedural powers of the board, including discovery, may be brought to bear upon the review of the protest. The board is required to make its final decision within forty-five days after the date of filing of the protest. Also, once a protest has been filed, the board has discretion to suspend, revoke or revise the procurement authority or the delegation of procurement authority under which the challenged procurement is being processed. Such a decision by the board stops the government action. The board can suspend even if the contract has already been awarded. However, the involved government agency can assert urgent and compelling circumstances that significantly affect the interests of the United States. If the agency position is persuasive, the board would hold the suspension in abeyance.
This procedure appears to be duplicative of the bid protest procedures established for the Comptroller General. The basic filing and suspension and hearing proce-

dures are similar. However, there is a distinction to be made because boards of contract appeals have tradition- ally been used only for the hearing and resolution of disputes arising out of a contract. In the case of bid protests no contract exists, and the nature of the consi- derations which must be given to the protest do not fall under the provisions of any contract. Rather, the pro- test procedure is a means for examining whether an agency has followed its regulatory requirements and complied with statutes as it conducted a procurement process.

CICA Definitions and/or Detailed Guidance

The CICA is different from many earlier statutory products in its detailed instructions and definitions of selected terms. In most earlier procurement legislation, the Congress has set its policies in broader terms, leav- ing details to the agencies, boards of contract appeal, and the General Accounting Office. Some examples of its work follow.

First, the statute states that architectural and engineering solicitations (which must follow congression- ally specified procedures), are to be considered competi- tive. This preserves a longstanding congressional view- point. However, objective analysts have argued for many years that the architectural and engineering procedures established by Congress are not fully competitive proce- dures. This subject is debatable because, under the existing federal architectural and engineering solicita- tion and award procedures, the competitive proposal on which source selection is based is limited to design or technical qualification issues; it excludes price.

A second detailed area in CICA is found in its treat- ment of unsolicited proposals, particularly ones involv- ing basic research. Often, basic research proposals are submitted to a government agency as a result of broad program planning announcements. Others are submitted without any agency announcement simply as an unsolicita- ted proposal for work which would advance knowledge. These proposals are generally unique in character and often are innovative contributions to the advancement of knowledge. Sometimes they include clearly proprietary

data, information, and concepts. The statute permits
award of such procurement without synopsis but does
require a justification for noncompetitive procurement.
Technology transfers must be avoided.

A third area where the Congress has defined its
terms is in its use of the term multiple award schedule.
For many years the General Services Administration has
been awarding contracts under what it calls a multiple
award schedule. These schedules have been based on negotiated contracts under which the supplier's product is
listed in the Federal Supply Catalog as a product which
can be obtained through a simple ordering procedure. The
order can be issued by any government agency authorized
to buy from the multiple award schedule. Most of the
products listed on the schedule are branded ones. Thousands of items are listed that may generally be classified as commercial items. In most cases the product can
be obtained only from the manufacturer or his authorized
distributors. Therefore, the items on the GSA schedule
are ordered under a restricted form of competition, not
in the normal sense in which that word is used in government contracting. The GSA schedule has been supported
for many years because, under the procedure, the agency
is able to negotiate very favorable benchmark prices for
government purchase of the items listed on the schedule.
Schedule prices are not always the lowest obtainable at
the time individual orders are placed but overall, they
are extremely favorable. Nevertheless, under the multiple award system there may be no immediate competitive
check of each price. By defining multiple award schedules as competitive procedures, the Congress has permitted GSA to continue to use this rather excellent tool for
purchase and distribution of products in government.

CICA distinguishes between sealed bid procurement
and competitive proposal procurement. In the past, these
terms have been associated, respectively, with formal
advertising and negotiated procurement. However, those
traditional terms do not appear in the new statute. Instead, CICA states that, with sealed bids, the process
does not involve discussions, whereas in competitive
proposal procurement, the solicitation and award procedure normally includes discussions. This congressional
distinction between the two procedures may be an effect-

ive way of distinguishing between them. However, one must be very careful in interpreting statutory language. The sealed bidding injunction against discussions does not mean that there should be no direct oral communication between potential bidders and government contracting officers during the solicitation and award phase of sealed bid procurement. In fact, it is vitally important that some communications channels be open, because there are frequent misinterpretations or errors in contract specifications or contract terms and conditions which require clarification. It is essential to the success of the procurement that competitors communicate with the contracting officer on such issues.

The term discussion continues in CICA to mean written and oral discussions. This language comes from the 1962 Truth in Negotiation Act (PL 87-653). Its meaning to government personnel sophisticated in the procurement process is discussions aimed at clarifying proposal details or concerning deficiencies associated with a proposal. The specialized meaning of discussions is important because CICA uses the term to perpetuate the structural rigidity of sealed bidding. The term also operates to limit the scope of discussions in negotiated procurement as practiced by the government.

A fifth definitional area is in the basic meaning of competitive procedure in government procurement. CICA declares that a competitive procedure involves "full and open competition," which it defines as permitting all responsible sources to make an offer. Apparently any restriction of the opportunity to make an offer would remove the procurement from competitive procedures, except in those cases where the Congress has, by definition, declared the procedure to be competitive.

All contract awards must be made to responsible sources with the possible exception of awards under the Small Business Act, Section 8(a). Perhaps the most explicit definition set forth in CICA is its definition of a responsible source, quoted below from Sec. 2731(8) of CICA.

The term 'responsible source' means a prospective contractor who:

1. has adequate financial resources to perform the contract or the ability to obtain such resources;
2. is able to comply with the required or proposed delivery or performance schedule, taking into consideration all existing commercial and Government business commitments;
3. has a satisfactory performance record;
4. has a satisfactory record of integrity and business ethics;
5. has the necessary organization, experience, accounting and operational controls, and technical skills, or the ability to obtain such organization, experience, controls, and skills;
6. has the necessary production, construction, and technical equipment and facilities, or the ability to obtain such equipment and facilities; and
7. is otherwise qualified and eligible to receive an award under applicable laws and regulations.

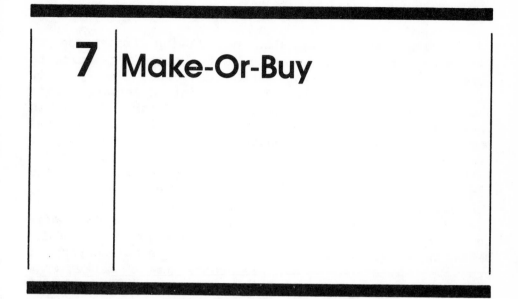

7 | Make-Or-Buy

The issue of make-or-buy is a pervasive matter, one that managers must approach regularly whether in the private or public sector. It arises early in any program and continues to be an issue as work progresses and change occurs. It requires decisions that strongly affect and even determine the character of the organization. The choice presented is whether in-house performance or out-of-house performance is to be embraced. This simple question affects many interest groups, is concerned with the future of the entities involved, and consequently is capable of raising strong opposition regardless of the decision.

Management may have work performed by its own employees or it can contract for others to perform it. There are no other options, although there are several approaches to each method. When contracting out, the options include purchase and lease. When in-house performance is intended, the options include application of existing capacity to the work, acquisition of operating entities that possess the capacity, and expansion of work force coupled with investment in facilities. Each approach has a place but every situation contains a unique complex of variables on the basis of which the manager selects action.

Irving Canton suggests the growing importance of make-or-buy decisions in his recent article, "Learning to Love the Service Economy," (HBR, May-June 1984, p. 89). He discusses manufacturers who enter into a services business as an additional profit-making venture that takes advantage of existing assets and skills. One of ten strategies he discusses is contract management and shared services. It is illustrated by the entry of producers of data processing systems into services associated with the use of those systems. The services are contracted out by the customer as a result of problems encountered in making systems perform. The systems producer may also offer to perform services for suppliers. The basis for these sales is knowledge and skills that are complementary to product transactions. This has become a major market segment in today's economy. Such sales involve a contracting-out decision by the purchaser.

This chapter approaches make-or-buy in several ways. First, it examines the potential relationships conceptually. How does the master-servant relationship compare with the buyer-seller relationship? Why does this definitional matter appear to be a greater issue in government procurement than in private sector procurement? The chapter then treats the elements of make-or-buy decisions. What causes the issue to arise? Who is involved? What are the alternatives? This discussion is followed by consideration of factors affecting the decision. Finally, the chapter examines the special policy problems encountered in government make-or-buy.

Comparison of Personal and
Nonpersonal Services Relationships

When a company or government agency decides to make a product or perform a service, its approach creates a personal services relationship with those who do the work. When the same organization chooses the reverse decision, and decides to buy a product or service, the relationship created with the performer group is contractual, or "nonpersonal." The distinction between those two types of relationships is best described as a legal one, relatively unimportant to most managers, particular-

ly in the private sector. The manager's principal concern is getting work done effectively. Nevertheless, the
distinction has important psychological as well as legal
significance, and when the work primarily involves services rather than material products, it has important
effects on behavior. It impacts the commitments of each
person to their respective organizations and the set of
objectives toward which effort is expended. For example,
the work of an employee is expected to benefit the program of the employer; its effect on external interest
groups such as suppliers or customers is the employer's
responsibility. By contrast, the same services performed
by a supplier's employee are expected to promote, in a
direct, measurable way, the program of the buyer as well
as that of the supplier. The distinction is a matter of
perspective of the parties, dedication of the individuals, and adoption of objectives in the view of each participant. The most effective way to view the difference
may be by examining the kinds of criteria to be applied
in determining when a personal services relationship has
been created. It should be noted that a personal services relationship is often characterized as the master/ser-
vant relationship or, more simply, the employer/employee
relationship.

The following factors seem to be most persuasive in
defining personal services.

1. Personal services are established at the discretion
    of the employer not his customer, that is, the
    employer selects the individual who will perform.
2. Personal services involve a significant degree of
    direct supervision and control by the employer over
    the individuals who perform the service.
3. The employer exercises the right or the power to
    dismiss individuals whose work is unsatisfactory.
4. In a personal services relationship, the employer
    furnishes the materials, supplies, facilities and
    assistance necessary for the employee to perform his
    service.
5. Payment for personal services is ordinarily on a
    time basis. Although incentive pay and piece-work
    payment plans modify the time basis for payment,
    such plans do not abrogate or fundamentally alter

the personal services character associated with employment. The basic responsibility of the employer is to compensate the employee for his effort, even though the amount paid may vary with units of output achieved.

6. When a personal services relationship is created, the employee's responsibility is to work on assigned products or services and his/her pay is primarily dependent upon the application of effort, not upon the completion of the product or service.

With respect to each of these six factors, the nonpersonal services relationship is the converse of that stated for personal services. The work is contracted out and the basic relationship between the sponsor and the performer is that of buyer-seller. Under that kind of relationship, the seller hires employees independently of the buyer; supervises, directs, and controls the application of effort by those employees; retains the right to promote, discipline, or dismiss employees; and is ordinarily responsible for furnishing the materials, facilities, supplies, and assistance that the employee may need. Furthermore, the seller pays employees on a time basis, but receives compensation as a contractor on a job basis. Job completion discharges or ends the relationship between seller and buyer but not between the seller and the employee. The buyer-seller relationship may be extended if additional end products or services have been encompassed by the agreement or are added to it.

The distinctions made in the foregoing discussion become important when the employer is a governmental organization subject to a civil service system and governed by laws established by a legislative body. This is the situation of the United States government. Under federal civil service rules, a federal position is established not only on the basis of work to be done, but also on the basis of the relationship between the government and the individual who performs the work. Thus, in general, the performance of work on a personal services basis by a person who has not been employed in accordance with the civil service statutes and procedures would be a violation of federal law. Nevertheless, there is no prohibition against the government having work performed by contractors on a nonpersonal services basis, and such work may be performed without regard to civil service laws. However, on several occasions, a problem has arisen in this area because the federal agency may have used the contractual method for creating a relationship between itself and the individuals who perform work which is tantamount to that of the employer/employee relationship.

In most areas, a public agency is able to determine whether to establish a civil service position or use the contract method in work performance. When an agency uses the contract method, it must be willing and able to entrust the performance of the requisite work to the contractor and forego the option of exercising detailed direct control over the workers. In effect, the government agency must be willing to abide by the terms of the contract, thus sacrificing a portion of its managing flexibility.

There are two background factors which must be recognized as affecting the administration of make-or-buy in government. The first is the potential that violations of the civil service statutes may improperly convert jobs from those available to federal employees, and federal employee unions, to ones which are not available to them. Therefore, a strong interest group is created which would generally prefer to see the work performed in-house by the government. In addition, the Congress normally establishes a stated personnel ceiling for government offices, and is, therefore, concerned with violation of those personnel limitations which might occur if de facto personal services are obtained using a contract. One consequence of these background possibilities has been litigation attempting to define conditions under which a government agency can or cannot contract out under the law. In addition to the public employee interest groups, private sector interest groups arise among potential supplier companies, their employees and unions, when the business of the company includes sales to the government.

In the absence of a government sales program, the personnel ceiling and personal versus nonpersonal service issues may not be of great importance to private sector firms. The availability of jobs is vital to them, and the broader organizational implications of make-or-buy decisions must be addressed in order to create the basis for ongoing management of any enterprise. The broader implications of private sector make-or-buy are important to public sector personnel for two reasons. First, government is concerned with its suppliers' make-or-buy planning. Under the FAR, part 15.7, government policy in this area is set forth in some detail. Secondly, greater insight into the peculiar structure of the government decision whether to make-or-buy will be developed through study of private sector perceptions of the issues.

Elements of the Make-or-Buy Decision In Industry

The make-or-buy decision is of deep concern at all levels of business organizations from top management offices to the working level. However, the nature of the interest varies with the responsibilities of the person considering the subject. For top management, the fundamental issues are: 1) determining the objectives and character of the organization, 2) deciding the composition of its in-house work force, and 3) formulating the public image of the company, that is, in what business is it engaged? To illustrate, companies which have developed a reputation as fabricators may be hesitant to extend their work into lines such as production of basic materials, extraction of natural resources, or distribution of completed products, yet each of these may be a possibility with respect to the future of the company. A similar example might be that of the production firm as it considers entering research and development. The efficient production operation may risk its competitive edge if it finances expensive talent, facilities and equipment necessary to new technological research. Conversely, the firm with an established expertise in sophisticated work may be ineffective when it moves into a production mode, where the nature of its staff and the character of its facilities may not lend themselves to efficient operations.

The make-or-buy decision may arise at lower levels in the corporate structure where the considerations may be of lesser magnitude and yet critically important to efficient operations. For example, if a manufacturer needs a newly designed piece part and could assign production of that piece part to his own fabrication units or subcontract for its manufacture, the decision usually will not involve the character of the corporation. Rather, it is a decision as to appropriate application of available resources. At this level, the decision may be simply a question of which is the less expensive way to have the product produced. Because of these different kinds of situations we must recognize that make-or-buy is a continuing question that arises regularly in the normal operation of the corporation.

Interest groups concerned with the make-or-buy decision include the purchasing department. As with all departments it seeks compatibility of its purchasing workload assignments and its personnel level. It has a special concern because it is acutely aware that suppliers are interested in a continuing line of business activity from their customers. The purchasing manager must deal with these interests and attempt to aid planning by supplier organizations. It is in this area that the integration of planning and forecasting activities with the make-or-buy decision requires careful analysis by the purchasing organization. The decision to buy makes a purchaser dependent to some degree upon suppliers and the system of suppliers that is developed. Yet the ability to develop an effective supplier system depends on the regularity and volume of business provided to suppliers. To a substantial degree, purchasing leverage is dependent upon the level of confidence that suppliers are able to place in the purchasing manager.

Elements which affect the make-or-buy decision become complex when, in addition to internal and economic issues, one considers the external political, social, and environmental factors which influence the private organization. These include legislative and regulatory policies and attitudes, and, when sourcing in today's economy, often involve a worldwide process. When this occurs, the buyer must become knowledgeable of political and social stability in each of the source areas from which products and services are drawn. Treating the international marketplace as a potential area from which products may be procured often provides the buyer with significant dollar savings and in some cases, quality improvements. These benefits accrue from properly developed make-or-buy studies because of the competition they introduce aided by the special interests of remote sources in capturing additions to their business base.

The real decisionmaking challenge in the make-or-buy area is the buyer's ability to deal with a wide range of alternatives. The alternatives may not be well defined initially, and the consequences of the decision may be unclear. Often there are many feasible alternatives. For example, a company may contract to buy a complete product which it will use, resell, or include in its production of a subsequent product. Alternatively, the company may consider the purchase of a component of that product instead of the entire product, or it may decide to manufacture both the product and its component and purchase only the material that is incorporated into the component. The make-or-buy question often addresses the level at which the company desires to bring its work in-house. At what stage does it want to assume the role of producer of the end product?

Many corporations have integrated their total operations by the technique of acquiring or investing in all of the stages of manufacture from the extraction of raw material to the retailing of final products. Integration on that scale may not be feasible for many firms in the future, but the need to choose from alternatives will continue. Often an entire set of make-or-buy questions will present themselves, each question related to the decision on another action. To act effectively, management must be thoroughly familiar with the entire set.

Important to good decisions and long term success in make-or-buy is management's recognition that the conditions on which its decisions are based change regularly. Consequently, a question that is best answered with a make decision in one period may, in a subsequent period, require a buy decision, even though management may be quite happy with its earlier decision on the same subject. As a consequence, reversals of the make-or-buy policy with respect to individual products can occur frequently.

A final element in the make-or-buy process is the type of analysis used in decisionmaking. Arguably, it should it be a systematic data collection and review procedure structured to ensure attention by key managers to clearly defined policy and criteria approved by top management. Because of the long range impacts of make-or-buy decisions, it is justifiable for a system to be developed by management so that the decision is carefully and properly made by people cognizant of all of the elements which influence the results. Nevertheless, make-or-buy is probably a decision which is made more often in the absence of systematic analysis than in its presence.

Factors Which an Organization May Consider in Make-or-Buy

Probably the most important issue in the make-or-buy question is the existence of sufficient administrative and technical expertise within the organization for performance and management of work. Whenever a "make" decision is made, it must be founded on the conclusion that the organization has or can acquire the expertise and talent both technically and managerially to introduce and successfully carry out the production process. Often some part of the manpower will exist in-house, but the balance requires hiring new personnel with the talent and expertise necessary to the new effort. Additionally, facilities investments may be necessary in order to successfully carry out the "make" decision. Beyond the bare existence of some part of the needed talent and expertise, there is a major question in many companies regarding the orientation and interest of inside talent in a particular production process.

A second major consideration in make-or-buy, often the most difficult, is that of choosing the least costly alternative. Cost comparison is not easy and is particularly difficult when comparing governmental and private organizations. While it can be argued that either make or buy could be the less costly way to produce a product, the particular assertion made in an individual case is often difficult to verify. The problems with cost comparison begin with accounting classification issues, encounter policy decisions such as full versus incremental costing of in-house work, and are aggravated by changes in the level of business activity currently being enjoyed by the company.

Companies often adopt a costing policy for make-or-buy analyses. An example would be costing the "make" option at an incremental cost level for the purpose of preferencing in-house production in order to maintain steady work levels for its internal work force. However, such a policy is not likely to be applied in all circumstances. An alternative policy, full costing of the internal work effort, would be a better economic criterion if the company prefers to minimize its total cost of production. By trading off "full cost" against competitive offers, the company stands to increase its own profit level or can improve its competitive position vis-a-vis alternative or competitive producers of the same product.

Cost comparisons involve many complexities in addition to the issue of incremental versus full costing of the in-house effort. These include consideration of direct and indirect expenses, variable and fixed charges, and measurement and allocation issues. Decisions may be subject to question and/or review as a consequence of their impact on the interest groups affected. A fundamental costing problem arises because internal costs of production vary with the level of production just as the expense of material acquisition varies with economic change. Neither can be reliably predicted very far into the future.

Perhaps more important than the cost comparison itself is the subjective impact of make-or-buy decisions on work force levels and retention of expertise on the part of the company. The decisions affect the future ability of every enterprise to perform. Yet variations in work levels (dependent upon the award of contracts and the behavior of the business cycle) regularly adjust the demand for a company's internal employment level. Therefore, a company sometimes may choose a "make" decision when it is more economical to employ a "buy" decision, simply because it wishes to retain capacity to accept future work. It may view retention of work in-house as the best method for financing the cost of carrying currently underutilized capacity, even though it is not cost effective for the specific product.

This same issue may be examined from an entirely reverse point of view--that of an effective purchasing manager who is concerned with the welfare of important suppliers. The purchasing manager develops a relationship with those sources of supply on which he depends for his regular material requirements. It may not be in his interest or his company's interest to cut back on purchases from an established, reliable supplier, if at the same time the supplier also is experiencing other adverse economic consequences. An aspect of the purchasing manager's responsibility is the internal articulation of important source of supply factors which advance the interests of both parties. Long range commitments are particularly important, and it is a responsibility of the procurement manager to provide a degree of protection to the interests of its most valued suppliers, just as other management personnel consider the interests and welfare of the internal production work force. Thus it can be seen that a tradeoff must occasionally be made between the relationship of the company with its existing suppliers and its relationship with its work force and/or unions.

Frequently a corporate make-or-buy decision will depend on the nature of the technology involved in the proposed work. The company will seek to protect its trade secrets and other confidential data. This becomes critical when the data must be provided to a supplier, as in a decision to buy an item which is based on proprietary material. The R&D capability of a company, its possession of technological assets, and its willingness to risk the confidentiality of its data may influence whether it is willing to buy an item in lieu of retaining its manufacture as an internal function. The degree of confidence a company has in its suppliers strongly affects this decision. Such a consideration could bring about a "make" decision even when the more economical method of production would be to contract out the performance of work.

A major factor frequently influencing make-or-buy decisions is the continuity expected with respect to future production. Products with only a short term production expectation tend to be "buy" candidates. Products that promise long term, continued, uninterrupted production processes are considered desirable products, ones to which any company would like to devote its investment resources. It is this very factor which may influence a company to enter into a new line of business activity. Whenever an item is to be produced which the company expects to be profitable over a protracted period of time, the motivation to enter into the production reaches its peak.

The relationship of anticipated work to existing work is often a strong factor in the make-or-buy equation. When production of a new product requires extension of existing capabilities and facilities, the company may be strongly inclined to make that move, partly because it is easier to predict a profitable use of its expertise and facilities, and partly because it is a comfortable, lower-risk decision. For the company to enter into a line of work in which it has no previous experience has converse implications. The relationship of new work to existing work is significantly impacted by the total investment required and the downside consequences associated with the new undertaking. To make a new item, the company must be properly financed, equipped and staffed to carry on the production process profitably. Resources are the limiting factor; they must be adequate to keep production operations in place long enough to realize a profit on the investment. The issue here is a fundamental capital budgeting decision, but it is colored in the make-or-buy context by the factors discussed in this section.

Government Make-or-Buy, an Evolving Productivity Enhancement Tool

We've seen how pervasive and important make-or-buy considerations are in private sector decisionmaking. Now we shall look at the government's attempts, over a protracted period of years, to contend with this same set of issues. It can be argued that the basic concerns of make-or-buy in government, such as the nature of the organization's work and objectives, and the cost of performing the work, are similar to those arising in the private sector. However, the government's attempts to treat the issues are clouded by varying political philosophies pertaining to performance of work and by the existence of a large government work force performing commercial or industrial activities.

A brief history of the federal approach to services contracting may be helpful in orienting the student to the nature of the problems that affect the system. For many years, Congress has restricted the ability of federal agencies in the area of excessive employment of personnel and in contracting for performance of services. The prohibitions have been directed at controlling the growth of the federal payroll, yet simultaneously precluding agencies from evading congressional intent through contracting for services. These attempts to control the growth of the federal bureaucracy culminated during the 1920s in a general attitude that contracting for personal services was wrong, because it appeared to contravene the civil service laws. The viewpoint seemed be that contract employees were less reliable than government employees, as indicated by the following quote from a Controller General decision.

> Personal services necessary in connection with governmental activities are for the performance by regular employees of the government who are responsible to the government, and such services should not be performed by contractors who cannot be held personally responsible for failure or misfeasance in the performance of their duties.[1]

The general governmental attitude against contracting for services changed during the Second World War. During that time the nation mobilized to carry on the war effort, and the basis for that mobilization was involvement of the resources of the entire private sector in the war effort. The successful use of contractors during that period, combined with substantial advances in the technological basis for conducting a war effort, resulted in a general opening of political thought toward the idea that performing work through contracts may be an important asset which government should employ. The changing attitude was reflected in a Comptroller General decision in 1952 in which he stated, "Where it is administratively determined that it would be substantially more economical, feasible, or necessary by reason of unusual circum-

stances to have the work involving personal services performed by non-government parties . . . " the requirement
to retain the job within the federal work force could be
disregarded.[2]

In 1954, President Eisenhower incorporated a policy
modification into his budget message to the Congress
wherein he announced, ". . . a policy of shifting from in-
house operations to state, local, and private enterprise."[3]   This effort represented the first major
attempt to establish a government policy to rely on the
private sector during peacetime for available goods and
services. The next major step in the development of that
policy was the Bureau of the Budget (later reorganized to
become the Office of Management and Budget) Bulletin No.
55-4 in which the following statement was included.

> It is the general policy of the administration
> that the federal government will not start or carry
> on any commercial activity to provide a service or
> product for its own use, if such product or service
> can be procured from private enterprise through ordi-
> nary channels. . .

The Bureau of the Budget policy was revised several times
during the late 1950s and early 1960s until a new circular, A-76, was issued in 1967. The use of a circular
instead of a bulletin tended to give greater permanency
to the policy. However, it would be an understatement to
say that the policy had little impact on either the federal bureaucracy or federal operations through the 1950s
and 1960s. This slow implementation may be attributed to
the lack of any clear statutory basis for the policy and
to the existence of substantial numbers of commercial/in-
dustrial activities being operated by government agencies
using government employees. This existing work force
seemingly would have been adversely affected by vigorous
implementation of the policy, and it appears that Congress tended to protect the federal work force against the
potential conversion of jobs to contract performance.

The government attitude toward nonpersonal services
was brought fully into focus by a 1965 Civil Service
Commission investigation and ruling that contracts
awarded by the Air Force at Fuchu Air Force Base in Japan

were illegal because of their creation of an employer/employee relationship. This relationship, in the opinion of the Civil Service Commission, violated federal personnel laws. Thus, the question of personal versus nonpersonal services emerged as a vital topic during the late 1960s. It was highlighted further by a case at Goddard Space Flight Center in which the Civil Service Commission ruled that Goddard contracts for scientific and engineering design and fabrication services rendered on-site at the center were improper. The basis for the ruling was that the contracts created what was tantamount to an employee/employer relationship between the government and the contractor's employees. The General Accounting Office concurred in this decision. It contained six standards known as the Pellerzi standards, named after the General Counsel of the Civil Service Commission at that time, Leo P. Pellerzi, who wrote that part of the opinion. His standards were to be used in judging whether a relationship created by a contract is equivalent to that of an employee/employer relationship. The six standards are paraphrased as questions below.

1. Is performance of the contract on-site at the government installation?
2. Does the government furnish the principal tools and equipment necessary to the performance of the work?
3. Are the services applied directly to an effort which is integral to the agency's work or to the organizational support that furthers the assigned function or mission of the agency?
4. Are services meeting comparable needs performed in the agency using civil service personnel?
5. Is is reasonable to expect that the type of services being provided will be required for longer than one year?
6. Does the inherent nature of the service, or the manner in which it is provided, require direct or indirect government supervision of the contractor's employees? This supervision would be reasonably interpreted to exist if it were necessary to adequately protect the government's interests or to retain control of the function involved, or simply to retain full responsibility for the function by a

duly authorized federal official.

The Pellerzi opinion required that all six conditions be present to find that an illegal contract on the basis of personal services did exist. A modification of that ruling by the Mondello supplement (Mondello was a successor Civil Service Commission General Counsel) indicated that all six of the elements need not be present in order to determine that the personal service existed. These rulings, initiated in 1967, seem to have governed the behavior of the federal agencies in this area through 1978.

In 1978 an additional ruling was made by the United States Court of Appeals for the District of Columbia on another NASA case which actually began in 1967.[4] This case was an important ruling because the court agreed with NASA that the contracts in dispute were legal. The Court of Appeals applied the Pellerzi standards as indicated above but interpreted them much more narrowly than the Civil Service Commission or the General Accounting Office had done previously. The Court primarily looked to the sixth standard for guidance regarding the existence of the employee/employer relationship. It held that in order for such a relationship to exist, there must be "relatively continuous, close supervision of a substantial number of contractor employees." The other standards were accepted as indicators of the potential that a personal services contract might exist but were not viewed as controlling with respect to that issue.

It is likely that the 1978 decision by the Court of Appeals reduced the significance of the personal/nonpersonal services distinction and brought about a more aggressive pursuit of OMB Circular A-76 as a means of testing whether a federal agency's performance of commercial/industrial activities is cost effective. The definitional issue receded in favor of a more pragmatic issue, that is, the economic impact of make-or-buy questions. As a result, the personal/nonpersonal services question is currently a background issue rather than one of critical importance. However, note that the definitional issue only receded, it did not disappear. Contracting out under A-76 involves nonpersonal services and should not create de facto employee/employer relationships.

Since the 1978 Court of Appeals decision, the effort of government agencies to implement OMB Circular A-76 has increased substantially. However, the question of contracting out versus performance within the civil service system has become, under the circular, only one possible outcome of the investigation of a commercial activity being operated by the government. The track record over the six-year period prior to this writing shows that many cost comparison studies have resulted in a continuation of performance in-house. When that outcome occurs after completion of a cost comparison, it is based on a conclusion that continued in-house operation is less costly than conversion to contractor performance. Such decisions are often attacked either on the basis that they were biased or that direct competitive comparison of government with industry is improper in a private enterprise economy.

Although the government make-or-buy decision under the A-76 guidelines is widely perceived by government personnel as a mechanism for contracting out the jobs which they hold, that is not the view presently held by government managers. Their view of the OMB circular and its implementation is that "the A-76 process should enhance governmental productivity" by comparing the cost of government-operated commercial activities with private sector bids for the same work. This view provides federal managers with an incentive to become more efficient through open competition with private businesses. Almost 1700 cost studies have been conducted since 1979, primarily in the Department of Defense, reportedly resulting in an average savings of 20 percent over the previous cost of commercial activity to the government. However, the savings often resulted from revised government operations rather than turnover of the work to contractors.

The program embraced by A-76 requires the federal agency to develop measurable performance output standards for commercial/industrial activity. Secondly, the program requires development of a quality assurance plan under which the agency's performance is measured and tracked to ensure that it maintains the required quality level. Third, the agency is required to conduct management efficiency studies under the revised output standards and quality assurance plans to enhance productiv-

ity. These studies may result in a redefined and modified government operation. The final phase of the study
program requires the agency to open the work to competition between its in-house operation and the potential
private sector performer. This competition is based on
the redefined governmental operation of the activity.

Under this approach, the agency gains insight into
the most cost effective method of having its work performed. The government wins approximately half of the
cost comparison studies made; the remainder are won by
the private sector. However, whether or not the government wins, the cost of performing the function is reduced
as a result of the studies and revisions of the work performance methodology devised during the study.

The government agency make-or-buy study is a highly
visible, controversial subject both within the government
and among the private sector competitors for government
contracts. One issue which arises in connection with all
of these undertakings is the political philosophy of some
commentators that government should not compete with private industry for work which can be done by the private
sector. While there is general agreement that certain
unique types of government work must be performed in-
house, defining the character of those jobs is problema-
tic and may not be adequate to resolve many contracting-
out controversies. It is argued that a federal function
should be performed only by a federal employee appointed
in the civil service by a federal officer. The issue
remains complex, however, because any nongovernment employee, whose work is viewed as a federal function and
who is subject to the supervision of a federal officer or
employee, may be considered a government employee.

It should be understood that the government policy
document, OMB Circular A-76, is defended by only a relatively small group of management and procurement-oriented
personnel. It is attacked by government employee unions
and by government employees in general, often on the
basis of fairness--some allege the retirement cost factor
to be too high. Contractor representatives see the cost
factors, and fairness in general, from the reverse perspective. Some have asserted that in-house competitors
are allowed to make adjustments after completion of the
bidding phase or may be allowed not to implement revised

work plans after winning. Some believe that a cost comparison study is inappropriate, that the government should not perform the commercial/industrial activity, and that the work should be competitively contracted out to industry with very few and limited exceptions. Perhaps the A-76 mechanism is to be viewed as a middleground position in the battle over the appropriate basis for government make-or-buy decisions. As currently implemented, the A-76 approach appears to substantially embrace the economic criterion of the least costly method of performance. However, for new commercial/industrial activities, it severely limits creating new in-house operations. The cost comparison is mandatory for the agencies, because significant overall cost savings and productivity gains are expected to result.

Notes

[1]G. Comp. Gen. 140, 142 (19264.

[2]G. Comp. Gen. 372, 373 (1952).

[3]U.S. President, Public Papers of the President of the United States (Washington, D.C.: Office of the Federal Register, National Archives and Record Service, 1954) Dwight D. Eisenhower, p. 79-81.

[4]Lodge 1858, AFGE, ET AL. v James E.l Webb, ET AL. No. 76-1821, No. 76-1934., U.S. app. D.C., Decided March 20, 1978.

8 | Procurement Management

The OFPP has devoted a substantial part of its resources to management challenges in the field of procurement. It gave detailed attention to the subject in its Proposal for a Uniform Federal Procurement System, dated February 26, 1982. In this chapter we explore the potential managerial role of procurement personnel. We shall first address the term procurement manager and the special circumstances making the practice of creative management particularly difficult in the field. The COGP and OFPP initiatives in the field are then presented, followed by an analysis of the reasons for the historically poor image of procurement personnel as managers. Suggestions for strengthening their management skills are proposed. The final section of the chapter addresses project management, currently the dominant managerial concept practiced by government for its major acquisition programs.

The Procurement Manager

Some ambiguity exists respecting use of titles such as procurement manager, contract manager, contracting officer, buyer, negotiator, and/or purchasing agent. In government procurement, the term contracting officer is extensively used throughout regulations and contract clauses. The term is well recognized as designating a person who has been delegated authority to act for the government in contractual matters, that is, to enter into and/or administer contracts for supplies or services on behalf of the government.

The term purchasing agent is commonly used in industrial organizations to designate persons authorized to act for a corporation in contracting and purchasing relationships with vendors. Buyers and negotiators are persons ordinarily employed under the supervision of a purchasing agent or contracting officer. Their work includes sourcing, solicitation, negotiation and other duties necessary for performance of the procurement function.

The term procurement manager is used in this book in a more general sense, referring to the person in an organization who is responsible for the planning, direction, control and staffing of procurement programs. That person may report to the general manager of a business unit or to the chief executive of a corporation. Within a government agency, the procurement manager may report to the agency head or to the head of a procurement activity within the agency and may report at lower levels of the hierarchy. The term is intended to designate that person who holds functional management responsibility for procurement, however, assignment of planning responsibilities for procurement programs is often divided or placed under cognizance of program managers. Management and direction of the function may be performed by a procurement officer (or by the contracting officer or purchasing agent in smaller organizations). Organizational level, title, and placement of procurement management responsibility is not uniform or consistent in government, although legal authority is consistently held by a contracting officer. Use of the designation procurement manager is important to the concept that the procurement process must be positively managed by persons knowledgeable of organizational objectives and interactions as well as contracting techniques and rules.

Great difficulty in government procurement arises in connection with the role of contracting officers within their organizations. Respecting its contractors, one point is well established--the government acts through its contracting officers. It is not at all clear what role (that is, authorities, duties, responsibilities and relationships) contracting officers exercise within their agency. The basic issue is whether contracting officers can function as procurement managers. In part, the lack of definition of roles results from the failure of the government to define levels of contracting officers, to consistently tie contracting authority to any specific organizational level, or to relate educational, knowledge or experience qualifications in any systematic way to appointments. The OFPP addressed this matter and adopted the term procurement executive to designate the lead responsibility for the function in government agencies. Entry and appointment qualifications, however, have not been agreed upon.

While some organizational positions, generally high level positions, are chartered to include contracting officer authority, a specific certificate of appointment, commonly referred to as a "warrant," is the normal procedure for most contracting officers. Chartering positions with authority is a problem in government because appointees often have no background in the field. OFPP has addressed this issue by advocating development of system standards that would include work force qualifications. Nevertheless, appointment as a contracting officer does not carry any clear relationship to organizational status. A contracting officer who exercises significant authority vis-a-vis a contractor may hold very high or very little stature in the agency's management.

Contracting officers are subject to the general constraint that their actions must meet all applicable requirements of law, regulation and other procedures. The specific effects of this general constraint are not easily measured, since the applicable body of such constraints includes statutes, executive orders, the FAR, and agency FAR supplements. Subpart 1.6 of the FAR vests contracting authority in agency heads and authorizes delegation to contracting officers only. In addition to the FAR, regulations issued by separate agencies (for example, the Department of Labor, and the Small Business Administration) and by various agency management instructions (or directives) are also part of this pattern of organizational control. For particular procurements, specifications and standards may constrain the process.

Regardless of the regulatory and policy material with which contracting officers are enjoined to comply, each procurement program demands exercise of judgment. Sample questions necessary for procurement planning and negotiation preparation are listed below:

1. How should a major project be subdivided and assigned for in-house performance and for performance by contractors and among contractors? What basis for subdivision should be used? How many performers are needed? (This question should not be confused with the make-or-buy issue covered in Chapter 7. When pertinent, the issue is associated with research and development and/or major acquisition programs. In such cases, it is a matter of competence and capabilities--not an A-76 type of cost comparison.)

2. Should a requirement be contracted as a system or as a group of subsystems?

3. Are the specifications and other technical documents definitive with respect to allocation of responsibilities and risks as between the government and the contractor?

4. Have all likely sources been included in the source list? Is a single source indicated? Should additional sources be sponsored?

5. Does the procurement plan allow for innovation and creativity by suppliers? Should it?

6. What criteria stand as the basis for source selection? Will data requested from offerors suffice for evaluations, including analyses requisite to negotiations?

7. What contractual arrangements (contract type and terms and conditions) are appropriate to the contemplated program?

8. Have issues necessary to negotiation been identified? A position developed?

9. Have all effects associated with a proposed change order been identified and evaluated?

Decisions on questions such as these are vital to the entire procurement process, and they require research, analysis, and judgment with respect to the procurement situation. The overlay of regulation, policy and management instruction guides the process of decision-making, delineates factors to be considered, and in very limited areas, proscribes a particular course of action, but solutions and decisions are found by assessment of the entire situation, not just the regulation.

The term "contract manager" is extensively used in general reference to government procurement. For example, the National Contract Management Association (NCMA) incorporated the term into its title. Personnel who are members of NCMA come from many types of interest areas—government, industry, nonprofit organizations, procurement offices, marketing, and the legal community. The term is widely recognized as embracing the management process that begins when the contract method is selected as the mode for performing a task. The administrative functions which contract managers must perform will be treated here as identical to those of the procurement manager. However, in many field organizations and in contractor organizations the contract manager may be primarily identified with obtaining timely performance, compliance and discharge of all obligations under contracts rather than planning, solicitation and award activities.

In general, the COGP was critical of the staffing practices and authority levels pertaining to procurement officials within both civilian and military agencies. It developed the theme that procurement managers should be in a position to articulate the needs and positions of their contracting offices at the general management level of the executive agency. The COGP position and the current planning of the OFPP are consistent in seeking expanded professional competence for the procurement work force.

Problems With Procurement Management

Purchasing managers are not well known for their managerial skills. Many have treated their field as a technology--as a tool to serve the demands placed upon it by other managers. This has resulted in a perception that buying is a technician's trade and in a tendency to group all purchasing and contracting activity into a single mold--the mold of the highly repetitive ordering process associated with small purchases. This perception has compromised the role of procurement managers and limited their creativity. Many of them share the perception and have tended to emphasize their relationship with suppliers to the detriment of their internal relationship with other managers. There is a need for change. Procurement needs strong, factually based planning for both near term and distant horizons. It also needs strong ties with financial, engineering, and production managers and access to top management. These needs cannot be recognized if purchasing managers continue to concentrate on processing orders while excluding strategic, forward-oriented, managerial thinking.

The poor image of procurement as a management discipline in government arises from several related factors. It is not clear which factors are causative, but the need for reassessment and realignment of priorities is evident. These factors are summarized in the following list:

1. The traditional organizational position of purchase and supply offices is remote from upper management.
2. Procurement evolved out of the purchase and supply function which is recognized as a support arm of every installation and office. Its role has expanded, so that today it makes large commitments of government resources, but that role has never been adequately differentiated from routine purchase and supply operations.
3. Highly structured purchasing techniques are embedded in traditional federal policy. For well over one hundred years, federal contracting was channeled through the procedurally complex, structured, sealed bidding or "formal advertised" procurement system. Only since the second world war has the negotiated procurement system with its increased ambit for exercise of discretion been practiced extensively. The image of channelized procurement decisionmaking con-

tinues. Enactment of CICA has modified this tradition but may have introduced new process rigidities.

3. Nonprocurement objectives have been imposed creating
   process complexity beginning with the depression of
   the 1930s. Government procurement has become an
   important vehicle through which Congress and the
   President have attempted to bring about social and
   economic change. Some of the initiatives have had
   measured success, others have had unexpected results, some have not worked, but all have burdened
   the procurement process by increasing its procedural
   complexity and diverting the attention of procurement managers from program objectives to social and/
   or economic objectives. As a consequence, many procurement personnel have become process oriented
   instead of end-result oriented.

4. Lack of attention to program oriented knowledge and
   training for procurement personnel persists in government. For a number of years government agencies
   have sponsored training courses with titles such as
   "Procurement for Nonprocurement Managers." They
   have yet to sponsor "Technical and Project Orientation for Procurement Managers." This, coupled with
   lack of meaningful qualification standards, has limited the potential for procurement personnel to embrace the substantive issues and complexities of the
   programs for which they write contracts.

5. Procurement is interdisciplinary in the subject
   matter with which it must deal, but procurement
   personnel often suffer the disadvantages of an interdisciplinary field without the accompanying challenges and advantages. The government contracting
   process requires expertise in business management,
   accounting, public administration, and law, as well
   as knowledge in technical or scientific disciplines
   that sponsor various projects. The combination of
   that breadth of subject matter in individuals is not
   easily found. For procurement the problem is magni-
   fied because federal policy has consistently avoided
   specifying what qualifications are demanded for
   entry into its procurement job series (1102). Similarly it has avoided specifying meaningful qualifications for appointment as a contracting officer. In-

stead it has adopted broad statements of qualifications that have no operational meaning. This approach has been coupled with low-grade entry level positions that have effectively limited the attractiveness of job openings. To date, federal policy has avoided specifying a college major as preferred or required for procurement personnel and has even avoided any requirement for college education.

6. Workload and schedule pressures often result in procurement personnel failing to think like managers. Instead they respond to pressures for immediate action on contracts that are behind schedule. Excessive workloads may be a contributing factor. Tardiness in early planning and documentation activities, and lack of qualified personnel may also contribute. Proactive management demands control over schedules, anticipation of coming events, and ability to move and acquire personnel to meet demands in an orderly manner. Securing ability to be proactive requires data (and use of it) that clearly demonstrates the necessity for resources to be made available. Workload analysis within the procurement office and comparison with other functional areas of the agency are vital. Resource needs of procurement managers must be asserted in timely fashion and with adequate evidentiary support. Too often this has not been done.

Improving Procurement Management

Solving the problems of the procurement management process has been a target for the COGP, the OFPP, and some federal agencies. Progress toward this goal has been slow. However, a sigificant number of military officers are being trained in the field. The emphasis of the military programs is project management. Furthermore, two of the services have established military occupational fields that allow career progression in project management. The civilian work force does not enjoy such luxury. Work force strengthening remains the key element in improving procurement management. A multifaceted attack is necessary to achieve significant progress. Under guidance of OFPP, the Federal Acquisition Institute (FAI) has proposed a broad approach to the needed improvement. Their program includes:

At the agency level:
1. Rework of procurement position classification
2. Wider adoption of agency intern/trainee programs
3. New training and education programs for procurement personnel
4. Better (higher) organizational positioning of the top procurement official
5. Delineation of qualifications for contracting officers
6. Proactive work force analysis and planning
7. Broad based recruitment of procurement personnel including college recruitment.

At the government level:
1. Establishment of a career board for procurement personnel
2. Creation of a central pool of interns
3. Establishment of training assistance at the inter-agency level.

These kinds of initiatives could achieve a significant improvement in management of procurement and, in turn, in the economy and efficiency of government sponsored programs.

The emphases of FAI were keynoted by the Commission on Government Procurement. Its concern with the role and skills of contracting officers was expressed in the following comments:

. . . Little direct top management attention is devoted to procurement or grant problems, and the lack of understanding of the importance of the procurement function by agency heads is apparent. . . .

. . . The failure to place procurement on an organizational parity with program technical personnel resulted in frequent comments that:

Technical personnel tend to dominate personnel engaged in the procurement process. Procurement personnel do not receive the management support they must have in order to bring their professional expertise into play in awarding and administering contracts, and, as a consequence, they must often bow to the desires of requisitioners who do not have expertise in procurement. . . . .

. . . The constraints under which procurement now operates in some agencies should be removed. If the function is to operate effectively and on a parity with other functional disciplines with which it must interface, it must be placed at a level in the organization which affords a high degree of visibility to the agency head. . . .

. . . The contracting authority being exercised generally resides in the "position" occupied. . . .

. . . The inadequacy of the delegation of approval authority to contracting officers is a major cause of the dilution and diffusion of his inherent responsibilities.[1]

OFPP's system proposal advocates several kinds of action to overcome the symptoms and causes indicated by the COGP report. Establishment of procurement executives by agency heads was a part of their program and Executive Order 12352 directed that action. The functions of the executive as advocated by OFPP include:

1. Participation in development of government-wide procurement policies, regulations and standards
2. Development of unique agency policies, regulations and standards
3. Evaluation of system performance in accordance with the approved system standards
4. Certification to the agency head that procurement systems meet approved standards
5. Enhancement of career management of the procurement work force
6. Act as the overall agency advocate for competition

The formation and administration of system standards

and work force improvements are significant parts of OFPP's management program. The program includes creation of clear lines of authority from the agency head to the operating level in each agency. Much remains to be done to bring about the reality of effective management practices in the procurement field, but these initiatives have expanded the opportunity for success.

Functional and Project
Concepts of Management

Approaches to organizing have been affected by the rise of project management over the last two decades. Similarly, management's decisionmaking is affected by the changed internal organization of buying entities. The importance of this change requires examination in some detail.

Organizational structures are nearly as varied in federal procurement as in private institutions; they depend on the creativity of agency leadership as well as the specific mission to be accomplished. However, the organization for procurement is constrained by statutory and regulatory requirements imposed on the procurement system. Because of its extensive and complex administrative requirements, procurement tends to encourage a specialized work force. A buying office performing the functions delineated in Chapter 3 is normally found within procuring activities. However, since the post-World War II period, intensive exploration for more efficient and effective organizational arrangements has been undertaken. One reason for this has been the establishment of giant undertakings such as space and major weapon systems programs.

The pure functional approach of traditional organizations using the accepted principles of hierarchical structure, line authority, unity of command, task specialization, span of control, line-staff division, parity of responsibility and authority, and so forth, becomes impossibly burdensome when combined with a unique, highly visible, complex procurement such as a space vehicle. Such projects involve coordination of hundreds of organizations and people.

Unique management concepts become essential whenever large, single-purpose projects cut across organizational flows of authority and responsibility. Such projects are a reflection of American society and technology as are the newer concepts of management. Organization of the federal government is also a reflection of the changing environment in which it operates. Recognition of these changes is central to an appreciation of the field of government procurement and contracting.

In the modern industrial community of the United States, most organizations are arranged, for purposes of their internal operations, along functional lines; that is, they are subdivided by the type or nature of the work and knowledge essential to performance. Similarly, organizations established to handle the government's procurement processes have been traditionally organized along functional lines. The policies and procedures under which the various procurement agencies work are formulated in a manner consistent with the traditional management concepts asserted by Fayol.[2] These concepts include pyramidal organizational structures, distinct superior-subordinate relationships, departmentation of functions, line and staff organizations and traditional systems of rewards and punishments. While the concepts may be valid they do not meet the demands for flexibility coupled with today's programs. Ability to apply intensive management attention to specific projects within the structure of large organizations mandates special configurations.

Regardless of the government's traditional structure, major federal procuring activities have adopted the new management concept--project management. This development has affected both government and industry. Project teams are clearly needed for large undertakings which seek to achieve measurable end results. In using the project approach, when the end has been accomplished, the team would be disbanded and the personnel returned or reassigned. This approach implies the existence of the parent or continuing organization that establishes the project, assigns the personnel, and disbands and reabsorbs the personnel.

Accommodation of the procurement organization to the demands for intensive management of special programs is done, in a sense, to help preserve the more traditional organization. The permanent hierarchical form may be unable to meet project demands, yet it remains essential for the long-run continuity of the institution. The distinctive feature of the new concept is that temporary, ad hoc groups are established to manage specific projects with definite goals and planned ends.

In any organization that undertakes severable, non-standard tasks, the group members, in order to accomplish their work, must deal horizontally, vertically and diagonally with peers and associates at different levels and in different functional elements both within the parent organization and with outside organizations. To follow a traditional chain of command in such circumstances appears to be unwieldy, time consuming, costly and in some cases, impractical. Both horizontal and vertical contacts are necessary to get the job done; they are difficult to chart formally, yet necessary for a smooth flow of work in the organization.

The acceptance of horizontal-vertical relationships among associates creates organizational stress. It requires changes in the existing procedures such as realignment of tasks, crossing formal lines of departmental authority, and acceptance of a hybrid organizational form. In major systems acquisitions, rigid hierarchical structuring has been supplanted by closely integrated project groups. The stress which managers experience is sufficient to indicate that a new outlook or viewpoint must be adopted. Cleland and King identified the principal ingredients of this new viewpoint.[3]

Acceptance of change as a way of life seems to be a key ingredient for success in project management. Projects are dynamic, while institutional elements do not change easily. The manager must accommodate these factors by accepting the fact that conflict exists and by recognizing that its resolution is a vital aspect of organizational life. A principal source of conflict in project organization is the inherent crossing of vertical lines of authority. A mark of the effective program manager is ability to make those crossings with a minimum of strife.

The project manager seeks to manage resources where ever they are available. They may be contractually ob-

tained;   human,   material or literary;   administratively
independent;   or they may be only temporarily available.
S/he integrates them into the project's fiber.

Seldom is the horizon of a project internal.   Its
support and objectives lie in the environment outside the
institutional or corporate setting.   The project manager
must visualize his role in this context and be prepared
to interact with field environments.

When project management is adopted, its purpose is
to provide the concentrated management attention that a
complex and unfamiliar undertaking is likely to demand.
At the same time, however, it should permit the rest of
the organization to proceed with routine business while
the project is underway.   The project management form of
organization has enjoyed success primarily because it
emphasizes a team approach to problems.   This has modera-
ted the problems of coordination which are found very
often in the traditional functional organization.

There are various ways in which the concept of project management can be adapted to a functional organization.   In each form, there are varying degrees of authority and responsibility which are assumed by the project
manager and which have been splintered from (or are
shared with) the functional managers.   Project organization may give the project manager complete authority over
an autonomous organization.   Conversely, it can provide
little or no authority over support personnel, in which
case the project manager serves as an information conduit
and as a negotiator seeking needed support for the
project.   The degree of autonomy and level of dedicated
support depends upon the charter granted to the project
manager by agency management.   Two general arrangements
are depicted in Charts 8-1 and 8-2.

Consider the project organization depicted in Chart
8-1.   This is a fairly typical arrangement, with the project manager acting as an assistant to the chief executive.   The project manager may be provided with clerical
help, but has no direct control over the functional departments.   In this instance, project work would be performed as routine work within the various departments to
which it is assigned by the chief executive.   The project
manager would be a coordinator, ensuring that work necessary to project completion was properly scheduled and per-

CHART 8-1

PROJECT MANAGER ACTING AS A STAFF ASSISTANT

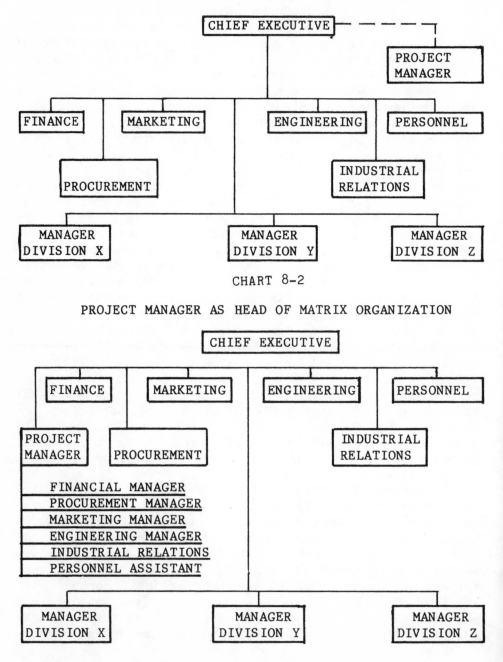

CHART 8-2

PROJECT MANAGER AS HEAD OF MATRIX ORGANIZATION

formed. The manager would have no authority over the establishment of priorities or the performance of personnel. S/he can recommend that action be taken when necessary, but general management makes the final decision. The project manager's influence would be derived primarily from personal ability, character, and proximity to the chief executive.

Conversely, the project manager can be placed in a line position as shown in Chart 8-2. In this example, the project manager has a staff assistant from each functional department. This method is sometimes referred to as a matrix organization because the traditional lines of vertical functional authority are maintained, yet the project manager has authority over assigned staff from the functional groups. S/he also exercises horizontal authority over associates in the functional departments. The functional managers thus become responsible to both their hierarchical supervisor and a project manager for support of the project. The project manager has authority as to the "what" and "when" of its functional support, and the functional managers determine how, where, and by whom the support is given. Clearly, the parties must collaborate.

There are various other ways (such as full projectization wherein administrative and technical personnel are employed directly by the project manager) in which the project management concept can be incorporated into a traditional functional organization. In addition, other factors influence the structure and relationships of project managed systems. Primary factors are the nature of the project, the internal and field environments applicable, and the personality of the project manager.

Because of its large number of unique programs, the federal government has embraced project management and requires its use by contractors. The Department of Defense led the adoption of the concept, but in numerous other areas, such as space programs, construction, and energy, it has been, and continues to be, utilized. Its appeal for important but unique national programs is its ability to focus attention on specific undertakings that are carried out within the larger institutional structure of agencies. Therefore, it has gained great favor.

Success in development, production and deployment of

major systems is primarily dependent upon competent people, rational priorities, and clearly defined responsibilities. Conditions for success are believed to be maximal when responsibility and authority for a project are held by a single person capable of integrating priorities, making decisions, and accepting responsibility. Program managers, accordingly, are given a charter which provides sufficient authority to accomplish recognized program objectives. Layers of authority between the program manager and component or agency head should be minimum.

To accomplish assigned responsibilites, the program manager must monitor the functional units involved in the project. Duties include ensuring that project funding is secured, technological challenges overcome, and contracts properly awarded and administered. In short, s/he coordinates the entire spectrum of activities. Government agencies and private industry employ various forms of project management but the highly formalized manner in which the DOD has embraced it may involve sophistication not needed elsewhere.

There are limitations to the project management concept. A list of some problems associated with it follows.

1. Project organizations tend to pursue their objectives single-mindedly, without regard for training.
2. Project managers demand the best functionally trained talent tending to drain the traditional organization of its strongest resource and of its ability to train new people.
3. As an overlay on the traditional organization, projects cause dispute and friction in defining the roles and continuity of the functional organization.
4. When the number of projects multiples, the ability of functional groups to support them is diminished.
5. Multiplication of projects tends to reduce their special status to a routine level.
6. Job insecurity becomes a problem as the project aproaches termination. This can result in efforts to obtain unnecessary extension of the project.
7. In a project environment, the workers tend to become isolated from their functional contemporaries and to

become project-oriented. They experience reduced contact with other functional or specialized personnel.

8. Problems of confusion and conflict occur when the project manager's charter and master plan fail to clarify delegations of authority and responsibility and interfaces with participating organizations.
9. Dual supervision of the worker occurs when the project manager intervenes at the worker level.
10. Total organizational costs may be increased because of duplication of skilled personnel needs. Both functional and project organizations have need for these specialists.

In most circumstances, a matrix concept prevails and the project manager accomplishes program objectives by securing support from other managers who are associated with functional disciplines. Under that arrangement, the career interests of project staff members are divided. They must maintain their allegiance to their disciplines while satisfying project demands. This raises a unique set of conflicts and challenges. The project manager holds explicit authority but only over major considerations involved in the project plan. One of his biggest problems is how to get full support when the functional people are responsible to someone else for pay raises, promotion and the other line superior-subordinate relationships. The project manager's authority, implied or explicit, is often dependent upon his persuasive ability, rapport with co-equal managers, and his reputation in resolving opposing viewpoints.

When project organization is overlayed upon the functional organization and the mixture of explicit and implicit authority is added, organizational problems are created as discussed above. Although the approach is well established, the concept and literature of project management is still evolving. Many forms of this management technique have been tried other than the models shown above.

In contrast with the above, the purely functional organization provides flexibility in the use of manpower. Personnel can be used in many different projects; specialists can be grouped so that knowledge and experience gained on one project is transferred to another. But the functional form of organization fails to provide the prime elements sought by project managers--project emphasis and responsiveness to project needs.

In the formulation of a plan for managing projects, the executive seeks to maximize effectiveness and efficiency. This may require some mix of project and functional concepts of management. While project management has become firmly embedded in federal management practice and will likely continue for an indefinite period, the thrust of this chapter is to point out the managerial needs of procurement and other functional groups and to gain recognition that project management is not without its costs.

Notes

[1] Report of the Commission on Government Procurement, Vol. 1, GPO, 1972, pp. 43-45.

[2] Henri Fayol, General and Industrial Administration. London: Sir Isaac Pitman & Sons, Ltd., 1949, p. 3.

[3] David I. Cleland and William R. King, Systems Analysis and Project Management. New York: McGraw-Hill Book Company, 1968, p. 152.

9 | Applications of Data Processing in Procurement

The federal government's efforts during the last decade to reform and update methods of contracting for goods and services have been discussed in Chapters 5 and 6. Coincident with those efforts the nation has experienced a revolution in information processing capabilities known as automatic data processing (ADP). Based on electronics, information is coded, moved, modified, compared, and interpreted in digital form. ADP's impact on management and on contracting methods promises to be far greater than that of the procurement reform effort even including the effects of CICA. To date, ADP's effects are only beginning to emerge.

Since 1980, the introduction of microprocessor-based computers and expanded application of data communications technology has filled gaps in potential uses of information technology that main frame computers alone could not reach. Today, distributed processing (this term is used to mean multiple processors, each with local systems software, connected by a communications network with other processors and/or a main frame computer) of information is available to all business functions that depend on text and numerical information. This factor so increases the flexibility with which the technology can be applied and so reduces its cost that greater use in all phases of procurement work is indisputably essential. For those working in the field, learning computer skills as a standard part of procurement expertise can only be described as tardy. While ADP has been broadly applied in financial, quality assurance, scheduling, accounting, and other business functions--including broad management information systems--its adoption by the procurement community has only begun.

Tardiness in adopting computer technology is probably caused by the fact that procurement requires large amounts of qualitative as well as quantitative information, and much of it originates externally from the buyer's organization. The result is an apparent resistance of the procurement process to the automation of its operations. Nevertheless, the procurement community has joined the revolution. The analytical and information search and processing powers lent by the computer must be mastered. This chapter examines potential applications of ADP in government procurement, reports on an applications survey, conducted by the author, of actual uses of ADP at the buyer/negotiator level in government, and includes brief descriptions of selected government procurement ADP systems.

Management, Statistical and Operational ADP Applications in Government Procurement

There are numerous individual ways in which automated data processing can enhance and improve purchasing. Some of the applications serve the manager's needs, others serve the buyer's or negotiator's needs, and still others serve the needs of procurement clerks and contract writers. At the management level ADP provides improved reporting and more timely awareness of activities going on at the operating level. In a fully developed system, the manager may observe enhancements to the productivity of the purchasing staff at all levels. However, in examining the benefits of automated processing, we must recognize that systems which aid the manager may not be of great practical value to the buyer or analyst. Conversely, systems which are of particular use to the operating level personnel may appear to be expensive and may have relatively little value to the manager for information and decisionmaking. Also, if not understood or not used effectively, ADP equipment investments appear not to be cost effective.

In government (as in all large organizations), there is a tendency to develop procurement automation first at a level which benefits the top management of the agency through generation of comprehensive management information. This serves the head of agency and the oversight levels of the government power structure.

The application of ADP in government procurement differs somewhat from applications in private sector purchasing organizations. The early applications in government were responses to government policy initiatives which require development of overall statistics regarding the placement of government procurement dollars. The statistical reporting supports evaluation of various social and economic oriented government policy actions. These have little direct relationship to the needs of an agency which sponsors a particular procurement action. One example of this type of reporting system is the Federal Procurement Data Center developed since 1979, which comprehensively gathers statistics and generates reports aimed at creating accurate government-wide and agency-wide statistical summaries. The statistics are valuable to many groups, but they are of little use to the procuring activity in its acquisition mission. The new statutory mandate contained in the Competition in Contracting Act for computerized recording and reporting of competitive and noncompetitive contract awards adds to the importance of this type of ADP application.

Potential ADP Applications in Procurement

The following listing is a summary of individual and specific aspects of a purchasing organization which could be enhanced or improved through automated processing of information. The listing is not intended to be exhaustive, but it should provide the reader with a general understanding of the varied applications and significant power which ADP will lend to the contracting community. It should also stimulate reflection on the potential for productivity improvement arising from more sophisticated application of information processing equipment and procedures. Although listed as independent systems, linkage and potentially full integration of the systems is feasible if based on a distributed data processing concept.

1. Source listing. A data base built through capabilities filings initiated by interested vendors, classified by products and services, and designed for generation of specific source lists.
2. Source research. A data base built through buyer-initiated market search using existing commerical and government information systems, survey research and other positive search techniques. Such a system could aim at extension of source qualification on a world-wide basis.
3. Supplier performance. A data base of objective information on performance of existing suppliers organized to capture purchase order results in areas such as timeliness of delivery, quality of products, service when problems arise, etc.
4. Purchase planning. Integration of purchase planning with cash management and schedule planning systems for the organization.
5. Operations measurement. A management system to record work assignment within the purchasing organization and to assess workload schedule and performance.
6. Workload planning. A system at the operating level which supports workload planning and scheduling and which generates status of work in progress. May be coupled with operations measurement.
7. Acquisition management information. A data base that supports management information needs at all levels for each phase of the procurment process including planning, solicitation and award, contract performance, and closeout of contracting documents.
8. Inventory analysis. An on-line data base focused on timely identification of requirements containing, as a minimum, inventory status, order status, lead time data, and customer demand schedules. Where feasible, this system would be part of a materials requirements planning system.

9. Purchase order generation. An on-line system based on automated sampling of inventory and source data automation for all requisitions. May be linked with the inventory analysis system.
10. Purchase analysis. A system containing models and analytical procedures for cost and price projections and comparisons.
11. Price comparison. An on-line data base containing analytical models and price schedules, organized by industry group and commodity or service items and based on research into the commodity and service categories used by the purchasing organization. Linked with the source research data base, this system will increase competition and drive productivity gains.
12. Document generation. A data base for generation of solicitation and contract documents built on a comprehensive analysis of regulatory requirements and established contract clauses.
13. Communications. An electronic mail system that provides electronic transmission of orders, expediting notices, invoices, payment advice and other routine information flow with established vendors.
14. Contract payments. A system that allows full control of payments based on electronic review of acceptance, billing, purchase order, and cash management information. Requires source data automation and communications arrangements.

Many of the elements of the listed information systems have been implemented or designed for various government agencies. However, at this point, the author knows of no government organization or agency that embraces all of these potential information processing modules in its procurement systems.

Survey of Automatic Data Processing Applications in Government Procurement Operations

During the summer, 1984, the author conducted an informal survey of fifteen government contracting activities for the purpose of determining what stage those activities had reached in their adoption and use of automatic data processing equipment. In conducting the survey fourteen specific procurement capabilities or procedures listed above were used as indicators of ADP applications. Each of the procedures appears to hold potential for substantial improvement and more economical performance of procurement work. The author interviewed contract specialists, negotiators, and/or supervisory personnel whose expertise was developed as negotiators or contract specialists in government procurement positions. Each was asked whether the capability or procedure existed and to respond only with respect to operations with which he/she was directly familiar.

Use of ADP techniques requires availability of equipment which may limit adoption of useful procedures. In conducting the survey the respondents were asked what equipment was available to negotiators and/or contract specialists. While several offices have a computer terminal or a microcomputer available, in only a few cases was it actually located at their desk or work station.

Furthermore, the existence of a terminal or microcomputer at a desk or available to the buying personnel does not, by itself, indicate utilization of that equipment for substantive contracting action. To a large extent, in surveying the government agencies, the degree of use was dependent upon the interest and initiative of the individual buyer or contract specialist. Little organizational emphasis has been placed on the adoption of skills in using analytical procedures, such as spread sheet analysis, which the computer might support. A number of agencies spoke of training programs in this regard, but the current status of training is sporadic, at best. From Table 9-1 it is clear that having a computer or terminal available is not a good indication of the level of use of ADP, although it is a necessary prerequisite.

The fourteen items used in the survey, with a tabulation of the responses to the questions, are listed on Table 9-1. The numbers and percentages in the table give a summary indication of the overall position of government agencies in their use of automatic data processing in the procurement field. However, the table data requires some interpretation and discussion in order to clearly understand the position of the government agen-

Table 9-1

Use of Automation in Support of Contracting Operations
By United States Government Procurement
Offices Fifteen-Agency Sample, August, 1984[a]

Procurement Procedures That Can Be Aided By ADP	Contract Offices with an Operational Capability	
	Number	Percent
1. Source listing	4	27
2. Source research	0	0
3. Supplier performance	4	27
4. Purchase planning	4	27
5. Operations measurement	10	67
6. Workload planning	3	20
7. Acquisition management information	7	47
8. Inventory analysis	2	13
9. Purchase order generation	2	13
10. Purchase analysis	5	33
11. Price comparison	3	20
12. Document generation	8	53
13. Communications	4	27
14. Contract payments	1	7
Aggregate	57	27

[a]Of the fifteen offices sampled, two had terminals or microcomputers readily available or at the desk of procurement personnel. Ten had such equipment in the organization and somewhat available to personnel. Two had initiated action toward greater use of the technology.

cies as a group. The following discussion treats each item by taking the most prevalently used ones first.

Operations Measurement

Of the several specific applications of information processing capability investigated in the survey, only one showed extensive actual use: item 5, operations measurement. Two-thirds of the agencies use some form of automation to track the assignment of work and its status for individuals within the purchasing organization. Most of the agencies batch processed on a weekly basis. Only two had on-line capabilities. Clearly, work status reporting as an aid to management and supervisory personnel is in use. Its use is not approaching that afforded by current technology, but it appears to be attractive for a strong majority of the government offices queried. Of the fifteen offices sampled, two had terminals or microcomputers readily available or at the desk of negotiation personnel. Ten had such equipment in the organization and available to negotiation personnel. Two had initiated action toward this objective.

Document Generation

The second most prevalent use of information processing equipment is in the generation of contract documents, item 12. All of the agencies have word processing equipment, but use of a computer data base of terms and conditions was limited to 50 percent of the agencies surveyed. Where an electronic data base existed it contained the standard clauses necessary to formulate a complete contract document. Some examples of this application follow.

The Air Force has developed a system known as the Acquisition Management Information System (AMIS) which features an application called Distributed Processing for Contractual Input (DPCI). AMIS will be discussed later in this chapter, but DPCI is of interest here because of its comprehensive contract document preparation capabilities. DPCI is designed to automate the writing and publi-

cation of solicitation and contract documents, while automatically capturing all pertinent contract information as
these documents are being prepared. It is considerably
more than a word processing system, because DPCI is built
upon a data base inclusive of FAR and DOD FAR supplement
clauses, as well as a vast array of historical data that
may be pertinent to the instant procurement action.

DPCI features simple question and answer computer
screens that explore the procurement situation by asking
basic questions, such as the dollar value of the action,
whether the contractor is large or small business,
whether government property is being furnished to the contractor, etc. Based on the answers given by the contract
specialist or writer, the system selects all appropriate
clauses, formats the document into the DOD uniform contract format, and prints it "free-form," that is, on
plain bond paper, ready for procurement action review or
signature.

DPCI is not designed as an aid for the preparation
of purchase orders and other simple contract documents.
Its purpose is to support the writing of contracts which
are complex because of size, lengthy time period, or
nature of the undertaking. DPCI is an operational system
with the advantage that procurement clerks, negotiators
or contract writers can easily prepare contract documents
with a minimum of training on the system. A similar system, which is known by the acronym PADDS (for Procurement
Automated Data and Document System), has been developed
by the Army.

The Air Force Office of Scientific Research (AFOSR)
has developed a system that not only prepares the contract document and selects FAR clauses, but also allows
for preparation of the purchase request (PR), statement
of work, contract data requirements list, and other narra-
tive attachments to the contract. As the administrative
process from generation of the PR to contract award is
accomplished, the action is tracked by the automated
system. At different stages of the process, different
members of the procurement team access the system, add
their inputs (such as the statement of work, line item
descriptions, prices, special provisions, and so forth)
and build the document to its final contractual form.
When the contract is being assembled for final review,

signature, and distribution, the contract specialist is able to "call up" all pertinent documents on one work station for editing and printing.

A less complex contract writing program has been developed by the Environmental Protection Agency. The EPA system is called Automated Procurement Documentation System or APDS. APDS is based on a series of questions which, when answered, allow the computer to select contract clauses which are contained within its data base including the Federal Acquisition Regulation and agency unique clauses. The system has been designed for use by clerks and other personnel in the writing of contracts, but the routine is considerably simpler than those which the Army and Air Force have developed.

Other contract writing systems using personal computers have been developed by individual agencies (for example, Goddard Space Flight Center). Commercial organizations have entered this field by developing software that aids preparation of solicitations and contracts based on the new Federal Acquisition Regulation system. One such system is known as FARA II. It is an inquiry system which allows the operator to respond to questions regarding the type of contract to be used, the method of solicitation, and the nature of the acquisition itself. The computer is then able to assemble the required document. Refinements of the document are incorporated by word processing and it is then transmitted to a printer.

The FARA II system has a number of interesting advantages. It is designed to run on microcomputers and is based on the standard MS-DOS, or CPM operating systems. It is also a system which can be tailored to the requirements of individual government agencies by the simple process of adding into the data base the agency's specific sets of clauses.

From these illustrations, it is clear that one of the modes in which the federal system is automating is in the preparation of its contract documents. Systems for that purpose appeal to government because of the multitude of regulatory clauses and rules for their use. The programs are relatively easily prepared, they act as an excellent checklist, and the resulting documents are current respecting regulatory changes--more orderly and more legible.

These systems probably should not be needed for the government's huge volume of purchase orders (orders less than $25 thousand) which can be based on a simplified set of terms and conditions; however, DOD agencies have developed extensive automated small purchase systems to process these relatively simple actions. For example, the Air Force's Customer Integrated Automated Procurement System (CIAPS) is an Air Force-wide base level procurement automation system that features computer-generated PRs, requests for proposal, delivery and purchase orders and management reports. It includes an automated bidders mailing list and selects sources from this list on a rotating basis to receive solicitations. CIAPS has been operational since 1971.

Defense Logistics Agency also has an automated small purchase system with much the same capability of CIAPS, known as the Standard Automated Materiel Management System (SAMMS), which automatically issues blanket purchase agreement calls and delivery orders up to $25 thousand and selects the lowest quotation for award of purchase orders. Notwithstanding these examples, however, many federal agencies are not yet using even this relatively simple form of automation.

Only these first three applications of ADP, operations measurement, document generation, and MIS, approach or exceed 50 percent use in the sample of procuring activities reported here, but these three areas are being rapidly expanded by the agencies.

Acquisition Management Information

Seven agencies included in the survey have developed an acquisition management information system. These systems vary widely in capability and magnitude. The most comprehensive is probably that of the Air Force Systems Command's AMIS (Acquisition Management Information System) with its comprehensive data base on a command-wide basis. Most other management information systems reported by respondents were local and were aimed primarily at schedule status. In this regard, each of the respondents was asked whether he/she inputted the system and, in addition, whether reports or other useful outputs were obtained by it. In most cases the operating level person inputted data but did not obtain reports. The Air Force AMIS system (discussed further in this chapter) with its on-line reporting capabilities does support inquiry by all levels of acquisition personnel.

Purchase Analysis

One of the major potential applications of the computer in support of procurement action is cost and price analysis. In this area, however, only one-third of the sample reported substantial progress. Respondents expressed great interest in use of such techniques as spreadsheet analysis and statistical projections but reported no strong agency-inspired thrust toward providing training and equipment.

Source Listing

Four agencies have on-line data bases which can be queried for bidders lists. In each case the on-line data base was based upon supplier initiated submission of data (Standard Form 129 or Small Business Administration, PASS system.) Two of the agencies generally did not create a bidders list, relying instead on their synopses in the Commerce Business Daily to generate their bids and proposals.

Supplier Performance

The creation and use of supplier performance information was surprisingly sparce among the agencies. Only four agencies create automated records of their suppliers' compliance with contract obligations in areas such as delivery, milestone adherence, reporting, timeliness, financial status, and other dimensions of the performance of contract work.

Purchase Planning

Relatively little use was made of computer technology in the planning of procurement activities. Only four respondents reported any effort to integrate the planning of procurement activity with agency financial and schedule planning conducted at other levels. In lieu of automated information bases, the planning activity generally was conducted by personal contact and hard copy communications.

Communications

Table 9-1 indicates that four of the agencies sampled had established some form of data communications. These were electronic mail systems. However, in three cases, these systems were new and rudimentary and were limited in terms of the number of stations served. Not found were fully developed on-line interactive message sending and receiving capabilities, coupled with queuing of messages for delivery upon the daily start up of each terminal. One agency had subscribed to a commercial electronic mail system and was fully operational but served only a limited number of terminals.

Price Comparison Data Base

Use of the computer to create data bases of pricing information is believed to hold considerable potential for improved pricing activity. Nevertheless, only three agencies had generated price data bases and all three were limited to the recording of prices paid and similar information drawn from prior contracts which the agency had awarded. There were no cases in which an affirmative effort had been mounted to use market research techniques to create a pricing data base for use in cost and price analysis activity.

Workload Planning

Although the use of operations measurement by ADP was one of the most extensively applied techniques, only three of the sampled agencies had provided ADP support of planning activities to the operating level negotiator, contract specialist, or buyer. To some degree, of course, these personnel are supported by management information systems or schedule reporting systems which facilitate assessing and projecting the status of work.

Inventory Analysis

Item 8 in Table 9-1 was included in an effort to determine whether government agencies have integrated their inventory and procurement responsibilities in a way to allow automated generation of requisitions. Of the respondents, only two reported any tie-in between the generation of procurement requests or requisitions and an on-line data processing system containing a base of inventory and lead-time information, order status, and other data essential to the initiation of procurement activity.

Purchase Order Generation

Might the entire purchasing process be automated by government agencies? As indicated by item 9, only two offices in the survey have adopted such a system. (The CIAPS and SAMMS systems were discussed previously under the heading "Document Generation.") Nevertheless, the concept of generating a purchase order by an on-line ADP system is important wherever high volume ordering occurs. Respondents recognize that the computer, if it has inventory, lead time, order status and supplier data within its data base, could be used to generate the purchase order automatically.

Contract Payments

Electronic transmission and verification of invoice

payments was surprisingly low in its rate of utilization. Only one agency had such a system. Although the Department of the Treasury has initiated electronic fund transfer for many government payments, the system is not generally supported in procuring agencies by electronic processing of the documents necessary to create a public voucher authorizing expenditure of government funds. Reliance on hard copy records of key documents such as invoices, contracts and modifications has not noticeably diminished.

Source Research

None of the surveyed agencies had initiated any proactive source research activities on a systematic basis, ADP or otherwise. The agencies rely on contractor initiative to file Standard Form 129 or to initiate contact in some other way. It is the author's observation that buyer initiative might be added to sellor marketing efforts as a way of broadening the industrial base on which government operations rely. Collection, organization, and retrieval of useful source data would be enhanced by ADP. Its value would be even greater if data communications allowed extension to query remote data bases.

Table 9-1 may be viewed as a quantitative measure of federal government use of automated systems in its contracting work. The sample size for the survey was fifteen, and the number of capabilities/applications queried totalled fourteen. Consequently, the data collected forms a matrix with 210 cells. With 57 cells filled, it may be said that 27 percent of the sampled use potential is being employed. While that statistic is debatable (it overstates the level of use in terms of current, 1984, technology), there is no question that a great deal must be done for government to secure the benefits of automation in this field. Even with respect to the data presented, a significant number of interpretive comments may be needed in order to reliably assess the current status of government agencies in their implementation of ADP for procurement purposes.

Selected ADP System Description: AMIS

At this time there does not appear to be any fully integrated purchasing management systems in the federal government.   However,   there are   several   examples   of advanced information processing systems in use.   Some of these   systems   have   very   large   data   bases.   One major example (already mentioned) of a government procurement-related information system is the United States Air Force Acquisition Management Information System (AMIS) which is headquartered at Wright Patterson Air Force Base, Ohio. AMIS is a product of the Air Force Systems Command.   It has been in development for over ten years and is operating   to   support   Air   Force-wide   acquisition   information needs.   It is an automated contract data repository and communications   system   with   information   on   over   60,000 active contracts.

At the present stage of its development, the AMIS system supports management needs for information on administration   of   contracts   and   delivery   of items.   It also provides for electronic payment of invoices.   Other than the   preparation   of   solicitation and contract documents, it is not currently supporting the solicitation and award and   planning   phases   of   the   procurement   process.   With further   development   and   through   integration   with   other independently   developing   information   systems,   the   AMIS will   support   comprehensively   the   acquisitions   process. In   the   case   of   an   organization   as   large   as   the   United States Air Force, the contracting functions are geographically   dispersed,   yet   must   be   coordinated   among   various entities   within   the   Air   Force   system.   Therefore they are dependent   upon   timely   input   of   accurate   information describing   the   end   product   and   status   of   the   contract under   consideration.

The   AMIS   will   generate   summary   activity   reports, respond   to   one-time   inquiries   from   an   acquisitions office, and support on-going dialogue with other contracting   functions.   It is a part of the management control process   of   the   Air   Force   Systems   Command.   It   captures data on all new contracts and is updated as contracts are modified   and   various   events   such   as   deliveries   and   payments   occur.   The   system   is   designed   to   be   able   to respond   to   the   myriad   questions   that   may   be   asked   about

the status and schedule of a contract during its performance period.

The AMIS has been structured by design to comply
fully with the Department of Defense uniform contract
format and with the uniform data exchange requirements of
the Military Standard Contract Administration Procedures
(MILSCAP). Because of this basic compliance with mili-
tary-wide formats and procedures, the AMIS is able to
converse with contracting agencies other than the Air
Force Systems Command. Specifically, it is able to
communicate with the Air Force Logistics Command, the
Army, the Defense Contract Administration Services
regions, and other government contract entities. It
should be noted however, that these organizations are not
generally fully MILSCAP compatible with the exception of
the Army. AMIS is intended to be a user-oriented system,
taking advantage of current technology to enhance both
its data input programs and its ability to respond to
inquiries and report requirements. In its strict functional definition, the AMIS is designed to be a command-
wide central repository of contract schedule data structured so as to allow current updating and immediate
communications for the entire command and for other authorized users. It is fully automated and allows immediate
access to the information contained within it by Air
Force Systems Command users at all levels including the
Air Force Systems Command contract payment functions.

As indicated by the foregoing discussion, the
effects of ADP on management and on contracting methods
within the federal government are just beginning to
emerge. A strong movement toward expanded use is discernable and some sophisticated systems are in place, yet it
should be clear that additional impetus is needed to
foster adoption of the technology. The movement needs to
be managed so that disruption of operations does not
occur and to prevent wasteful duplication of effort and
expenditure of funds. A first step toward this integration has been the establishment of the Procurement Automation Council (PAC) under the auspices of the Office of
Federal Procurement Policy. The PAC is comprised of
representatives from federal agencies. It meets twice
monthly to discuss fundamental issues in procurement automation. New and ongoing efforts within the agencies,

plus lessons learned from past experiences, are shared
among council members in hope that costly mistakes won't
be repeated. Formation of the council may well be the
first step toward creating a comprehensive, integrated
federal procurement automation systems concept.

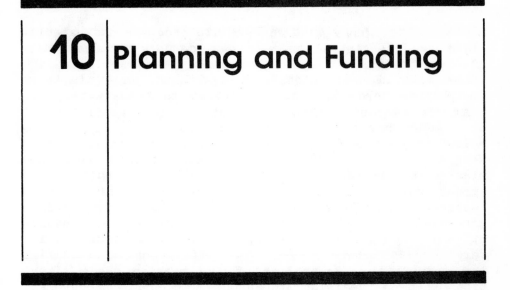

10 | Planning and Funding

Setting objectives, planning, and funding, important processes in government procurement activities, are addressed in this chapter. The first topic is the role of top management in setting objectives and in planning and securing resources. To accomplish these goals, a team of specialists prepares the plans and statements of requirements necessary for individual acquisitions. The chapter then turns to a discussion of acquisition planning factors. This is followed by an examination of basic features of technical documentation necessary for the solicitation and award process. Execution of the federal budget is treated next, but only in terms of its relationship to contract funding. Funding of contracts and a treatment of contract finance complete the chapter.

Setting Objectives
and Securing Resources

As agencies approach decisions to undertake projects or work efforts, they encounter various situations, some of which require reexamination of their congressional charter to determine the scope and definition of their mission. When the undertaking is within its established mission, the agency must analyze its programs and capabilities to determine whether it has adequate manpower, facilities, funds, and other resources necessary to fulfill those mission commitments. This kind of review is known as mission needs analysis. Through this analysis, program and resource gaps that exist in the capabilities of the agency are identified, and program needs may be perceived or capabilities sought that will fill these gaps. When the analysis of needs discloses that a redefined mission or new program authority will be required, the agency must seek additions to its responsibilities by seeking approval of the Congress. When the agency already possesses adequate mission definition and capabilities or resources, it can proceed. It will define its requirements and generate a work effort that will fulfill the commitment. Regardless of the mission needs situation when a decision to proceed occurs, procurement action is often necessary.

Questions of mission and capabilities do not arise for ordinary activity. For example, logistics and supply requirements are generated by a review of inventories, and rates of consumption of those inventories, as the agency pursues its normal operating plan. Similarly, an agency may possess an item of equipment which is performing its work, yet may need repair, overhaul, or design modification. The perception of these needs precipitates initiation of a purchase action. Sometimes, an agency may identify the need for new equipment or services to be rendered and as a consequence, will have to define, for purposes of an acquisition action, the detailed description of the necessary equipment or services. The normal result of such analysis is the generation of a purchase request.

In the situation of an agency with a research and development mission, the discovery of a weakness in existing hardware for which it is responsible may precipitate a new research, design or development effort. Again, this discovery normally generates purchase actions to fill the need. Depending on their magnitude and relationship to the agency's current program, these decisions may require the specific approval of higher levels within the agency or perhaps approval of the Congress prior to the initiation of action, but they do not involve mission needs analysis.

The discovery of gaps between mission and capability may be the first step toward a major systems acquisition. For example, in the military, a review of potential enemy threats may reveal the need for a new or improved weapon. Such a conclusion may lead to a decision to seek a new technological capability and the initiation of a technological/conceptual review intended to define an undertaking to meet the threat. This may be performed as an in-house activity, but frequently will be performed principally as a procured activity. Substantial agency resources are devoted (using both in-house and contractual performance methods) to the regular and continuing review of capabilities and needs.

When mission need has been identified and defined, the agency establishes a program office to manage further development and to secure approval of the necessary plans and budgets. Approval of major acquisition programs is obtained one stage at a time, as the magnitude of commitments increases with each step. Acquisition planning and strategy development are specifically designed to ensure that expenditures will fulfill the agency's requirement. In planning an acquisition, agency management must subdivide the work and allocate resources to each subdivision. Sources of capabilities could be internal or external to the agency. The outline of sourcing alternatives is an essential part of acquisition planning. Similarly, the sequence and the schedule for carrying out each stage of the necessary work must be made part of the plan. Perhaps most significant, the acquisition plan must include preliminary cost projections to formulate the basis for initial decisionmaking. These initial steps toward the start of a procurement process must be brought to a conclusion by the presentation of an initial budget.

Planning Factors

A key to successful procurement planning is a system that achieves comprehensive internal coordination. No single office can be staffed to hold expertise in all of the disciplines essential to place and administer a major procurement. This is a result of both the complexity of government policies regarding expenditures through a contract and of the need for a mixture of technological, financial, business management, and contractual fields of expertise. The principal organizational creation that attempts to facilitate this internal coordination requirement is project management, which was discussed in Chapter 8.   matrix

In addition to the use of project management, government agencies have developed the concept of a procurement team to perform contract planning and negotiation. The team concept developed because functional groups such as procurement are not always part of the project office, yet coordination must continue throughout planning and negotiation processes. Each relevant disciplinary group should contribute to formulation of the plans. Each must ensure that an understanding of factors important to their area of responsibility is developed as an agreement is approached. This requires use of the procurement team approach.

Employment of the procurement team is a challenge, because the numerous disciplinary groups may hold widely variant perceptions regarding technical and management factors. Coordination for purposes of contract negotiations, usually under guidance of one functional manager (a contracting officer), is in many respects coincident with the broader coordination duties of the program or project manager, who is assigned responsibility for the system. If these individuals work smoothly together and are successful in securing and considering the inputs of all members of the procurement team, the likelihood of project success is enhanced. Often the necessary level of cooperation and coordination is elusive.

Most of the procurement-critical decisions must occur prior to the start of PALT (Procurement Administrative Lead Time). PALT marks the point of transfer of responsibility for procurement action from the initiator (or requestor) of a procurement action to the contracting unit for the solicitation and award process. Requirements must be defined, funding secured, and procurement planning accomplished prior to the start of PALT. The pre-PALT phases of work are almost invariably under control of a project manager whose definitional, funding, and planning decisions must be compatible with the demands of the solicitation and award process and with the nature of the contractual interface once a contract is established. During the PALT interval, principal responsibility shifts to the contracting officer for preparation of required justifications and management approvals, solicitation, contractor proposal evaluation, pricing, negotiation, and award decisions. The duties of project manager and contracting officer, though distinguishable, interact and directly affect their mutual success.

It is evident that the transfer of responsibility for procurement action at start of PALT should not be the beginning of consultation between members of the procurement team. Early participation by all members of the team greatly enhance both the PALT and contract performance phases of a program.

The Federal Acquisition Regulation addresses procurement planning in general at subpart 7.1. Under the FAR supplements, specific, implementing detail is added at the discretion of the agencies. In the Department of Defense FAR supplement, a formal procurement plan has been required for development procurements over $2 million and for production procurements over $5 million. However, the general use of such plans is encouraged whenever it is considered advisable by management and, under CICA, mandatory formal procurement planning requirements will increase.

The use of a comprehensive plan is not pertinent to individual contracts of small dollar value. However, a formal plan should be developed for projects which include numerous contracts of varying values. The planning factors to be treated are:

1. program, item or system description--including applications and related in-house efforts
2. funding plans and cost estimates
3. delivery requirements with attention to any overlap of development and production efforts
4. relationships with planning, programming, budgeting documents, and review requirements
5. historical summary of the procurement
6. risk analysis: technical, cost and schedule
7. logistics support planning over program life cycle
8. relationship of cost objectives and design factors

including consideration of economic change projections and learning factors

9. consideration of life cycle costing
10. reliability and maintainability factors
11. status and planning for tests and evaluation
12. management systems, information and control requirements
13. schedule for key decisions by general management
14. government-furnished property issues, including any plan for breakout of components
15. cost study methodology pertinent to the procurement
16. detailed milestone analysis and schedule
17. updating considerations for the procurement plan
18. identification of persons participating in preparation of the procurement plan
19. identification (for each proposed contract) of the procurement approach, including:
    a. description of the item
    b. cost estimate
    c. competitive status and expected sources
    d. procedure for source selection
    e. discussion of contract type
    f. basic authority for negotiation
    g. data requirements and intellectual property rights as they relate to competitive reprocurement
    h. policy considerations affecting the procurement
    i. milestone analyses.[1]

Specifications and Work Statements

Central to definition of a requirement for procurement action, technical documentation is developed and approved within program or functional technical offices of executive agencies. These documents must convey sufficient understanding of requirements necessary for the contractor to prepare estimates and perform the work. They must also delineate or provide the basis for interpreting responsibility for work efforts and results pursuant to the contract. It is normally assumed that the parties comprehend the work imposed, but such assumption may be precarious. Frequently the full impact of required work is not appreciated until after performance begins or even later. The documents must also be adequate for the solicitation and award process. However, the nature of that process depends primarily on technical documentation.

Management problems during performance of government contracts often are rooted in ambiguities or defects of the work statement or specification. Many of these problems begin with issues that could have been avoided by better technical documentation.

The administration of changes, terminations, inspection and acceptance of contract end items, interpretation of government property questions, and even the determination of allowable costs are related to proper and complete interpretation of the controlling technical documents. If those documents fully express the need of the government, if they are unambiguous and fully adequate to performance, and if performance by the contractor is fully consistent with the requirements of the controlling documents, contract administration should be relatively straightforward.

Too frequently a government requirement is not adequately expressed by the controlling documents, or the contractor may encounter difficulty achieving the requirements. A combination of these two problems may be encountered with the consequence of greatly complicating the contract administration process.

Perhaps one of the most important aspects of specification interpretation is the determination of the basic nature of the document. Traditionally there have been two primary types: performance documents and design documents. More recently a third type has emerged for government use, the functional specification. All three are mentioned in the Competition in Contracting Act.

A performance document expresses its criteria or standards of performance in terms of functions to be performed, such as degrees of precision or capability levels. Other examples of performance requirements would be speed of a vehicle, reliability standards (such as mean time between failure), accuracy of a measurement instrument, or ability of an end item to withstand environmental conditions. A multitude of other performance standards or requirements could be listed.

By contrast, a design document is one which details what is to be done in terms of physical characteristics. These include size, shape, delineation of component parts, diagrams of wiring or other physical parameters, specification of materials to be used, and many other factors. A design is often specified by inclusion of drawings and parts lists, or by supplying a sample item which is to function as a product standard. The use of a design specification implies that the government is seeking the reproduction of an end item already in existence, or similar to existing items.

The obligations and responsibilities imposed on a contractor differ depending on the character, performance or design of the controlling document. When a design document is used, the contractor is obligated to manufacture and produce an end item which is identical to, or interchangeable with, the item described. The document will include a description of the quality features which are characteristic of the item, and the contractor is responsible for achieving that level of quality in production. When this type of document is used, the contractor is not held responsible for design adequacy. In other words, he is responsible only for duplication of the item which the government has already designed. The sufficiency of that design with respect to the desired use is the user's responsibility.

When a performance document is used, the contractor is responsible for achieving the performance outcome as specified in the document. In research and development work, it is normal for the contractor to encounter a performance specification and other documents which define measurable outcomes and require design and qualification effort. The character of his responsibility is entirely different from that of the producer under a design specification. Acceptance of the end product is dependent upon fulfilling the performance achievement imposed by the document. If the document was properly prepared and expressed operating, environmental, reliability, or other standards of acceptability desired by the government, the contractor becomes responsible to verify achievement of those end objectives.

These distinctions between a performance and a design document are important conceptually. However, it is extremely difficult to distinguish between the two types of characteristics. Many performance requirements have overtones with respect to design, and design constraints may impose limitations on performance outcomes. Furthermore, it is normal for the controlling technical document to contain both performance and design parameters. It is difficult to separate the two.

A functional specification is similar to the performance specification in its omission of design detail. It differs because it sets forth the intended use or application for which the product is bought in lieu of specifying capabilities or performance standards to which the product might be tested. The purpose of the functional specification is to encourage government purchase of commercial products on a competitive basis. Any product meeting the stated functional uses of the agency could compete under this type of document.

An additional factor in procurement is cost. It is more costly to perform the design and qualification work necessary to produce an end result than it is to copy or reproduce work which has been done previously. Yet frequently government end objectives can be achieved only partially by specifying proven designs, and will, in part, require new designs.

Ordinarily, the procurement of an item for which the government has a complete and adequate design document could be most economically accomplished by the use of that document. On the other hand, when a design document is to be used which has not been fully qualified or repeatedly proven in past experiences, or has been changed (which may alter the sufficiency of the document), it may become costly to write a contract requiring the contractor to reproduce only that which is specified. The problem of costliness arises when it is discovered that the document is ambiguous, defective, or where performance is impossible. Conversely, use of a "proven" document may be uneconomic if it specifies an item which is technologically antiquated, even though the procurement itself may be administered without difficulty. This factor is important with respect to currently evolving government policy favoring use of functional specifications for commercial items and performance, rather than design specifications for other acquisitions.

When a government contract imposes upon the contractor a controlling document containing both design and performance parameters, an anomaly may be created. It results when an end item which conforms exactly to the design requirement cannot meet the intended use and performance levels imposed by the performance requirements. Avoidance of this situation should be one of the major objectives of procurement managers.

Interpretation problems arise in government contracting for many reasons. Predominant among the reasons is the tendency to buy advanced technological devices (often ones not proven through repeated production) and the propensity to change the precise description of its end objective after the contract has been awarded.

Another major source of problems in interpretation is the general and intensive pressure of the government to obtain competition in its procurement early in the cycle of procurement action. Much of what the government buys is new in character, or different from that which has been done before. This is true whether it is buying hardware, software, or simply research products. In any case, an intensive effort is mounted to obtain the benefits of competitive procurement processes.

These efforts frequently result in the use of newly developed specifications in competitive procurements, when the new document has not been proven. Each competitor in the procurement process interprets the document and, if a winner of the contract, will proceed to perform in a manner consistent with that interpretation. If the procurement was highly competitive, and the resultant contract was for a fixed price, the contractor who won the award probably did so by interpreting the specifications as requiring the minimum effort and, therefore, the least expensive effort. Once the contract is awarded, the ability to successfully complete the contract profitably may involve intensive cost-cutting during performance.

The supplier is normally allowed to accomplish the work in his own way. Choice of the least expensive method of performance is allowed, provided an acceptable end product is delivered. The government responsibility for adequately and accurately describing its objective or end item is vital to successful contracting and a major element in effective planning for procurement.

Budget Execution

Control over budget execution is exercised by the Office of Mangement and Budget (OMB) through apportionments and by executive agencies in allocations and allotments of each apportionment. These techniques ensure that expenditures of the different parts of the appropriations occur within designated periods. Accounting records, required both during the spending process and upon its completion, result in establishment of hundreds of thousands of separate accounts, making the process complex.

The fundamental steps required for budgetary control consist of planning, scheduling, detection of variances from the plan, analysis of their cause, revision of the plan, and enforcement and continued review. To accomplish these steps, the government agencies develop specific procedures which, in general, can be summarized in four statements:

1. Schedules of estimated obligations must be developed and approved within the management channels of the agency. Generally the schedule must be distributed by calendar quarters within the fiscal year.
2. The apportioned amounts must be subdivided and responsibility for maintaining obligations within these subdivisions must be assigned.
3. The execution process is monitored through the review of status reports on obligations and accrued expenditures.
4. Revised schedules of estimated obligations are developed as their need is indicated. This process is called "reapportionment."

When Congress has appropriated funds, the agencies and departments must initiate action to secure release of their spending authority from OMB. To do this, they review and revise their budgets in accordance with congressional action and submit requests for apportionment to the OMB. The request details the agency's need for funds over the coming fiscal year and proposes a quarterly apportionment schedule. An apportionment on the basis of specific program activities may be used to supplement the time-based proposal.

A review process (generally similar to the budget preparation cycle) is used to provide a basis for the apportionment request. Justification material is based only on the original estimated requirements, but is updated to reflect conditions which have changed since the original estimates were submitted and on the actual dollar availability.

Upon completion of review by OMB, the agency is notified of the funding schedule it will receive. At the end of each month, the agency must make a report of the current status of its appropriations and authorizations, showing the cumulative apportionments, obligations, expenditures, unliquidated obligations and unobligated and unexpended balances. These reports (sent to the Treasury and the OMB) provide the ability to perform continuous monitoring of the apportionment status. Agencies may initiate requests for change in apportionments as necessary. These changes are approved by the OMB in the same manner as the original request.

The second step in the budget execution cycle is the allocation process; it extends obligational authority to administrative units within the department or agency. (In some departments the procedure described here is termed allotment. The term is not standardized throughout the executive branch. Used interchangeably, both terms are defined as the authorization to incur obligations or to make expenditures.) In this step, the agency head extends obligational authority to subordinate administrative units and may limit the authority in terms of objects of expenditures, activities, or organizational units, as long as the allocation is in accordance with the agency's apportionment.

Obligational authority is further extended to subordinate organizations by the allotment process; it is used to divide the allocations assigned to major operating agencies within the department. The allotment provides the organization (at the operating level) with the ability to carry out its assigned mission by authorizing it to obligate the government to pay for required goods and services.

Within operating agencies, control over funds to be obligated by contract is exercised by a financial management officer. Control is established by requiring certification of procurement requests that funds are available. Coincident with this certification is commitment of a portion of an available appropriation to the specific procurement action. The commitment reserves the funds for that action and reduces the available obligational authority with respect to other actions. The funds are obligated when a contract is executed, and the appropriation account is adjusted to reflect the remaining obligational authority.

Incurring obligations does not necessarily mean that an immediate expenditure of cash occurs. In some cases, the obligation and the expenditure of funds may coincide; in others, there may be a considerable passage of time before expenditure occurs. In the purchase of existing assets or in the procurement of services (particularly those of government employees), the expenditure occurs close to the time of commitment. When the government contracts with the private sector (for purposes such as construction, development or production), the lag of expenditures behind obligations may be substantial.

Contract Funding

Contract funding refers to the obligation of funds through contractual action. It constrains but does not include payments to contractors. Contract finance refers to the contractor's need for working capital during performance. Payments to contractors are treated in this chapter under Contract Finance. In government, the procurement manager has responsibilities in both areas. The subject is treated in FAR subpart 32.7.

Normally, contract funding creates a government obligation through bilateral signature (contractor and contracting officer) on a contract or modification. It is a type of action that occurs frequently.

While many contracts are fully funded at the time of their original award, some are not. Most fixed-priced contracts for work to be completed within one year will be fully funded at the outset. This is the simplest arrangement, and reflects a conservative financial management on the part of the federal agency. However, full funding of the negotiated amount of contracts at their outset is not likely when large dollar projects (particularly ones which will extend over a period of several years) are the subject of the procurement. Several factors which cause this should be recognized.

First and foremost, the Congress appropriates monies annually; funds for subsequent years of a contract's life often will not be appropriated at the beginning of the project. This will be true even for research and development funds, although such funds are appropriated largely on a no-year or multi-year basis. This type of funding differs from funding of procurement and production work by annual monies. The annual monies must be obligated within their fiscal year of appropriation, but this is not true of no-year and multi-year funds.

When contracts are not fully funded at time of award, a major responsibility of procurement managers is maintaining currency with respect to the funding of ongoing work. The funding status of a contract is defined by the relationship between the amount of funds allotted to (obligated for) the contract and the amount of cost incurred by the contractor. Ordinarily it is expected that the amount of funds allotted and obligated should exceed the amount of costs incurred.

Funding status is not directly concerned with the question of contract pricing. The price, or estimated cost of a contract, is the subject of a pricing agreement between the contracting officer and the contractor. Funding status pertains to the relationship between the amount of the government's legal obligation and the amount of the contractor's incurred costs.

Funding status reflects, and is a product of, financial administration of the agency and its planning, programming, budgeting and budget execution processes. A current awareness of the status of all contracts (especially those that are incrementally funded) is vital. It is important that contracts not fall into a deficit situation. To maintain a current awareness of contract status the contractor must make required financial reports, and the agency must review them to be alert to any additional changes in the expected funding schedule.

The contractual basis for this ongoing effort is the

inclusion of incremental funding provisions--specifically the Limitation of Funds or Limitation of Cost clauses. When an incremental funding clause is used, agency management must regularly review the rate of expenditure of funds and should program funds to cover the contractor's expenditure rate. While funding clauses establish the legal basis for scheduled obligations, it remains the responsibility of the agency to ensure that the funds are appropriately budgeted and available in accordance with the schedule.

The incremental funding clauses obligate the contractor to notify the contracting officer whenever incurred costs are projected to exceed, within sixty days, 75 percent of the total amount allotted to the contract (this percentage and number of days can be varied within limits). The purpose of the notification is to ensure that additional obligations can be met on time. While the government does not have any legal obligation to add additional funds to an existing contract which has been incrementally funded, the contractor is not obligated to continue performance of the contract when allotted funds have been exhausted.

The use of an incremental funding clause increases the agency's managerial responsibilities. Maintenance of contractual funding schedules is a constraint on agency propensity to use available funds to simultaneously carry on the maximum number of projects possible. This may cause management to schedule small allotments of funds to many contracts. By this approach, the least amount is tied up in obligated, but unexpended, balances on contracts.

Funding, whether simple or complex, acts as a limit on payments, since no amounts can be disbursed unless obligations are first established for a sum equal to or in excess of the payment. Ordinarily, payments follow the contractor's incurrence of costs and disbursements as he performs. Funding is directly tied to execution of the federal budget and involves development of financial plans to perform approved programs, and subsequently, to review performance. A key objective of agency management is to ensure that limitations on available funds are not exceeded in accomplishing the plans.

Government personnel are enjoined not to encourage

contractors to perform work beyond the amount of contract obligations. However, there is no legal prohibition against a contractor expending an amount greater than the obligation. Such expenditures are at the contractor's risk since the government's legal liability is limited to the obligated sum. Historically, significant risk capital has been expended by contractors in connection with some high priority projects.

Contract Finance

Funding, whether a simple, single-sum obligation or a complex schedule of obligations, is associated with contract finance only as a limit on payments to the contractor for amounts expended by him. Managing payments and determining payment schedules are vitally important to contractors since they affect the company's working capital position. Contractors are responsible for financing their working capital needs during performance of the contract but seek to reduce capital needs through payments. Like funding, payments may be in one sum or in increments over time. However, they are normally made after performance, whereas funding actions should occur before performance. Several mechanisms exist whereby the government will aid the contractor in financing working capital. This subject is covered in FAR part 32.

As part of an effort to encourage competition and to provide the broadest possible competitive basis for procurement, the government has adopted a policy of providing financial assistance to a contractor. Contract financing is regarded as a tool to be used for the benefit of the government by aiding and expediting performance and delivery. The basic objective is to support procurement and production and to foster small business policy by providing necessary funds to enable contractors to perform.

Government financing should be provided only to the extent that it is reasonably required for prompt and efficient performance. It is not ordinarily authorized for purposes other than the working capital needs of the contractor. Thus, it is normally precluded when the purpose of financing is to allow the expansion of contractor facilities. In addition, an order of preference exists in the financing techniques on which contractors may rely. Private financing is the first and simplest technique. It implies one payment after delivery and acceptance. Partial payments are similar. Agencies normally permit a liberal policy in making partial payments for partial deliveries of a contract's total performance. By this approach, the contractor's commitment of private capital, as well as the government's need to provide financing, is minimized.

Basic financing policy dictates that agencies facilitate making contract payments. Congress set a standard for payment of contractors in the Prompt Payment Act (P.L. 97-177, approved May 21, 1982) by directing that payment be made within thirty days after receipt of a proper invoice. Payment of interest for delay beyond the payment due date was also directed by the statute, but only if the delay exceeds fifteen days (time intervals differ for food products and agricultural commodities). Administration of interest payments remains complicated because of numerous arrangements and variables associated with them.

To take advantage of a contractor's ability to secure working capital from financial institutions without government aid, the Assignment of Claims Act of 1940 is significant. It enabled government contractors to assign claims for payment under federal contracts to banks, trust companies or other financial institutions. For many contractors, this authorization enhances borrowing capacity. Under the act, government payments are made directly to the lender, thereby increasing assurance of repayment of the loan. In 1951, the Assignment of Claims Act was amended to provide protection to the assignee (that is, the bank or other financial institution) against setoffs of assigned funds resulting from unrelated financial obligations of the contractor to the government. A setoff is essentially a reduction of the amount of funds due by the amount of funds owed.

There are four methods by which the government provides contractors with working capital. Listed in their preferred order of use, they are: customary progress payments, guaranteed loans when authorized, unusual progress payments, and advance payments.

The preferred method is customary progress payments based on cost incurred by the contractor. (For construction or shipwork, progress payments are based on percentage or stage of completion rather than cost.) Progress payments are normally authorized when lead time from contract award to first delivery is six months or more (four months for small businesses). The customary payment rate is 90 percent of total cost incurred (95 percent for small businesses), but may be for a smaller percentage at the discretion of the agency. Any higher rate is considered an unusual progress payment and is restricted to special circumstances and must be approved by the head of the procuring activity. The DOD also has adopted a system of flexible progress payments.

Solicitations frequently provide for customary progress payments. The provisions covering them may be included in solicitations whenever the contracting officer believes that the period from the beginning of work to the first delivery of production quantities will exceed six months, or if he considers that the progress payments will be useful and necessary on the basis that substantial accumulation of predelivery costs could have a material impact on the contractor's working funds.

Although not used extensively in peacetime, contractors involved in the national defense may be authorized to use a guaranteed loan. Under the guaranteed loan procedure, a financing institution loans the needed funds directly to the contractor only after the loan is guaranteed by the government. The loan is guaranteed through the Federal Reserve Board on the authorization of the procuring activity and a fee is charged for this service. Its advantage lies principally in making available to a contractor private financial sources otherwise unavailable. Government funds do not become involved in this type of arrangement unless the contractor is financially unable to meet his commitment to the lending institution.

If necessary, a contractor may be authorized unusual progress payments. When this occurs, it involves either a payment in excess of the percentage limitations required for customary progress payments or shorter lead time than required for customary progress payments, or both. They require special justifications by the contractor prior to authorization.

The least preferred method of government financing of a contract is advance payments. This method of financing differs from the other techniques in that funds are paid into a special bank account in advance of performance. The contractor pays contract accounts by drawing on the special bank account. Advance payments are made in anticipation of and for the purpose of complete performance under a contract or contracts. They are expected to be liquidated from payments due the contractor incident to performance of contracts. The primary uses of advance payments are for the financing of research or research and development contracts with nonprofit educational institutions and for the management and operation of government-owned plants.

Notes

[1]The FAR Subpart 7.1 details planning factors for acquisitions, however this listing was based on DAR 1-2102.

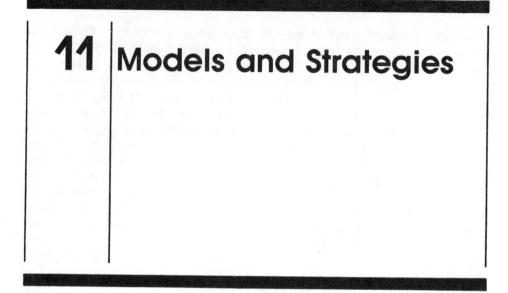

11 | Models and Strategies

Three models of the procurement process are presented in this chapter. Each contributes to understanding procurement by placing emphasis on particular aspects. The first model, prepared by the COGP in 1972, has become the most widely recognized model of the federal procurement system.[1] Following that, a generic model developed by the author is offered. The third model is one that the Office of Federal Procurement Policy prepared in 1976 and published as its "Major Systems Acquisition Cycle."[2] The OFPP model summarizes the procurement methodology instituted by OMB Circular A-109 and characterized in this book as technological/conceptual procurement.

The chapter focuses next on procurement strategy. It distinguishes between acquisition and procurement strategies, developing the thesis that the principal objective of procurement strategy is optimal source selection, whereas the principal objective of acquisition strategy is mission fulfillment. Nevertheless, the two are interdependent. While four different solicitation and award processes are discussed in the context of procurement strategy, the chapter asserts that procurement management must devise a strategy appropriate to each particular acquisition.

Finally, the chapter brings together the diverse activities and relationships discussed in Chapters 10 and 11 by setting forth a cyclical analysis of procurement process interrelationships.

Models of the Procurement Process

COGP Model

As part of its report, the COGP published the model shown in Chart 11-1 which embraces the principal concepts associated with the federal system of procurement. The statutes and regulations, depicted on the perimeter of the model, are important to the manager because they define the unique environment within which each decision is formulated. In Chapters 2 and 5, many facets of the environment were discussed. Understanding the environment is as important to the manager contemplating a sale to the government as it is to the manager who selects the procurement strategy to be followed by the government.

The statutes and regulations define, in depth, the government's concept of a procurement competition, and they also limit competitive behavior. Specific limitations include solicitation and award procedures, mandatory minimum labor rates for certain contracts, preferences in award of contracts for specified groups, directed sources for acquisition of specified materials, and many others. Acceptable competitive behavior, such as independent, confidential responses to competitive solicitations, is delineated in great detail. Within the guidelines of the statutes and regulations, selection of solicitation method and of sources is left to the procurement manager, just as selection of marketing strategy is left to the prospective contractor.

At its core, the COGP model identifies the procurement work force. Upon examination, however, one finds the work force is not well defined. Many disciplines and functions, as discussed in Chapters 3, 8 and 10, participate in the process--some regularly, some occasionally. Many of the involved disciplines do not perceive of their role as procurement oriented, even when performance is to be achieved by contract. Other members of the work force

CHART 11-1a

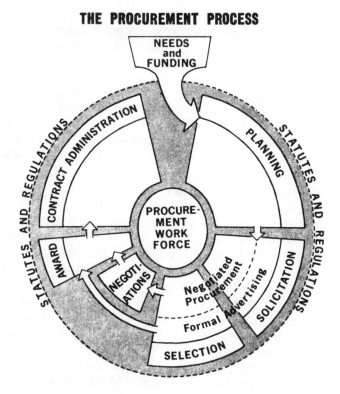

THE PROCUREMENT PROCESS

aThe Commission on Government Procurement published this model in its report in 1972. It has been widely accepted as representative of the federal procurement process. With approval of the Competition in Contracting Act of 1984 the terminology used by the commission to represent the two principal methods of procurement could be changed to read sealed bidding and competitive proposals. Regardless, the model is an accurate repesentation of the system.

become totally involved with a facet of the process such as requirement definition or price analysis. Some (hopefully the top level decisionmakers) develop a comprehensive view of procurement and an understanding of the strategies, objectives, and practices that make it work.

The model begins by identifying the perception of needs and their funding. All procurement, large or small, routine or complex, must be initiated by identification of current or predictable need. The nature of the need and its relationship to the economy becomes the principal guiding force in development of the procurement strategy. At this beginning point in the model, a principal factor to be determined is whether procurement, that is, acquisition from an external source, or in-house fulfillment of the need is indicated. Management must decide this question after evaluation of the issues and consideration of make-or-buy policy as discussed in Chapter 7. Whether make or buy is the decision, general management must also have available both manpower and funding resources to give effect to the decision.

One aspect of the needs-determining process that may cause confusion is the distinction between routine support requirements and special or nonroutine generation of demands. Procurement action may be precipitated as a regular and continuing activity for many types of needs. These arise regularly as a result of established programs like inventory replacement, ordinary operating procedures, maintenance, and repair. On the other hand, needs arise that are unique, unexpected, or a part of major systems development. In these situations, funding problems, strategy selection, and source decisions may be complex and may involve substantial management effort, technical expertise, and time.

The planning phase is principally where procurement strategy is developed. Critical to the strategy decisions is the translation of perceived needs into detailed statements that will be incorporated into one or more individual procurement actions. During the planning process, each procurement action is defined so that it fits the capabililties offered by the marketplace. This drawing of relationships between defined needs and perceived sources and capabilities enables the manager to develop a procurement strategy.

In the model, the segment identified as solicitation, selection and award conceptualizes the execution of
procurement strategy. The model indicates only two technologies in this area, that is, formal advertising and
negotiated procurement. With implementation of the Competition in Contracting Act, the terminology should be
revised to sealed bidding and competitive proposal procurement, but the model remains accurate. These two techniques plus small purchase procedures summarize the three
recognized government procurement methodologies. In this
chapter, we will expand on these methodologies by identifying four general themes around which procurement strategy is developed. The effective manager will become fully
knowledgeable of each. The importance of the proper
development and execution of procurement strategy cannot
be overemphasized. It is the key to creation of a sound
and manageable business relationship. It leads to the
joining (for a particular undertaking) of independent
entities with divergent as well as coincident interests.
Its product, the contract, is always important to the
success of the undertaking, but its criticality to the
organization varies with the magnitude of resources
involved and with the length of the resultant business
relationship.

The final segment of the model, identified as contract administration, represents the time frame within
which outcomes are reached and the success of the strategy is discerned. This final segment often has a far
greater time frame than other segments of the model. During the contract administration phase, management action
occurs and most procurement resources are consumed. Also, within this time frame, many additional procurement
actions may be generated, defined and executed. Each new
action employs or fits into the procurement strategy, is
the subject of supplier marketing strategy, and is critical to the involved independent organizations.

Generic Procurement Model

The COGP model, as discussed above, establishes a
general conceptual framework for the procurement process.
The administrative stages and decisionmaking steps essen-

CHAPTER 11: MODELS AND STRATEGIES 221

tial for purchase action are depicted more specifically in the Generic Procurement Model, Figure 11-2. This model represents the life cycle of procurement beginning with recognition of a need. It identifies the stages through which the procuring agency must proceed and emphasizes the planning phases and the administrative actions following the contract award. It is entirely consistent with the COGP model but does not attempt to identify the alternative patterns or methodologies of solicitation and award.

The generic model views procurement as a continuum not completed until use of the acquired goods and services has reached the point of disposal action. While it begins with needs perception, as does the COGP model, it focuses on the key sourcing decision--whether to buy externally or to perform required work in-house. In government, this decision varies from industrial make-or-buy deliberations as indicated in Chapter 7.

Requirement definition is also a focal point of the generic model. Large commitments are made to carry out this work. When needs are perceived, they are not ready to be set forth in a contractual work statement. The translation of a need into a defined requirement often entails extensive technical effort--in some cases, work that must itself be contracted. In a sense, government research and development contracting is a process of defining requirements. The fundamental importance of this focal point is that a fully successful contract cannot be written without a good definition of the requirement in terms interpretable by the parties to the contract.

Resource allocation is also highlighted by the generic model. It is a vital issue involving governmental budgeting and budget execution and it is treated in Chapter 10 and later in this chapter as part of the cyclical analysis. Its criticality is seen again in Chapter 15 in the discussion of technological/conceptual strategy.

Solicitation and award is summarized as one item on the generic model. The centrality of these processes to procurement is recognized and discussed rather fully in Chapters 12, 13, and 14, but the generic model treats it as it is--one step in a complex system of activities.

CHART 11-2

GENERIC PROCUREMENT MODEL
(Material or Services Acquisition)

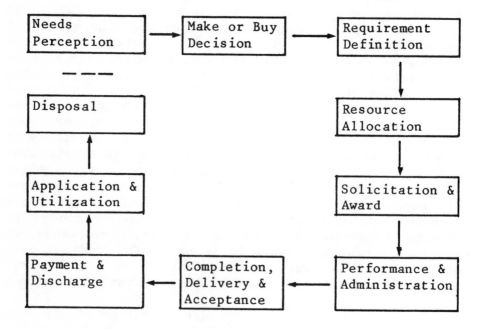

Performance and administration represents that part of the procurement process in which the contractor is the principal actor and the part in which major resources are consumed. The purpose of the procurement is achieved at this focal point--or not achieved. The government is involved through surveillance, may act in an advisory capacity, and may be forced to take a disciplinary or directive role if performance lags. Responsibility for contract outcome lies with the contractor, but administrative contractual actions may be taken by the government to ensure successful outcomes. This focal point is vital because the interactions of buyer and seller can operate to homogenize responsibility. Nevertheless, the clear objective during the focal point is completion in accordance with the contract requirements.

Completion, delivery and acceptance are set out as a focal point in the generic model because they are the objective of the contract. Together, they also represent the end of productive work under the contract. Unfortunately, completion can occur without delivery and acceptance, usually signifying an unsatisfactory outcome. Default, convenience termination, cancellation or exhaustion of funds could result in completion without delivery and acceptance.

Payment and discharge are set forth because they represent the fulfillment of the oblilgations of both parties. They also represent an administrative review which can involve substantial negotiation, property, audit, and adjustment activity.

The model focuses on application and utilization. This represents the satisfaction of acquisition objectives--fully, partially, or not at all. It is the reason for the procurement process. The continuum of the model includes the point at which goods and services reach disposal, which completes the life cycle of a system or equipment. Throughout the life cycle of any system, at every focal point, individual contract actions--each following in its own way the generic model--are initiated, performed, and completed. In this sense, the model is constantly reenacted.

A-109 Model

Chart 11-3 is the model for major systems acquisitions prepared in 1976 by the OFPP. It summarizes the principal activities and events necessary to plan and make decisions for large projects. The circled numbers on the chart represent decisions that must be made by the agency head. Seven activities are also specified in the model which, together, delineate a unique and complex acquisitions strategy. The model does not identify elements of the solicitation and award process. However, each of the seven activities, with the possible exception of mission analyses and needs evaluation, would require contractual action, including solicitation and award. The full implication of mission analyses, alternative systems exploration, and competitive demonstrations should become clear under the discussion in Chapter 15, Technological/Conceptual Strategy. The model is intended to apply to projects classified as major by an agency including projects to acquire hardware, equipment, software, construction, or improvements to real property. The A-109 model differs from the COGP and generic models because it is based on a specific policy innovation that was designed to achieve the following:

1. Top level management attention to the determination of agency mission needs and goals
2. An integrated systematic approach for establishing mission needs, budgeting, contracting, and managing programs
3. Early direction of research and development efforts to satisfy mission needs and goals
4. Improved opportunities for innovative private sector contributions to national needs
5. Avoidance of premature commitments to full-scale development and production
6. Early communication with Congress in the acquisition process by relating major system acquisitions to agency mission needs and goals.[3]

CHART 11-3

MAJOR SYSTEM ACQUISITION CYCLE

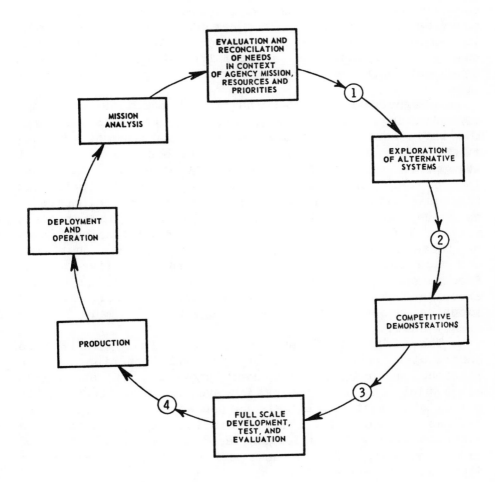

Procurement Strategies

As managers approach decisions, they seek a methodology that reduces the risks inherent in their decisionmaking. They seek information that approximates the set of outcomes resulting from the decision, or set of decisions, for which they are responsible. In dealing with uncertainty, procurement decisions are similar to those faced by management in other contexts such as in staffing or investment or, as in government, choosing programs to be supported from all those proposed. For purposes of our discussion here, we will assume the selection of programs has occurred. Procurement strategy development is concerned with devising a sourcing plan that will ensure fulfillment of acquisition objectives. It is dependent upon each agency's mission, goals, and policies.

In government, determination of missions and goals is made largely by the Congress, although it is supported and influenced by executive agencies and others. Strategy formulation (that is, devising methods for attainment of goals) is largely performed by executive agencies. The process of formulating strategy is the principal responsibility of general management, but all elements of an agency must contribute to this task. It is a process heavily influenced by social or economic policies. Many of these policies are determined by Congress, but they are made operational by elements of the executive branch. Procurement strategies generally are formulated within executive agencies at a program office level, but the adoption process (for major programs) is made by the agency head.

The Office of Federal Procurement Policy (OFPP) has contributed much to defining the relationships between missions and goals, procurement programs, and strategies by issuing its policy on major systems acquisition. Its policy statement was largely patterned after the recommendations of the COGP. The commission report contained a comprehensive and challenging approach to acquisition of major systems.[4] OFPP's new policy put the commission's approach into effect.

OMB Circular A-109 addresses the subject of acquisition strategy in some detail. It defines strategy formulation as the initial task of a program manager and as a task that requires thinking through all factors relating to the program and treating each so that all program objectives will be achieved.

Procurement strategy, as defined in this book, focuses on the principal decision problem of buyers--the identification, qualification and selection of sources. In many respects, this is coincident with acquisition strategy, except that the focal point is source selection instead of program completion or fulfillment, or acquisition objectives. In effect, procurement strategy is treated here as a subset of acquisition strategy. Additionally, this book postulates that there are four general strategies pertinent to government procurement. The use of a strategy depends upon the nature of the procurement and competitive circumstances. Source selections are the starting point for discovery of the set of outcomes to which the organization and the manager are linked through their commitment to an acquisition strategy.

The procurement strategies are distinguished by their respective approach to employment of competition in selection of source and in award of the procurement contract. The manager is in a position, initially, to select a strategy that reflects the type of competition that the world presents, given the particular need that is to be fulfilled.

To place procurement strategy into the context of the federal procurement system, it is useful to recognize that longstanding statutory/regulatory terminologies exist. These terminologies are useful primarily because they are familiar legal descriptors. The objective in this discussion is to place them in a management decision-making context. For example, sealed bidding is a well known procurement procedure; the manager, however, has no interest in that particular procedure. The manager is interested in the effect of sealed bidding on the immediate objective of source selection and on the broader objective of mission fulfillment.

The strategies pertinent to procurement are stated in summary fashion at this point. Each is the subject of a following chapter which explains its use in detail.

Price-Directed Strategy

The traditional and most widely recognized procurement method is based upon price-directed strategy. Under this strategy, the manager approaches his procurement in a manner calculated to allow (in fact, to force) the market to act as a decisionmaker through competitive bidding. The objective is to take advantage of vital market forces in which price directs source selection.

There are three techniques that employ this strategy: one, not normally used in public procurement, is the familiar auction; the second, primarily developed as a public procurement technique, employs the sealed bid, and has been known as formal advertising; the third is competitive bidding with non-price selection criteria. In government procurement, the second and third techniques are widely used. Selection between them requires assessment of procurement objective and competitive situation. Competitive bidding with non-price selection criteria is a price-directed bidding technique but allows non-price factors to influence source selection. One example of non-price factors is the substitution of life-cycle cost guarantees for price guarantees. A second example is introduction of social/economic factors which modify the price criterion to favor protected groups in the economy. Chapter 12 discusses price-directed strategy.

Classical Competitive Procurement Strategy

More widely employed but less widely recognized than price-directed strategy is classical competitive strategy. In government terminology, this strategy requires negotiation rather than formal advertising, and the assumptions are more complex. The strategy uses competitive price bidding but not as the principal source-determining force. The manager employing a classical competitive strategy designs his procurement to allow non-price considerations to enter into, and potentially to govern, source selection. In this strategy, the number of non-price factors is expanded, so that a manager may formulate decision criteria unique to the individual procurement. A fundamental part of this strategy is the existence of viable competitors seeking the award. It is treated more fully in Chapter 13.

Limited Source Procurement Strategy

Less widely recognized, yet prevalent, is procurement strategy built upon a limited choice of sources. A limited choice exists in numerous situations because there is a particular source that is so dominant that only an extraordinary set of events would cause the manager to employ a new source. Procurement under these conditions employs cost-based pricing processes, since the force of competitive price offers is missing. The most widely recognized techniques under this strategy are: (1) the unsolicited proposal, (2) the solicited non-competitive proposal, (3) the change order and, (4) the regulated industry purchase procedure. Limited source strategy is examined in detail in Chapter 14.

Technological/Conceptual Strategy

Finally, and perhaps only qualitatively different from classical competitive strategy, is procurement of major systems designed to take advantage of the full range of technological/conceptual capabilities offered by private enterprise. This strategy, associated with major undertakings of substantial complexity, is based upon the assumption that the potential sources, not the buyer, should conceive and delineate systems to meet the buyer's need. The strategy involves several stages and contemplates awarding a set of contracts, one with each of several sources, but all provided with the same systems objective. Each source, funded through a sequence of contracts, develops and refines its technological/conceptual system. The work is based on the buyer's mission need statement--competition is financed by the buyer, with each source striving to win award of the major contracts for operational systems development and/or production. Final source selection is based on the alternative ideas developed. Under this strategy, selection of sources for the "sequence of contracts" is based upon classical competitive or limited sourcing strategies, but these are interim selections of limited dollar magnitude. (This strategy is the subject of OMB Circular A-109 and will be treated more fully in Chapter 15.)

The procurement manager should develop expertise in the detailed techniques and procedures by which these alternative strategies are applied to each procurement. If appropriate to the nature of the undertaking and to the type of market being faced, these strategies can greatly enhance the effectiveness of the procuring activity.

Procurement Process Interrelationships: Cyclical Analysis

One approach to gaining an adequate perspective of the procurement process is to view it as the interaction of several ongoing activities. The most critical activities in the federal system are cyclical; they occur repetitively and to a degree, predictably. In this section, five cycles are conceptualized that encompass the entire process. They are the system life cycle, the acquisition cycle, the research and development cycle, the procurement cycle, and the fiscal cycle. Chart 11-4, Objectives Determination and Resource Mobilization, identifies the principal elements as cycles, subsystems, organizations, offices and documents. Although each government agency uses its own nomenclature and procedures, Charts 11-4 and 11-5 use nomenclature of the Department of Defense, because it is the largest, most extensive and best documented system. All nomenclatures cannot be used, but with adjustments for mission and technology, the interactions depicted by these two charts represent the techniques and issues with which all agencies must grapple.

At the front end of its procurement process, an agency sets its objectives and secures resources. It does this through planning and budgeting activities shown in Charts 11-4 and 11-5 as subsystems and identified as the Joint Strategic Planning System (JSPS) and the Planning, Programming and Budgeting System (PPBS). JSPS and PPBS make up the fiscal cycle in Chart 11-5. In practice, they draw technical, schedule and financial informa-

Chart 11-4

ACQUISITION PLANNING SYSTEM
OBJECTIVES DETERMINATION AND RESOURCE MOBILIZATION

Cycles	Sub Systems		Documents			
		JSPS	PPBS		Acquisition Management	
Life	JSPS	JIEP	JSPD	MENS	TEMP	
Acquisition	PPBS	JLREID	CG	SDDM	TCP	
R & D	Authorize &	JLRSS	POM	IPS	RDPS	
Procurement	Appropriate	CRDOD	JPAM	MRF	R&TWUS	
Fiscal	Acquisition	JSPD	IP	DCP	SAR	
	Mgmt.	JPAM	PDM	AS	JMSNS	
	Apportion-	JSCP	SR			
	Ment		DPS			

Organizations	Offices (DOD)
Congress	SEC DEF
Budget Committees	DAE
Authorization	DSARC
Appropriation	DIR T&E
OMB	CAIG
DOD	S/SARC
Component	Component Head
	Project Manager

LIST OF ACRONYMS

Planning, Programming Budgeting System (PPBS)

JSPD	Joint Strategic Planning Document
CG	Consolidated Guidance
POM	Program Objectives Memorandum
JPAM	Joint Program Assessment Memorandum
IP	Issue Papers
PDM	Program Decision Memorandum
SR	Status Report
DPS	Decision Package Set

Chart 11-4, Continued

Joint Strategic Planning System (JSPS)

JIEP	Joint Intelligence Estimate for Planning
JLREID	Joint Long-Range Estimative Intelligence Doc.
JLRSS	Joint Long-Range Strategic Study
CRDOD	Commander's R and D Objectives Document
JSPD	Joint Strategic Planning Document
JPAM	Joint Planning Assessment Memorandum
JSCP	Joint Strategic Capabilities Plan

Acquisition Management System

MENS	Mission Element Need Statement
SDDM	Secretary of Defense Decision Memorandum
IPS	Integrated Planning Summary
MRF	Master Reference File
DCP	Decision Coordinating Paper
AS	Acquisition Strategy
TEMP	Test and Evaluation Master Plan
TCP	Technology Coordinating Paper
RDPS	Research and Development Planning Summary
R&TWUS	Research and Technology Work Unit Summary
SAR	Selected Acquisition Report
JMSNS	Justification For Major System New Start

Offices

SEC DEF	Secretary of Defense
DAE	Defense Acquisition Executive
DSARC	Defense Systems Acquisition Review Council
DIR T&E	Director, Test and Evaluation
CAIG	Cost Analysis Improvement Group
S-SARC	(Service) System Acquisition Review Council
CH	Component (military) Head
PM	Program Manager

Organizations

OMB	Office of Management and Budget
DOD	Department of Defense

tion from the research and development, the acquisition and the procurement cycles, and they address the system life cycle.

External constituancies are vital to agency objectives and resource decisions, and the focal point for the decisionmaking process is found in the Congress. The planning and budgeting process is an interaction of organizations, offices and personalities and includes events distributed over a period of three years, normally longer. A brief treatment of the principal cycles, subsystems, documents, organizations and key offices follows.

Key segments of an agency's bureaucracy are devoted to objectives determination and resource mobilization efforts. Successful performance of these tasks is a principal responsibility of agency heads and their senior management personnel. Beyond the senior groups, technical, scientific, operational, and research leaders and their support staffs perform the information-gathering and analysis functions. Identification, definition, and prioritization of objectives, coupled with cost projection and budget formulation, are the main functions of the agency's headquarters bureaucracy and the upper echelons of its field organizations.

The cycles identified in Chart 11-4 concern widely different aspects of the procurement process. The fiscal cycle may be viewed as an annual cycle culminating in annual appropriations, but in reality, it is a three-year effort with three separate cycles proceeding simultaneously, one for the current year and one for each of the next two. The fiscal cycle in its totality is made up of the JSPS, the PPBS, the congressional authorization and appropriation system, and the apportionment system. Within the fiscal cycle, objectives are proposed and negotiated initially under the JSPS and more broadly, by the interaction of the five systems.

All of the organizations specified in Chart 11-4 are involved in the fiscal cycle. The interactions of those organizations are formalized in hearings at each level—Congress, OMB, and executive agency. Nine offices are identified in the chart (DOD offices are used for illustration purposes), each of which is a focal point for planning and analysis in support of decisions on objec-

CHART 11-5

PROCUREMENT PROCESS – INTERRELATED CYCLES –DOD

SYSTEM LIFE CYCLE	CONCEPTION → DEVELOPMENT → PRODUCTION → OPERATION → RETIREMENT				
ACQUISITION CYCLE	ACTIVITY	TECHNOLOGY BASE	CONCEPT EXPLORATION	DEMONSTRATION AND VALIDATION	FULL SCALE DEVELOPMENT	PRODUCTION/ DEPLOYMENT
	DECISION POINTS		O	I	II	III
RESEARCH AND DEVELOPMENT CYCLE	ACTIVITY	RESEARCH	EXPLORATORY DEVELOPMENT	ADVANCED DEVELOPMENT	ENGINEERING DEVELOPMENT	OPERATIONAL SYSTEMS DEVELOPMENT
	FUNDS	6.1	6.2	6.3	6.4	6.6 PROCUREMENT
			6.5 MANAGEMENT & SUPPORT			
PROCUREMENT CYCLES		P A A S	P A A S	P A A S	P A A S	P A A S
FISCAL CYCLES		JSPS PPBS		JSPS PPBS		JSPS PPBS

tives and/or resources. To carry on the decisionmaking
process, supporting organizations and offices are extensive at subordinate levels, mostly within the military
services or DOD. Of the many documents that contribute
to the process, twenty-six are specified in Chart 11-4.
The documents are important ingredients of the process;
they change through updating, reissuance, and as a result
of negotiations. Many are generated anew for each program or specific event, while others pertain to the
entire program of the agency for a given year. Preparation of each is manpower intensive. The documents listed
belong to three systems, JSPS, PPBS, and acquisition
management. Working interactively, they establish the
basis for procurement and contracting action. Many additional documents would be added if the chart extended to
the internal processes of the military components. However, the items shown give excellent insight into the
complexity of the systems and seem adequate for illustrative purposes.

Chart 11-5 depicts the relationship of the five
cycles in terms of the procurement process. The life
cycle is a concept that includes the entire period of
existence of a system from its conception until its
retirement. In the aggregate, it is a period that may
exceed thirty years. The life cycle includes acquisition
cycles, research and development cycles, procurement
cycles, and fiscal cycles. The life cycle of a system is
meaningful for decisionmaking purposes primarily in terms
of fiscal, acquisition, R&D and procurement documents,
and actions. Chart 11-5 illustrates this thought by showing that procurement cycles (planning, solicitation,
award, and contract administration) are frequent and
recurring; each is related to the others. The fiscal
cycle is also a frequently recurring cycle, but in most
circumstances, since it embraces a three-year period, it
is accomplished less frequently than the procurement
cycle. In practice, both cycles overlap. For major
projects, the complete procurement cycle, including
performance and administration of contracts, is often
several years in duration.

The research and development cycle identifies
several phases through which new technologies proceed as
they are reduced to operating systems. It is a cycle

that may be supported through a series of procurement and fiscal cycles. Appropriations associated with each phase of R&D activity are identified by the last two digits of the appropriation designator. They are often cited and are included in Chart 11-5 for identification. The acquisition cycle is an independent management process that establishes key decision points for new systems development and production. Its phases are analogous to the R&D cycle phases, but it is more specific because the structured decision points are pertinent to major programs requiring formal agency head decision. The decision points are identified as milestones 0, I, II, and III on Chart 11-5.

The reader should note that a modification of DOD acquisition policy effective with the March, 1982, revision of DOD Directive 5000.1 retained the four decision points as on Chart 11-5, but tied the systems acquisition reviews into the PPBS process. In addition, it delegated decision point III (production) to the service secretary. It required a new document, a Justification for Major System New Start (JMSNS), to be forwarded to the Secretary of Defense along with, or before, the POM (see Chart 11-4).

It should be stressed that the period of each of the five cycles is variable, except for fiscal cycles which must coincide with annual budget instructions. Length of the life cycle depends on the nature of a system and the emergence of alternatives. The period of the acquisition cycle depends on the specific system and its management. The length of the R&D cycle is affected by technological progress. The procurement cycle length depends upon the nature of the work needed, the procurement strategy adopted for the project, and managerial leadership. Numerous procurement cycles are initiated in support of each phase of the acquisition and R&D cycles. The phases of each procurement cycle as represented in Chart 11-5 include planning, solicitation, award, and administration. They are accomplished anew for each defined need, resulting in the formation or modification of contracts. Some cycles are completed in days; others have performance periods exceeding five years.

Notes

[1]Report of the Commission on Government Procurement, Volume I, GPO, 1972, pp. 2 and 159.

[2]"Major System Acquisition," OFPP Pamphlet No. 1, August 1976, p. 4.

[3]"Major System Acquisition," p. 2.

[4]Report of the Commission on Government Procurement, Volume II, GPO, 1972.

12 | Price Directed Sourcing

The techniques described in this chapter take advantage of market forces so that priced offers determine source selection. Under price directed sourcing, independent offerors, operating freely in an open marketplace, make priced offers (bids) in an effort to win contracts. The offers are treated as being reasonable based on the operation of the free enterprise system. The principal government procurement technique under this strategy is sealed bidding.

While sealed bidding is designed to generate prices that reflect the reasonable cost of performing the required function, the auction technique, not generally applicable to government procurement, generates prices reflecting current values. In slightly modified form, price directed sourcing can also employ a life cycle cost (LCC) criterion to generate offers that minimize the buyer's total cost of ownership. Each of these techniques allows competitive market prices to be determined by the solicitation and award process. The three techniques have important differences which are discussed in this chapter.

In government procurement, an historical procedure has been pursued with diligence--especially at the federal level. That procedure has been known as formal advertising. With implementation of CICA, the term "sealed bidding" was adopted, but the two terms refer to the same process. The sealed bid system has severe limitations but can be an effective method for taking advantage of price competition. It assumes that the lowest bidder should be awarded the procurement. In price directed procurement, sealed bids involve an entirely different concept from that of bidding based on the auction technique. With auction bidding, repetitive competing bids are sought; with sealed bidding, one bid is allowed.

Under LCC, the buyer seeks to award procurement on the basis of the total cost of ownership of the end items acquired. LCC can be employed in the same procedural environment as the sealed bid procurement process, but the basis for contract award is no longer price. Instead, life cycle cost becomes the award criterion but price remains a significant element of the LCC.

Sealed Bid Model

The design of the sealed bid technique, although rooted in historical actions of the Congress, can be analyzed by examining the procedures required. The essential design objectives are: award of the purchase on the basis that all bidders have an equal chance to receive the contract; selection of the winning bidder based on the lowest bid received (from a responsive and responsible bidder who is capable of performing the undertaking); selection of a contractor (the key decision) through a public procedure in which a public record of the decision is made available to any interested party.

Federal procurement is not the only type of procurement to employ sealed bid purchasing. It is used extensively at the state and local level and in a modified form, is known as competitive bidding in the industrial purchasing community. However, it is highly structured and proceduralized in the federal system.

While sealed bidding is an effective technique, it is not necessarily any more effective in creating competitive price behavior than other less rigorous combinations of competitive bidding and negotiation as conducted within the private sector. Furthermore, certain limitations on the effectiveness of sealed bid procurement have been identified by the work of the Commission on Government Procurement and by subsequent writings.

Criteria for the Use of
Sealed Bid Procurement

While sealed bidding is an effective technique for use by government procurement managers, it is certainly not a system that can be used without due consideration of all factors associated with the technique. The procurement manager's decision to use the model requires each of the following elements:

1. A conclusion that there will be more than one qualified supplier willing to compete for and to perform the proposed contract.
2. A decision that the requirement is adequately defined to allow competitors to bid for the procurement on an equal basis. Under CICA, a conclusion that it will not be necessary to conduct discussions with offerors appears to replace the previous "adequate specification" prerequisite.
3. A conclusion that sufficient time is available to allow the purchase to be accomplished through an orderly solicitation and award process.
4. A conclusion that price can be used as an adequate basis for determining the source to be awarded the contract.

Since price competition is the heart of a sealed bid procurement, the method cannot be employed if price is governed by law or regulation. Also, the technique applies only to acquisition that will be accomplished within the limits of the United States and its possessions. However, foreign sources can compete for advertised procurement.

The first element, adequacy of competition, is not always evident. Clearly, it would be useless to publicize a procurement and to request competitors to bid, if it were known that competition could not be obtained on

the open market. The conclusion that there is competition has to be made before the solicitation is issued.
It requires the availability of at least two capable
sources to compete for the award. Furthermore, the
nature of the work, the relationships among the potential
producers, and the current status of their businesses
should be examined in order to determine that a competitive environment does exist.

The second element, that no discussions will be
needed, implies the need for adequate definition. This
has historically referred to specifications or other technical description. It has probably been the most difficult requirement for the government to fulfill. The
support given by CICA to use of the functional type of
specification may reduce the difficulties associated with
specifications. Otherwise, formal advertising requires a
precise delineation of the government requirement. In
the absence of either the functional specification or a
detailed description, it is impossible for the offerors
to accurately prepare bids and for the government to evaluate them on a common basis.

The third requirement for sealed bidding, adequate
time, refers to the minimum period of time needed to
communicate the requirement to bidders, for them to
prepare and deliver bids, and for evaluation and award to
take place. Under CICA the statutory waiting times associated with publication of synopses applies equally to
competitive proposal and sealed bid procedures. As a
consequence, time may be less important than in the past
as a prerequisite for use of the system.

The time element should be kept in perspective.
Many negotiated procurements require a much longer lead
time than the normal sealed bid procurements. However,
in urgent circumstances, negotiated procurement--espe-
cially noncompetitive negotiated procurement--may still
be carried out in a shorter period than the minimum
required to carry out a sealed bid procurement. Urgent
actions arise regularly because of emergencies and other
events. The negotiation procedures that allow faster
response do so by allowing work to be initiated, even
though the final price decision cannot be agreed upon
until later. With sealed bidding, price must be decided
before work is authorized to begin.

The fourth prerequisite, the requirement that price be an adequate basis for making the award decision, stems from the fact that, under normal conditions, a sealed bid procurement is awarded to the responsible supplier who presents the lowest bid for the procurement. Because of this the marketplace determines the source selection decision. If considerations other than price are critical, and if such factors cannot be fully defined and specified in the invitation, sealed bidding would not be a feasible method for conducting the competition.

Historical Summary and Policy Considerations

Until enactment of CICA, procurement by sealed bid was mandated by public law. It is covered in Part 14 of the FAR which is the primary source of guidance to personnel for this method of contracting. Some modification of Part 14 will be implemented by FAR changes mandated by CICA. The philosophy underlying the historic general requirement for sealed bid procurement is embodied in the following quotation from the decision of the United States Supreme Court in the case of United States of America vs. Brookridge Farm, 111 F. 2d.461 (1940).

The purpose of statutes requiring the award of contracts to the lowest responsible bidder, after advertising, is to give all persons equal right to compete for government contracts, to prevent unjust favoritism, collusion or fraud in awarding government contracts, and to secure for the government the benefits which flow from free and unrestricted competition.

The first statute which included clear provisions for formal advertising was the Civil Sundry Appropriations Act, passed in 1861. That act specified the four major provisions for formal advertising which are still pertinent to sealed bidding today. These provisions were: first, a written invitation for bids must be prepared which includes all necessary information for each bidder to prepare his bid; second, the invitation must be issued to all known sources of supply; third, the bids in response to the invitation must be received and opened in public, at a time announced in the invitation; and fourth, the contract must be awarded to a responsible bidder who submitted the most favorable bid to the government.

Whenever sealed bidding is used, these requirements impose administrative processes which may be too time consuming to accomplish the procurement needs of the government. As a result, the requirements were suspended during periods of major wars. For example, under the First War Powers Act of 1941, Congress authorized the War Department to use negotiation during wartime, in lieu of advertised procurement. Furthermore, at the end of World War II, Congress passed the Armed Services Procurement Act (ASPA) of 1947. That act stated that the formal advertising method is required, but it included seventeen exceptions to the requirement whereby procurement by negotiation could be conducted even during peacetime. Two years later, Congress enacted the Federal Property and Administrative Services Act (FPASA) of 1949. Procurement is discussed in Title 3 of that act, and the structure and language set forth is similar to that of the Armed Services Procurement Act. The FPASA permitted negotiated procurement under fifteen specified conditions but retained mandatory use of formal advertising. General reversal of the mandatory use of sealed bid procedure did not occur until 1984.

Nor did the elimination of the preference for formal advertising eliminate the preference for competitive procurement procedures. It has reinforced it. Federal policy assumes that a competitive market acts as a limitation on an offeror's price. The assumption is that each offeror will, in seeking to win, adjust his performance processes so that he will be at least as efficient as the most efficient competitor. Under this assumption, effective price competition will ensure the reasonableness of a bidder's cost.

Open competition is seen as achieving two principal goals of the government. One goal is to gain the benefits of full and free competition; the second is to ensure that all qualified sources have an opportunity to bid on an equal basis against their competitors. Sealed bid procurement continues as an important basis for achieving these objectives.

It is the creation of this equal basis for competition that has required the development of detailed procedures for carrying out a sealed bid procurement. These procedures largely evolved out of court, contract appeals board, and/or Comptroller General decisions. They are often thought of as being rigid and mechanical. While the procedures may so appear, they should not be thought of as substitutes for the exercise of good judgment and discretion by the procurement manager. The technique is dependent upon use of proper specifications; good structuring of the invitation to eliminate ambiguities, good judgment in revisions, amendments or cancellation of the invitation, proper timing, prebid conference management, and handling of questions arising during the solicitation and award processes.

Formality of Sealed Bidding

Sealed bidding became highly proceduralized and formal, probably as a result of the requirement that the bids be opened in a public place. A public opening requires that the bids be sealed and then held by the contracting officer until the appointed time. This procedure guarantees that each bidder independently arrive at the bid price submitted to the government. It is designed to ensure that no person other than the bidder knows the bid price until all bid prices are disclosed at the public opening. At the public opening, the bids are abstracted. That is, the price offered by each bidder is extracted from the bid and posted. The bid document is reviewed by those present at the opening.

Timeliness in submitting a proposal is important because of the public opening requirement. It is defined in terms of the day and the appointed hour for the public opening. All bids must be submitted and in the hands of the contracting officer by that day and time. Furthermore, under CICA, in order for an adequate number of competitors to be in a position to compete for the award, the solicitation document must be publicized fifteen days in advance of issuance, and the contract cannot be awarded less than thirty days after publication. The mandated form of publication is a synopsis in the U.S. Department of Commerce newspaper, Commerce Business Daily (CBD). It is assumed that persons interested in competing for federal contracts will be subscribers but receipt of the CBD is not essential for bidding. Any potential bidder who requests a copy of a solicitation document is provided a copy (to the extent available) and permitted to submit a bid.

In addition to publication in the CBD, procuring agencies can (but seldom do) use other forms of advertising and publicity to obtain competition and to notify industry of proposed procurement actions. Normally, agencies are expected to develop adequate bidders mailing lists that include the known producers of the item to be procured.

Potential bidders are included on pertinent bidders lists if they have submitted an application (Standard Form 129). Also, firms are included on pertinent lists whenever the procuring activity considers them to be capable of filling the requirements of the particular procurement (regardless of submittal of application forms). The lists may be developed by obtaining names of potential bidders from various trade directories.

The Firm-Bid Rule and
Award to the Low Bid

The firm-bid rule requires that a bidder whose bid is among those present when bids are opened remain in the competition through the period during which the government evaluates bids and determines the winning bidder. This rule is important because, at the time of bid opening, all bidders learn the prices of their competitors. In the absence of the firm-bid rule, any of the bidders could then withdraw or modify their bids if, for example, the bid was a little too high to be a winner, or was a winning bid, but was too far below the next low bid. To allow a bidder to withdraw or modify bids at will would defeat the sealed bidding system.

The firm-bid rule may be enforced by requiring bidders to file a bid guarantee. The bid guarantee is used primarily in construction contracting and may be filed in the form of a bid bond, postal money order, certified check, or other acceptable monetary form of assurance that the bidder will, upon acceptance of his bid, perform the required work. Bid guarantees, however, are required only when the IFB specifies that a contract must be supported by performance bonds (under which the surety guarantees performance) or performance and payment bonds. Payment bonds ensure that subcontractors and workmen are paid by the contractor. Bid guarantees in combination with performance bonds, or performance and payment bonds when used, provide the government with a reasonable amount of time to analyze bids and select the most favorable. The firm bid rule applies to sealed bidding even in the absence of bid bonds.

Ordinarily, a contract winner has the lowest bid. However, the concept of the low bid must be understood to be the bidder with the lowest evaluated bid. The order of preference from low bid to high bid, revealed by examination of the abstract of bids prepared at time of bid opening, is not necessarily the final order of preference of bidders in the sealed bid system. Often, a solicitation incorporates factors for adjustment of bid prices to reflect certain government costs incurred when business is conducted with the contract winner. Other factors also play a role in award. These will be defined in the section entitled Processing Bids.

Contract Types Used in Sealed Bid Procurement

Sealed bidding is designed to allow the marketplace to determine a price at which the government acquires its materials and services. The type of contract becomes an essential part of the technique.

The principal applications of sealed bidding are construction, materials and/or services that are clearly defined and usually comparable with items available in the commercial marketplace. As a result, it is believed that price should be firm at the time of award, and that risks associated with performance should be borne by the supplier. Consequently, the firm fixed price contract is used to define the business relationship. The supplier, under this contract type, guarantees to perform the contract effort on time.

Because the guarantee includes price, the supplier carries the risk of cost changes during the period of performance. However, if provided for in the solicitation, a contract clause can be included that allows price adjustments based on economic change. The philosophy of such clauses is that only contingencies of an industry-wide nature or cost changes beyond the control of the supplier would actuate the price adjustment process. By removing this element of risk from the bidding, it is believed the competitors will remove contingency factors from bid prices.

Constraints on Communications Between the Parties During Sealed Bidding

During the sealed bidding process, communication between the government and potential offerors is formal. The system is designed so that there should be no need to communicate except on a formal, written basis using the solicitation and the bid. Any information informally communicated to a bidder could create a preference or cause another bidder to believe that there is unfair competition. Often a prebid conference is employed to overcome the constraints on this communications process.

The prebid conference provides for an equal and simultaneous disclosure of information to all parties. It is used in complex procurements to brief the prospective suppliers and to explain specifications and requirements. Care must be taken during the process to avoid disclosing certain kinds of information to the bidders. As a matter of policy, information which should not be disclosed includes the name and number of firms solicited, any special terms and conditions received from individual bidders, any proprietary data included in bids, and any information that may create a claim of prejudice or preference caused by government action.

Regardless of the design of the system, it is vital that communications channels remain open. For example, a bidder may identify deficiencies such as an ambiguity or defect in the specifications. When this happens, the bidder is obliged to inform the government. If the contracting officer agrees that a deficiency exists, the specification should be amended and the amended portion communicated to all recipients of the IFB.

Processing Bids

A critical phase in the sealed bid model is the period from receipt and opening of bids to contract award. The government is responsible for carrying out four major processes during this time period. Those processes are:

1. Evaluation of bids for responsiveness
2. Determination of the price order of preference
3. Evaluation of bids for any non-price evaluation factors
4. Determination of the responsibility of any bidders to whom an award is to be made.

For practitioners, the preparation of the IFB, the evaluation of bids, and contract award is a routine function. Nevertheless, it requires an acute sense of the conditions existing in the industrial sector being solicited, the effect on competition wrought by the timing and provisions in the IFB, the handling of questions and amendments prior to opening, and the processes of evaluation after opening. Very difficult questions relating to the adequacy of specifications, the responsiveness of bidders, the nature of mistakes and other matters arise. The required decisions may affect one or more of the evaluation phases identified above.

Under the sealed bid model, a bidder must be responsive to the government's invitation, and it is the duty of the contracting officer to determine the responsiveness of the bidder. The bidder is not permitted to deviate or to take exception, in any substantial fashion, from the precise requirements which have been expressed in the solicitation document. Therefore, responsiveness can be defined in terms of the IFB itself.

The IFB contains the instructions to bidders, specifications, quantities to be delivered, schedule, and numerous terms and conditions. If the bidder is not responsive in each of these areas, the contracting officer declares the bid nonresponsive, and the bidder is excluded from further consideration. The basic criterion is whether the bidder offers to do what the government has required. The issue of a bidder's responsiveness has been the subject of hundreds of bid protest decisions by the Comptroller General.

If a bid conforms with the essential requirments of the IFB, the contracting officer determines its position in the price order. Certain adjustments may be necessary for this purpose. For example, a contractor's offer often includes a discount structure. The contracting officer, in determining the price order of preference, will discount the price offered by the amount of the discount, provided the conditions of the discount conform with the IFB. Normally, the most important consideration is the time period required in the government's payment process. If that period of time is equal to or less than the bidder's discount period, the government can secure the benefit of the discount. Where such a case exists, the discount is deducted from the bid price, and the net price is evaluated and compared with the competing bids. This adjustment is made for all bidders.

Other price adjustments, some of which are additive, are made for factors such as transportation costs, government inspection costs, government property considerations and other elements that have been identified in the IFB. It is critical to the sealed bidding system that any adjustment of a bid price for a determination of price order of preference must be in accordance with the requirements specified in the invitation for bids. By using this technique, all bidders are on an equal basis, since all are on notice that evaluation adjustments may be made to their bids. Bidders must consider these factors when establishing a bid price.

Bids may also be evaluated by non-price factors. For example, qualified products, delivery schedules, the availability to the government of proprietary data, or similar items may constitute non-price evaluation factors if they have been specified as such in the IFB. Not only must the invitation identify these factors, but it must also identify the weight given to them in the evaluation process. Application of the evaluation factors must result in the objective determination of the winning bidder. Non-price evaluation includes certain priorities applied under small business and labor surplus area set aside programs, and unless waived, the Buy American Act. These are discussed in Chapters 17 and 18. The effect of these programs is to determine award on the basis of price competition among the bidders within the preferenced groups. Finally, award may be determined by drawing lots if equal bids are received. (Absence of collusion is vital and should be verified in this situation.)

The last area of consideration during the processing of bids is the determination as to whether an offeror is a responsible contractor. Government policy dictates that a non-responsible contractor cannot be awarded a government contract. Responsibility is defined in many ways. The first is the ability of the contractor to perform the work, including compliance with the government's delivery schedule and other terms and conditions of the IFB. The second is the ability to finance the costs of work until payments begin. These two elements are known as capacity and credit. In addition, the contracting officer must identify the contractor's tenacity in pursuit of successful performance and the perseverence needed to successfully complete the contract regardless of any difficulties encountered. The supplier's past performance is an element in making determinations of responsibility to the extent that past behavior can be considered indicative of future performance. Suppliers must be able to demonstrate possession of adequate business integrity to be awarded a government contract. Ordinarily this can be assumed in the absence of past dishonesty or violation of trust. In the case of construction or research contracts, the supplier must possess adequate facilities, equipment, technical skills, and quality assurance expertise to be considered for award of contracts requiring such specialized capabilities. (Note: Ability to secure these capabilities, rather than possession, will suffice for most categories of procurement.)

Acceptance, Rejection, and Award

A sealed bid procurement should be awarded to the supplier whose bid is most advantageous to the government, considering price and other price-related factors as specified in the solicitation. The process by which the contracting officer makes this selection is indicated earlier in the chapter. The successful bidder is given a properly executed award document or a notice of award in a format determined by the procuring agency. If the award of a contract cannot be made during the specified period as set forth in the IFB, then the contracting officer should obtain an extension from each bidder. The contracting officer should support the selection of source by preparing a statement which indicates that the award went to the low bidder or, if not awarded to the low bidder, listing all lower bids with individual reasons for rejection.

An IFB is not always followed by the award of a contract. Reasons may arise to justify cancellation, but the reasons should be validated in light of the important signal that IFBs give to industry to invest time and money in bid preparation. Some of the valid reasons for cancelling an IFB and thereby rejecting all bids are:

1. Indications of collusion among the bidders
2. Ambiguous or defective specifications
3. The supplies or services are no longer required by the government.

When all bids have been rejected, a contracting officer is obligated to notify each bidder and state the reasons, but the government is not liable for bidding costs simply as a result of the rejection of all bids.

At times, individual bids may be subject to rejection. This differs from mere lack of success in capturing the contract award. During the evaluation process, prior to award of a contract, bids may be rejected if:

1. The bid fails to meet the delivery requirements specified in the IFB
2. The bid fails to conform with the specifications contained in the IFB

3. The low bid is from a non-responsible concern
4. The bidder fails to state a price or includes a qualification that renders the price offer unenforceable at time of delivery
5. Any qualification is stated which jeopardizes the finality of the price at which the award is made.

Rejection of a bid for these or any other reason is the responsibility of the contracting officer.

Mistakes

All of the foregoing elements of sealed bidding are brought into focus by mistakes. Mistakes are claimed by bidders after bid opening and can raise issues such as those discussed earlier under Firm Bid Rule. Once bids are public, acceptance of a bidder's representation that a mistake has been made raises issues that could jeopardize the integrity of the bidding system. The problem is the possibility that no mistake actually occurred and that the representation is merely an effort to reposition the bidder in the ranking of bids. Regardless, bona-fide mistakes can be grounds for correction or withdrawal of bids, and contracting officers cannot ignor claims of mistakes. Important possibilities are that an award would be made at an unconscionably low price (the mistake results in an unintended low bid) or that a bidder other than the true low bidder is selected.

When a low bid is received that differs significantly from competing bids or from the government's estimated price, the contracting officer must solicit bid verification. If s/he fails to obtain verification and makes an award, the contractor will usually be relieved from any obligations established on the basis of a mistake which the contracting officer knew, or should have known, to be likely.

An apparent bid mistake discovered after the opening but before the award of a contract can be handled by:

1. allowing a correction of the bid
2. allowing a withdrawal of the bid
3. refusal to allow withdrawal or correction of the

bid.

A correction is allowable if it does not result in a displacement of other bids, provided the existence of the mistake and the actual intended bid can be shown through clear and convincing evidence. In the event the correction of a bid would alter the relative standing of bidders, correction is limited to those circumstances where the evidence is obtainable from the invitation and bid documents without further reference to other documentation. This constraint generally limits corrections to errors of a clerical nature. On the other hand, allowing withdrawal of a bid normally requires only clear and convincing evidence of the existence of the mistake.

Once a contract has been awarded, correction of bid mistakes is much more difficult, because at this point, a correction of a mistake amounts to reformation of the contract. The contracting officer can take this action if it results in a more favorable contract for the government. Other possible actions are rescission of or amendment to the contract. Actions to reform, rescind, or amend a contract without consideration to the government are procedurally complicated and generally require agency decision after full review of the circumstances.

Under certain conditions, action to rescind or reform a contract because of a mistake can be decided under the Extraordinary Contractual Adjustments authority conferred by Public Law 85-804. However, this authority is available only to those government agencies authorized to use it by the President. This type of adjustment is discussed in Chapter 3 under Contract Adjustment and is fully treated in FAR, Part 50.

Two-Step Sealed Bid Procurement

The two-step sealed bid procurement is a method through which the government can obtain the benefits of price-directed strategy when the existing specification or other documentation of the government's requirement is not adequate for a normal sealed bid procurement. Essentially, two-step sealed bidding incorporates certain advantages of negotiated procurement. The first step is a negotiation procedure; the second step is a modified sealed bid procurement procedure.

To employ the two-step process, the contracting officer must issue a request for technical proposals (RTP) to industry. The RTP specifies that proposals include technical data only, not pricing data. The request is based on a government specification sufficiently developed to delineate a set of criteria to determine if technical proposals are capable of providing the desired end result. The set of criteria is not as detailed and not as complete a description of the objective as the normal type of controlling technical documentation essential to a successful sealed bid procurement.

When the RTP is issued, respondents are given sufficient time to develop their technical approach. The technical proposals must include the engineering approach, any special manufacturing processes or testing techniques, and related information such as management or manufacturing plans or facilities information necessary to carry out the procurement work.

Upon receipt of technical proposals, the contracting officer initiates a technical review and evaluation. This review and evaluation determines if any of the technical proposals are acceptable for further consideration in the procurement process. Acceptable proposals are included in the second step. If the technical evaluation results in determination that particular proposals are unacceptable but capable of being made acceptable through addition of necessary information or clarification from the contractor, the contractor will be invited to discuss the proposal and submit to the contracting officer any additional information and/or clarification needed. Final decision respecting which proposals are acceptable completes step one.

When all technical proposals have been classified as either acceptable or unacceptable, the contracting officer may initiate step two of the procedure. Step two is a sealed bid action conducted through the normal procedures of a sealed bid procurement, except that solicitation is issued only to those sources whose technical proposals are acceptable. The invitation will include a statement barring the consideration of bids from other sources. It will also state that the supplies or services rendered must be in accordance with both the government specifications and the bidder's accepted technical proposal. Synopsis in the CBD of the step-two solicitation is done to reveal the names of the firms that have submitted acceptable proposals. However, publication in the CBD is provided solely for the benefit of prospective subcontractors.

In summary, the first step of the two-step sealed bid procurement is a procedure whereby sources are prequalified for participation in the second step. The second step is a modified sealed-bid procedure. In the two-step method, prequalification differs from that used with a qualified products list (QPL). Two-step prequalification identifies and defines engineering and technical competence for producing an item or a service, whereas the QPL prequalification is based upon an actual review of a qualified product already in existence. Under CICA, with elimination of mandatory sealed bidding and adoption of the discussion, no-discussion distinction between competitive proposal and sealed bid procurement, the advantages of two-step may diminish.

The foregoing explication of the federal government's sealed bid procurement procedure has been in considerable detail. Nevertheless, substantially more detail on this procedure is included in the respective procurement regulations and in decisions of the Comptroller General related to award protests. As a model for securing price-directed procurement decisions, the sealed bid process is relatively effective. However, the procurement manager must not be misled. The model has only limited applications and, in its highly structured format, is not capable of being put into effect for complex acquisition programs.

Suboptimization Problems With Sealed Bidding

CICA may prove to be an effective response to the suboptimization problems that have been associated with the government's historic preference for the formal advertising system. That system has been challenged as to whether it enhances the overall economy and efficiency of government purchasing. The challenges have arisen because effective sealed bid procurement has demanded that the buyer prepare a specification against which all offerors can compete on an equal basis. This has been interpreted to require detailed design specifications under control of the government. Whenever the end objective of the procurement is to buy items obtainable from the commercial marketplace, this approach eliminates most competitive commercial products, because they will have unique design. The approach has generated producers of government unique end products, ones that meet the government specification requirement. It has also resulted in creation of a government unique distribution and support system for those products. The CICA has eliminated the basis for this by clearly authorizing use of functional specifications. This should open the government market to commercial items, generally gaining access for government use of proven and often superior commercial items. Such items may be available through normal commercial distribution channels which reduce the need for government inventory and supply systems.

The Auction

In order to explain the relationship between sealed bid purchasing and the other major price directed technique, the auction will be briefly reviewed. Within our economy, there are a number of auction markets. These markets provide a forum for repetitive public bidding for the purchase of those items traded in accordance with the rules or practices of the particular market. The most well known of these markets include the secondary trading of common stocks on the organized stock exchanges and trading of commodities on the organized commodity exchanges. Directly analagous are well established practices in the sale of antiques, used automobiles, livestock, works of art, tax sales, gold, currencies, and many other specific items, when interested buyers are given the opportunity to compete in an open forum and to competitively and repetitively bid against each other. Markets are often established with a set of rules or practices which regulate the bidding.

The federal government, as well as any other buyer,

is entitled to participate in auction sales. However, in every case, the subject of an auction sale is an existing product or other valuable item. In the case of the stock exchange, the item of value is a share in the corporation traded. In the commodity exchange, it may be a contract for current delivery or future delivery of a commodity. The commodity traded is a well-defined, homogeneous product. Each trader has a common understanding of the nature of the commodity which is bought or sold. This characteristic, preexistence of the items which are to be traded (plus homogeneity for ubiquitous materials), is prerequisite to an effective auction. It is a characteristic which is absent in nearly all procurement by a federal agency except small purchases. (Price support operations of the Department of Agriculture and currency or gold transactions of the Treasury are not considered here.)

Most government procurement seeks performance of work rather than acquisition of a preexisting item. Procurement may solicit the production of a material end item or the rendering of services. The operating circumstance is that work has yet to be performed at the time of the contract award. In this type of situation, the use of auction techniques is not considered effective and could result in the creation of unconscionable contract relationships. When trading existing items, the willingness of the owner to transfer ownership at a given price is a value judgment which may be unrelated to the cost of creating the item. It could be substantially below (or above) the cost of creating the item, as in the auctioning of most used automobiles. Ordinarily, used automobiles are sold at very low prices relative to new ones except in the case of antiques. The value attached to the automobiles even if they qualify as antiques is clearly far below the cost of establishing a production line to produce those same automobiles. Similarly, in auctioning works of art, the cost of originally creating the work may be significantly different from the value attributed to the art by the marketplace. The procurement manager should be cognizant of these circumstantial differences between the auction and the sealed bid. Both are price-directed transactions; both are included in price-directed strategy. They are not applicable in the same situations.

Price-directed strategy is not limited to seeking acquisition objectives. It may also be employed to influence costs and/or prices. At top levels of government, numerous policies are found which are designed to enhance or protect segments of the economy. These policies have the effect of placing a floor on costs and, therefore, on prices. Certain social and economic policies associated with federal procurement have this effect (see Chapter 18). Similarly, in the auction markets, strategy is expressed in policy actions of the government. Auction markets and prices generated by them are influenced by actions such as stockpiling, price-supporting purchases of commodities, and regulation of exchanges. Currency values, interest rates, and values of securities are strongly influenced by policy decisions of the Federal Reserve Open Market Committee concerning government buying and selling in financial markets. Policy actions of this kind affect procurement prices but are not normally viewed as part of the procurement operations of government, even though they involve purchases and sales.

Life-Cycle Cost

A variation of the sealed bid technique is found in the life-cycle cost approach. Under this approach, a solicitation may be issued to initiate a sealed bid procurement which incorporates a provision requiring the bidder to specify a computed total life-cycle cost, rather than price, as the criterion the contracting officer will use to select a source. The lowest life-cycle cost wins the award. This technique has been employed in the purchase of certain nonrepairable end items such as aircraft tires by the Air Force and batteries by the Army. For these nonrepairable items, the basis for the life-cycle cost award has been the computed cost to the government per unit of service obtained.

Some experimentation has also been conducted in the procurement of repairable items on a life-cycle cost basis. Repairability introduces complexity, since calculation of life-cycle cost must consider the variables associated with maintenance and repair.

The concept underlying this approach to competitive bidding is to encourage more cost effective products to be offered. The technique asks for a guarantee that life-cycle cost of ownership of the selected item will be at the expected level. The guarantee is important, since the technique substitutes the life-cycle cost estimate of the contractor for his bid price as the award-determining factor, but realization of the LCC can only be measured after delivery.

The appeal of the LCC technique is that it may acquire a superior product which takes advantage of the latest technology without the necessity of the government developing its own specifications to define the latest, best and most cost effective end product. Where pertinent, this technique may be of great value to any procurement manager. LCC experimentation with repairable products has been primarily conducted within the National Bureau of Standard's Experimental Technology Incentives Program. Under that program, GSA has procured room air conditioning units using fuel efficiency as a life-cycle cost factor. Even though life-cycle cost action differs from procurement in which price directly determines the award, the technique is treated here as a price-directed strategy, since the award decision is made on an open solicitation using an objective criterion. The award price influences selection, since it remains a significant factor in the total life-cycle cost. This strategy has great potential value to procurement managers in all fields, but actual experience with the concept is limited.

Complex LCC models have been developed for major systems acquisitions. This application involves substantial complexity and would not fit our concept of price-directed strategy since source selection would be dependent on many factors in addition to lowest life cycle cost.

13 | Competitive Negotiation

Procurement managers in the federal system have found that sealed bidding cannot be used for most procurement. Instead, negotiation is needed to achieve federal acquisition objectives. Table 13-1 presents current (1983) statistics on negotiated and sealed bid procurement. It is evident from the table that sealed bidding accounts for only one-tenth of total procurement awards. An analysis of Chapter 12 reveals the reasons for this, particularly the prerequisites for use of structured bidding. Chapter 12 also identifies the recently emerging recognition that in the field of commercial products, use of formal advertising has forced the government into uneconomic specification of its needs. Negotiation is a more effective method for most procurement because it increases the ambit for procurement managers' exercise of judgment. Our purpose now is to examine negotiation strategies in order to discover their essential characteristics, limitations, and advantages. Although CICA abandoned the term negotiation in favor of competitive proposal procurement, it remains a viable term for reference to a class of actions and will be used in this book.

The three negotiation strategies are distinguished on the basis of approach to competition. The first, classical competitive strategy, is treated in this chapter.

It includes four competitive techniques. In general, the strategy of all four techniques is founded upon a classical procedure, that is, government specification of its requirement in terms of performance or design, or both. Development of the specification is followed by solicitation of potential sources and selection of a contractor.

Classical competitive strategy and price-directed strategy differ in two principal respects: classical competitive negotiation strategy allows for factors other than price-related ones to determine source selection, and it may employ cost-based analysis to determine price. These two procedural elements, source selection and price agreement, may be independent decisions under this strategy, whereas in price-directed strategy, they are coupled.

Negotiation strategies employed by the federal government have substantial problems. One is the traditional interpretation that federal procurement has only two fundamental methodologies. One of these, sealed-bid procurement, has been treated under price-directed strategy; the other, negotiated procurement (partially treated in this chapter) has, until CICA, been viewed as undesirable. This judgment, historically rooted in the preference of Congress for sealed bid procurement, appears to have changed, but an explanation of the basis of the preference for the sealed bid method is important to the understanding of the general structure of federal procurement operations.

The government has resisted using negotiation because of one central issue associated with the concept. While our economy and our government are deeply committed to the free enterprise system, and while there is the general commitment to allow a private contractor to earn a profit under government contracts, there is a continuing fear that profit on publicly funded contracting activities may be excessive. Associated with that fear is a concern over the degree to which public managers should be allowed to exercise judgment regarding the expenditure of public funds. That concern is heightened whenever expenditures are made through the contracting process. When expenditures are made for work that is to be conducted in-house by federal employees, the issue of profit

does not arise. However, when a contract is made with a
private organization, the issue of profit (particularly
the amount of profit associated with the cost of performing the work) is engaged.

Under the sealed bid procurement model, the issue of
excessive profit is minimized, since the winner of the
competition has won in an open forum which is publicly
verifiable. Negotiated procurement, however, is subject
to criticism. Source selection and price level determination are decisions which must be made through the judgment of managers, and their objectivity in this regard is
subject to question. Also, these key decisions--source
selection, price level, and risk allocation--may be complex, involving numerous factors other than direct cost
to government. Potential for disagreement over outcomes,
however, may be minimized if the classical competitive
negotiation strategy is employed. This chapter addresses
the models under that strategy.

Competitive Negotiations Overview

In advance of our discussion of competitive proposal
techniques, it is necessary to place the federal approach
to negotiations in perspective. First, the general meaning of negotiations may be captured by reference to statements from authoritative sources. For example, Bouvier's
Law Dictionary defines negotiations as, "the deliberation
which takes place between parties touching a proposed
agreement." Black's Law Dictionary defines negotiation
as "deliberation, discussion or conference upon the terms
of a proposed agreement; the act of settling or arrang-
ing the terms and conditions of a bargain, sale, or other
business transaction."

The term negotiation generally implies that a series
of offers and counteroffers are made in a conference situation continuing until a mutually satisfactory agreement
is concluded by the negotiating parties. However, under
federal procurement, the term includes solicitation of
proposals, conduct of written or oral discussions when
required, and making and entering into a contract. Thus,
it would appear that negotiation in federal procurement
includes a number of events that occur from the issuance

TABLE 13-1

PROCUREMENT METHODS, FEDERAL GOVERNMENT
FISCAL YEAR 1983[a]

Procurement Method	Actions		Dollars	
	Thousands	%	Billions	%
Sealed Bidding	44.6	10.7	9.0	5.9
Competitive Negotiation	172.0	41.4	45.7	30.0
Noncompetitive Negotiation	176.7	42.3	87.6	57.5
Procurement for Foreign Governments	6.7	1.6	6.2	4.1
Procurement from Regulated Sources	15.2	3.7	3.7	2.5
Totals	415.2	100.0	152.2	100.0

[a]Table derived from "Total Federal Snapshot Report" (Individually reported actions--excludes small purchase orders). Federal Procurement Data System, Fiscal Year 1983, dated January 26, 1984, p. 17.

of a solicitation until a contract has been established. A key element in negotiations which has been recognized by the federal government is that offerors may, during the course of negotiations, amend their proposals without invalidating the solicitation or the resulting contract.

The concepts just expressed convey the idea that competitive negotiations are a principal system of procurement, that they involve discussions, and that the discussions are an important part of the decisionmaking process. Therefore, it must be determined when, what, and with whom to discuss a planned procurement, and how to end discussions once they are initiated.

Competitive negotiations are initiated by solicitation. Under CICA, "all responsible sources" are allowed to submit proposals. The normal document for solicitation is the Request for Proposal (RFP) which is similar in form to the Invitation for Bids (IFB) used in sealed bidding. The RFP initiates a somewhat more flexible procedure because it contemplates discussions between each offeror and the government concerning the project. Some adjustments of price and conditions can result from the negotiation and a number of types of contracts may be considered. The process is covered in FAR, Part 15.

Both the RFP and the IFB should delineate all matters which are of significance in generating competition among suppliers on an equal basis. For RFPs these matters include, but are not limited to, a closing date for receipt of proposals, the factors on which evaluation for source selection is to be based, the work statement or specification, delivery schedules, the proposed type of contract, and appropriate terms and conditions. Additionally, the RFP includes a declaration that a contract award may be made without discussion at the discretion of the government. The contractor's proposal must be an offer to provide the supplies and services defined by the government's RFP. It should describe a work effort under which the contractor believes s/he will be able to successfully perform the required work.

The Statutory Authority
for Negotiations

Since 1947, the principal authorities for negotiations have been listed as statutory exceptions to the advertising requirements of the Armed Services Procurement Act, 10 U.S. Code 2304, and the Federal Property and Administrative Services Act, 41 U.S. Code 252. As has been discussed in Chapter 6, CICA has eliminated the mandate for using sealed bidding, and, consequently, the exceptions.

Competitive negotiations require internal approvals of negotiation plans and agreements, but the procedure allows a somewhat flexible bargaining process. The contracting officer (or negotiator/negotiation team under his guidance) bargains with those offerors whose proposals are potentially acceptable alternatives. In carrying out this process, the government representative is strongly committed to observing impartiality to all offerors.

Affirmative Guidance for Negotiations

Prior to 1962, government negotiators were permitted to carry out the negotiations process without any substantive guidelines enunciated by Congress. In that year, however, Public Law 87-653, widely known as the Truth in Negotiations statute, was enacted. This statute provided guidance to negotiators in two significant ways: first, it required contracting officers to conduct discussions with offerors; secondly, it required prospective contractors to furnish cost or pricing data to support negotiation of contract prices (with some exceptions). While the statute applied to military procurements only, its substantive provisions were adopted by the Federal Procurement Regulations System for civilian negotiated procurements. Under CICA it applies by statute to all executive agencies.

The Competitive Range

The competitive range is a term drawn from Public Law 87-653. The law requires the contracting officer to hold discussions with all offerors within the competitive range.

Congress' affirmative guidance in this area was a strong impetus in causing procurement managers to consider competitive proposals. In particular, the competitive range requirement has great significance in the communications and negotiations process leading up to source selection and pricing of negotiated procurement. As modified through CICA, the statutory language establishing the competitive range concept (cited from Section 303B (d)(1) of CICA) is:

(d)(1) The executive agency shall evaluate competitive proposals and may award a contract—
(A) after discussions conducted with the offerors at

any time after receipt of the proposals and before the award of the contract; or

(B) without discussions with the offerors (other than discussions conducted for the purpose of minor clarification) when it can be clearly demonstrated from the existence of full and open competition or accurate prior cost experience with the product or service that acceptance of an initial proposal without discussions would result in the lowest overall cost to the Government.

(2) In the case of award of a contract under paragraph (1)(A), the executive agency shall conduct, before such award, written or oral discussions with all responsible sources who submit proposals within the competitive range, considering only price and the other factors included in the solicitation.

These requirements are modified for procurements in amounts less than $25 thousand which are to be awarded using "special simplified procedures" for small purchases. The purpose of these procedures, provided by regulation, is to promote competition to the maximum extent practicable.

With specified exceptions, government agencies must use competitive procedures for all procurement. These procedures are defined as including only "full and open competition" which is further defined as a procedure that permits all responsible sources to submit sealed bids or competitive proposals.

The procurement manager's objective in this process is selection of the offeror whose performance is most likely to meet government needs. In approaching this objective, however, s/he must ensure that each competitor is treated equally. Upon receipt of proposals, the first major problem is to determine which ones fall within the competitive range.

The competitive range may be decided by evaluating each proposal in light of all elements specified in the solicitation, including (but not limited to) cost and price, evaluation criteria, work statement, and specifications. The key decision is whether, in the agency's judgment, the offeror has a reasonable chance of being awarded the procurement. The determination that an offeror is not within the competitive range excludes him from further consideration. Furthermore, exclusion from consideration may occur at any point prior to the completion of negotiations with the successful offeror. Initially, when it determines that a competitor is within the competitive range, the procuring agency must include him in subsequent discussions. Offerors who are clearly within the technical range will be determined by the technical evaluators to be acceptable and will be included in subsequent negotiations, unless cost or price is so high as to render the proposal infeasible. However, offerors may be determined to be unacceptable--yet potentially capable of becoming acceptable--through meaningful discussions which might result in the improvement of their offers. Wherever this possibility exists, the offeror cannot be excluded from the competitive range without further written or oral discussions.

In conducting written or oral discussions, the contracting officer must point out to each offeror the ambiguities, uncertainties, or deficiencies that may be contained in the offeror's proposal. The contracting officer should then allow the offeror a reasonable opportunity to clarify, correct, or further support and improve his proposal, but must avoid identifying areas in which other offerors have apparently achieved better or more highly evaluated concepts and ideas. In effect, the contracting officer is responsible for helping an offeror understand the deficiencies of his proposal without conveying information contained in competitive proposals.

A complex problem related to this required procedure is whether the contracting officer should conduct discussions with any offeror. CICA requires that all RFPs reserve a right for the government to accept a winning proposal without holding discussions. This can be done if the decision will result in the lowest overall cost to the government, but it is permitted only if there are no discussions with any offeror. It is infrequent that proposals will be adequate for such a decision on major contracts, but in all cases the competitive proposal process must eventually narrow the field of competitors to the selected winner.

As a practical matter, conducting discussions with all in a large field of competitors could be burdensome and expensive for all parties. Consequently, contracting officers need to systematically narrow the number of competitors, yet to to show that the lowest overall cost to the government has been obtained. The Comptroller General has made many decisions in developing guidelines for doing this which contracting officers must observe as they approach decisions for each procurement. Accepting a winning proposal without discussions simplifies the whole process, but the contracting officer must ensure that no significant omissions or deficiencies exist in the proposal of the winning offeror, and that any award made without discussion does not alter the basis for competition or otherwise deny the government the benefits of maximum competition.

Competitive procurements raise difficult questions respecting the cutting off of negotiations (ending the discussions process). Many protests have been filed with the Comptroller General dealing with this matter, and it has been held that a notice should be issued by the contracting officer to effect a cutting off of negotiations. The notice must include advice that negotiations are being conducted, that offerors are being asked for their best and final offer (BAFO), and that any revisions or modifications of proposals must be submitted by the closing date which is specified. The intent of this set of criteria is to preserve competition. Problems associated with this procedure are discussed under "Dual Negotiations" in this chapter.

✓ Selection of an offeror for award of a contract involves considerations similar to the determination of competitive range. Evaluation criteria stated in the RFP should specify in each case what those considerations include. The evaluation criteria are applicable to both the competitive range and source selection decision. Clearly, when more than one offeror remains in the competitive range at the point of receipt of the best and final offers, a selection of one winner is expected (with the exception of some cases in which a multiple award of contracts may be made). The selection of a successful contractor is made from among the offerors who remain in the competitive range at the conclusion of written and oral discussions. The proposal is selected which offers the greatest advantage to the government, in terms of price and other factors, based on the judgment of the contracting officer (or other designated official).

Cost and Pricing Data Requirements

The second key policy established by the Truth in Negotiations statute and reinacted in slightly revised form in CICA, is the cost and pricing data requirement. Under it, prospective contractors must submit cost and pricing data before award of contracts or modifications valued at or above $100 thousand. The requirement does not apply to sealed bid awards but does apply to modifications thereto. At the discretion of the executive agency the requirement can be applied to lower dollar value awards. These cost and pricing data requirements apply to subcontractors if the subcontract or modification is expected to exceed $100 thousand. The data submitted must be accurate, current and complete as of the date of the agreement on price, and the contractor or subcontractor must certify that the data meets these requirements. The contractor must agree to a contract provision under which the government has the right to reduce the price of the contract by any amount determined by the agency head to have been increased because cost and pricing data was noncurrent, inaccurate or incomplete. Finally, the agency obtains the right of audit for purposes of determining whether the cost and pricing data submitted in connection with the negotiation of the contract were accurate, complete and current at the time of the certification. The requirements do not apply if the price is based on adequate price competition, is set by law or regulation, or is based on an established catalog on market price of commercial items sold in substantial quantities to the general public. In general, these data requirements attempt to give the government buyer an ability to analyze the relationship between cost and price and through negotiations to verify the validity of proposed prices by questioning elements of cost or price data.

Taken together, the competitive range and data requirements policies have created a unique form of negotiation pertinent to government procurement operations.

It is intended that submission of data will place the two parties on equal ground respecting vital cost and price information. The requirement is believed to aid negotiations when competition on a price basis does not constitute a major factor in selection for award of contract. It is a cumbersome and administratively expensive procedure justified by the need to ensure that public funds are not paid in excessive amounts to individual contractors. Since price competition often does not meet the standards of objectivity set by the Congress, the data requirements are imposed virtually as the norm in government negotiated procurement. With respect to overall economy and efficiency in government, this broad application of the competitive proposal procedure has never been subjected to objective verification of its cost effectiveness. The policy may have reduced profiteering via overstated costs by suppliers. It does not capture any other type of cost savings, and it is hardly arguable that the cost of personnel and other administrative factors imposed on both government and contractor organizations for 355,000 contracts every year totals a smaller sum than the savings from reduced profiteering.

Dual Negotiations

The concept of dual negotiations arose with Public Law 87-653. One of the constraints associated with competitive proposal procedure is that an agency cannot effectively assign two separate teams of negotiators to conduct discussions simultaneously with different offerors, yet the purpose of the procedure is to include competitors in the discussion process and to keep all competitors on an equal basis. It is virtually impossible to keep them on an equal basis if separate teams negotiate the contract. As a result, the agency must conduct "dual" negotiations. Effectively, it can only appoint a single team to carry on discussions.

Since negotiations are a bilateral process, only one competitor can enter negotiation at one time. As a result dual negotiations, that is, sequential negotiations, are required. The government team negotiates first with one competitor, then with a second, a third, and so on, until all competitors in the competitive range have negotiated a complete and final contract. This negotiation process becomes impracticable in terms of time required if very many competitors are competing at the time that final negotiations are initiated.

In addition to the administrative problem of conducting dual negotiations, there is a danger of transferring technical information central to the proposal of one competitor into the hands of another competitor. If such a transfusion of technical information takes place, the positions of the competitors are compromised. Furthermore, if the buyer team encourages such transfusion, there is a tendency for the independent ideas of competitors to become homogenized so that through proposal revision, each competitor offers the same technical/ management package. When this occurs, the buyer may initiate price discussions in such a manner that each offeror's bid is traded off against the others, creating, unofficially, an auction. Such a development contravenes stated policy positions of the procuring agencies and could violate rights in intellectual property of the competitors. It also might be perceived to be a violation of the proper employment of an auction procedure as has been discussed in Chapter 12. Nevertheless, in the interest of increasing the amount of competition present in public procurement, competitive discussion has become a standard procedure in government procurement.

Models Developed for
Competitive Negotiations

Pre-1962 Model

The requirement for discussions with all offerors in a competitive range was an innovation of the Congress in 1962. It has been reinforced by CICA. Underlying the passage of the original requirement was a perception of the Congress that many offerors in competitive negotiated procurement were not being fully considered for the award of contracts, even though they had responded to an RFP. The statute was intended to increase the level of competition by requiring the contracting officer to consider more fully all offerors through the required competitive range discussions.

An understanding of this requirement is placed in better perspective by reviewing the general practices followed for major procurement prior to 1962. During that period, proposals received in response to a solicitation were evaluated in one step for both source selection and negotiation purposes; the source selection decision would normally be made prior to the initiation of any negotiation. By that process, the procuring agency could unilaterally (and perhaps without consideration of all relevant factors) exclude from negotiations all offerors except the one selected for award. Negotiations and discussions under those practices were undifferentiated.

With the passage of Public Law 87-653, procuring agencies were no longer able to exercise that degree of discretion. They were effectively required to expand their evaluation processes to determine which offerors are in the competitive range and to carry out discussions with all who qualify.

Award without discussions was permitted and is still permitted by CICA under limited specified conditions, but for most negotiated procurement, award of a contract without discussions is impractical due either to complexity of the work or to its lack of definition adequate for price competition. As a result, most negotiated procurement requires the expanded discussions procedure. Subsequent to the 1962 enactment, agency procurment managers began to develop implementation procedures. Out of this, agencies generated different general interpretations of their negotiation responsibilities.

NASA Model

In interpreting the new requirement, the National Aeronautics and Space Administration (NASA) considered discussions and negotiations to be two different processes. As a consequence, upon receipt of proposals in response to a competitive negotiated solicitation, NASA first conducted an evaluation of the proposals to arrive at an initial determination of the competitive range. It proceeded, as necessary, to conduct written and oral dis-

discussions with all offerors believed to be either acceptable or through discussions potentially capable of becoming acceptable.

These written and oral discussions continued until the agency concluded which offerors were within the competitive range for purposes of requesting a best and final offer. Upon receipt of those offers, the agency selected one or more offerors for negotiation of a contract. Analyses of proposals (as modified by the best and final offers) for purposes of detailed cost and price negotiation were carried out by the agency, and the selected offeror(s) invited to negotiate.

Out of those negotiations, a final contract agreement was determined and an award made. The award was based on the earlier selection of a single contractor for negotiations, or if more than one continued in competition through the negotiation process, a final source selection was made. This interpretation of the statute allowed the agency, in most cases, to limit the incidence of dual negotiations and possibly avoid some of the resulting pitfalls.

DOD Model

Under the DOD interpretation of the Truth in Negotiations statute, the term discussions, as used in the statute, was interpreted to mean negotiations. Under this interpretation, written and oral discussions and negotiations resulted from the initial receipt of proposals. When proposals were received they would be evaluated for both source selection and negotiation purposes and discussions followed. During written and oral discussions, some offerors initially included in the competitive range may later be considered unacceptable and, therefore, dropped from the competitive range. Written and oral discussions, including negotiation of contractual details, continued with other competitors. This procedure required sequential (dual) negotiation sessions with each offeror. Upon completion of this process, the contracting officer requested best and final offers from remaining competitors.

If technical transfusion has taken place, and if

repetitive requests for best and final offers are issued
by the contracting officer, an auction appears to (or
actually does) take place. In any event, the negotiation
process results in a completely negotiated contract with
more than one competitor, and the final source selection
decision is made from that group.

Scope of Negotiations

In competitive negotiated procurement under the
government system, interactions with offerors include
discussions and/or negotiations. It is intended that
part of this process should provide advice to the offeror
of the proposal of deficiencies found by the government
during its evaluation. It is also contemplated that
cost, price, technical, and other matters which might
generate revision of proposals should be a part of the
discussions. But discussions are constrained by the
objective that information concerning a competitor's
proposal or relative position in the competition should
not be disclosed by the government representative.

One product of discussions is change. A contractor's proposed approach or plan may be modified or the
government requirement may be modified. In the event
that government requirements are modified, all remaining
competitors must be notified and an amendment of the solicitation issued. Changes in work plan or approaches that
do not alter government requirements normally would not
require amendment and, in fact, should not be communicated to competitors if the effect were to create a technical transfusion of information or an auction.

Any change in requirements having substantial impact
such as to require complete revision of the solicitation
should result in cancellation of the solicitation and
initiation of a new procurement action. These comments
highlight a very critical area for exercise of judgment
by the procurement manager. To what degree and in what
ways can negotiators be allowed to modify a procurement
without compromising the competition? Definitive answer
to that question will not be attempted here. Instead,
the sections which follow attempt to outline the subject
matter negotiators need to consider while avoiding any

compromise of the competitive process. The actual level of attention to any of these areas will vary depending on the nature of the procurement, its magnitude, its antici- pated longevity, peculiarities of the overall program of which it may be a part, and so forth. In general, the larger the procurement, the more attention should be paid to each area.

Deliverable Item Description

Deliverable items in a government contract should normally be written as a listing in an article of the con- tract schedule. The list should be in the RFP and is established by the procuring agency; however, in research, development, or systems procurement, the poten- tial contractor(s) may contribute significantly to its development. Furthermore, in such procurement, a complete listing of all deliverable materials may be extremely difficult. An understanding of the list and of any area where doubt may exist should be developed during negotiations. Even with relatively common deliverable items the requirement may be adjusted during negotia- tions, if economic quantities or breakout decisions indi- cate the need for a change, or if government requirements are altered. The impact of such adjustments on proposed schedules and costs can be complex.

The likelihood of negotiated changes in the list of deliverable items depends on the complexity of the job and the completeness of planning prior to the solicita- tion or negotiation sequence. A particularly sensitive area is the list of deliverable data items. In procure- ments where extensive data is to be prepared by the con- tractor, it is likely that definitional work including exercise of judgment as to the government's needs and possibly including planning, design, and quality issues may be subject to change. When the contractor carries this type of responsibility, a concomitant flexibility in procuring agency planning is likely to exist and may affect the contractual arrangement of the procurement.

Technical Description of Work Requirement

With respect to negotiations, the normal presumption is that the specification, or other description of work, is fully defined prior to the issuance of an RFP, preparation of a proposal, conduct of evaluations, and negotiations; however, the facts often reveal that this is not the case. One reason for negotiated procurement is inadequacy of specifications because of complexity either in the work or the acceptance standard. In the areas of research, development, and major systems, failure to recognize complexities can result in end item failures, normally reflected later by cost growth, schedule delays, reduced acceptance standards, or cancellation. While technical agreement on the work requirement may be reached in prenegotiation conferences, responsible negotiators recognize that the dollar and schedule agreements at negotiations put form and meaning into any technical understanding. As a result, the negotiation conference can be successfully concluded only if the basic work agreement, which is reflected by the dollar and schedule agreements and risk allocations, is brought to the attention of the participants during cost and price negotiations. Factors of particular importance are:

1. Specification in the work description as to precise fit or function, performance goals committed, application of standards of cleanliness, reliability, maintainability, environmental exposure, and other cost-generating requirements.
2. Definition of quality, inspection, test, or documentation standards for acceptance purposes.

The negotiator must verify, essentially by use of effective questioning, that the work description is fully understood and that cost agreements are matched to it. This is the heart of a successful negotiation. Contract type, price, incentive arrangement, warranties, and other contract provisions are keyed to it and dependent upon it. Timely performance, contract management complexities, profitability to the contractor and the project image depend on it.

Schedule

Even when end product delivery objectives are un-changing, detailed planning and scheduling is a process that is dynamic and extremely resistant to stabilization. It is geared to work statement variables and management planning or reprogramming. During the interim between RFP, proposal submission, and negotiations, planning activity continues, and the negotiator must be current as to the schedule, its implications, and the reasons for any updating. When sequence of work, milestones or deliv-erable items change or are rescheduled, the impact on cost and work plan may be critical. A realistic schedule is directly affected by government-furnished items and by interorganizational relationships as discussed below. The negotiators should examine this area systematically and in depth.

Co-Contractor and
Subcontractor Relationships

Performance of large or critical segments of a program by independent organizations adds measurably to negotiation variables. With regard to subcontractors, the prime assumes responsibility for coordination of effort and performance. Nevertheless, the sufficiency of this effort and the adequacy of data provided to the government regarding the subcontractors is the negotia-tor's concern. The problem of discovery of underlying faults regarding the subcontractor's work or cost and pricing data is greater than with the prime, yet verifica-tion is no less important to the success of the project.

The procurement manager's problem with subcontract relationships is not as complex as with co-contractor relationships. Co-contractors may all be prime contrac-tors to the government, may have no privity of contract with each other, yet may be dependent on each other for the interfacing of subsystems or major components of the overall project. Contractual and subsequent administra-tive problems inherent in this relationship are:

1. Division of liability for mutual responsibilities

2. Division of mutual costs of coordination
3. Responsibility for timely performance
4. Arrangements for exchange of data.

This relationship is exemplified by the employment of a prime operational system contractor whose design and fabrication effort is constrained by the work and progress of one or more subsystem or experiment contractors who are also prime contractors, and who, in turn, are constrained by the system contractor. The negotiators bear a responsibility for ensuring that these interfaces are properly negotiated. The challenge of this problem lies in the fact that these relationships almost defy clear cut contractual expression.

Government-Furnished Material, Data and Approvals

The contractor's obligation to perform major contracts may be dependent upon government-furnished property (GFP) including material, facilities, and/or data. A listing of GFP doesn't cover the complexities involved, since listings of material and facilities are subject to changing demands and availabilities. With regard to government reservation of the right to approve contractor actions, it is often impossible to forecast the full scope of the problem. At negotiations, the parties should identify all requirements in general, establish specific demands where possible, and document all critical schedules and dependencies as far as possible. The negotiator should verify arrangements for managing this interface as well as the availability of required items in accordance with the schedule. One of the challenges at negotiation is that the negotiators must ferret out unstated assumptions and expectations of all parties, resolving any conflicts concerning availability and use of property whether physical or literary.

Management Planning and Systems

Organization of work by the contractor and his inter-

nal management systems is vitally important to his success. Traditionally, management would not be projected
into negotiations extensively, since the source selection
process was assumed to have selected capable contractors.
Currently, however, government demands for improved
management have made it mandatory to go beyond the surface and discover the effectiveness of management plans,
organization and systems. A full understanding of government expectations and contractor intent must be achieved
in this matter.

Particularly significant systems subject to these
questions are: cost accounting, estimating, schedule
planning and control, technical status monitoring and
reporting, subcontracting and purchasing, management
information, budget and financial control, and when applicable, configuration and data management. Review and
verification at contract negotiations of any of these
systems or of the contractor's plan for organization of
the work is essential. (DOD policy pertinent to major
systems contracts is expressed in the Cost/Schedule
Control Systems Criteria of DOD Instruction 7000.2).

Specialized Personnel Capabilities

Proposals normally include resumes to indicate to
the customer the general capacity of the contractor's
personnel. During negotiations an understanding of the
capabilities which will be applied in performance of the
contract may be very significant. This is particularly
true where areas of new technology are involved or where
performance standards are critical. While relatively few
contracts are written requiring application of specific
individuals to the work, the need for verification of
approaches and technological capacity is present whenever
success is dependent upon unique or highly qualified individual abilities. Therefore, the negotiators must be
prepared to determine the extent to which the talents
reflected in resumes will be applied, when they will be
applied, alternative manpower resources at the contractor's command, and the true availability of such manpower. Negotiation in this area differs from the standard approach that concerns quantities and mix of the

labor hours proposal. Except for the partial coverage afforded by "key personnel" clauses, understandings in this area remain just that--understandings.

Cost, Price and Funding

Central in the scope of negotiations is agreement on cost and price. Achieving that agreement is inseparable from negotiation of all of the foregoing as well as consideration of contract terms and conditions. In practice, the extent of actual discussion of the elements of the dollar breakdown depends on the magnitude of the differences between the buyer and seller, the sufficiency of information on which to base negotiations, and the level of analysis and evaluation of the proposal performed by the procuring agency. The attitude of negotiators, as well as their capacity for analysis, will govern their point of focus in discussion.

Prime costs, indirect expenses, subcontract costs, profit and other elements of the cost structure will normally be examined, but the allocation of negotiation time depends on problem areas. While cost analysis is most common for large procurement actions, positions may be based on price analysis or on comparison of competitive offers when feasible. Positions may also be based on prior experience, adjusted for dissimilarities of the current work with the previous work, and projected into the current time period. They may also be developed through use of learning curves and parametric estimating techniques. However, the use of such techniques requires examination as to validity of the application.

A subtle but significant aspect of many negotiations is the rate of funding of the contract. Numerous contracts are written that are incrementally funded because of the long-term and high-dollar nature of the work and the limited availability of current-year funds. The cost of performance may be affected by this factor if the schedule of work is constrained by it. The responsibilities of the contractor for performance within the allotted funding as scheduled must be clearly understood and reflected in the contract.

Terms and Conditions-
Type of Contract

While the negotiator must apply numerous clauses required by law or regulation, alternative clauses and unique terms and conditions are often written to reflect the project in question. These alternative or unique aspects of a contract cannot be fully enumerated, but a representative group would be: deliveries, warranties, key personnel, GFP list, make or buy plan, performance requirements, management systems requirements, incentives, special financing, data acquisition, waiver of patent rights, and advance agreement for reimbursement of specified cost elements. In negotiations, a working knowledge of all of these areas should be developed.

Division of risk between the buyer and seller are determined by: terms and conditions written especially for the procurement, boiler-plate terms and conditions, technical descriptions of work required, and type of contract. In general, fixed-price and incentive-type contracts place responsibility for performance and financial risks associated with delay or nonperformance on the contractor. However, the function of contract type in allocating risk is directly related to, and must be consistent with, the adequacy of the specification or other controlling data in the contract and to the degree of surveillance or control to be exercised by government contract administrators. These issues are discussed in Chapter 16.

Flexible-price contracts are essential in many procurement situations, especially in research and development, systems work, and in the performance of services or other work where the government controls significant decisions. Firm pricing arrangements or incentive arrangements increase responsibility and risk of the contractor if the governing contract work statement is definitive in terms of required performance. Nevertheless, the manager's confidence in on-time, within-estimate performance is dependent upon more than the type of contract instrument agreed upon. For example, a broadly written performance specification may dictate extreme care in negotiations to avoid contractual commitment to perform, for a fixed price, some unanticipated new achievement that is

beyond the realizable achievement costed into the contract price.

An overly detailed performance and design con-
straints-type of specification may inhibit the contractor's ability to make decisions without changes or direction from the customer. The negotiators should ensure
that the agreement is based upon understanding in the
fullest sense with regard to all details of the specification. They should adjust the contract type and terms
and conditions to reflect the situation.

All of the foregoing topics are a part of the scope
of negotiations; perhaps other areas should be identified. However, the complexity of reaching valid and
current agreements to be represented by the contract has
been indicated. To be successful in reaching such agreements is the challenge which should inspire the procurement manager to excellence. The challenge is to achieve
competence in the diverse negotiable elements to a level
that enables employment of the expertise of the negotiation team. The end objective is to ensure that the
contract reflects the job and facilitates its successful
completion.

14 | Noncompetitive Negotiation

    Competitive approaches to negotiation are not usable for a large number of procurement actions. Inability to employ them arises in several contexts, each of which meets a fundamental need in our competitive economy. In this chapter noncompetitive negotiation and limited source strategy are used interchangeably to label several widely encountered techniques. These techniques as used by the government are substantially changed from those pertinent in competitive negotiations discussed in Chapter 13. CICA has strongly discouraged use of noncompetitive procedures and has imposed new justification requirements as discussed in Chapter 6. The treatment in this chapter is directed toward understanding the need for noncompetitive actions and the processes available for them. It is not intended to advocate or discourage their use where applicable.

    In using limited source strategy, the government seeks supply or service from sources whose established prior position in the market dominates the source selection process. In effect, the limited source is the only source available, unless extraordinary measures are employed to create an alternative. Throughout the government this category of procurement approximated $97.5 billion in fiscal year 1983. (Please refer to Table 13-1.

The cited amount is the sum of the last three items in that table.)

The general strategy in these circumstances employs administrative processes to simulate or to substitute for competitive pressures. It is oriented toward government control over cost without distruction of properly constructed competitive advantages which the free enterprise system recognizes as essential to progress. The strategy relies on cost-based analysis and negotiation as a substitute for competitive pressures to establish a degree of government control over prices it pays to contractors.

Limited source procurement is carried out in a number of specific circumstances; all are important to the market situation in which they occur. Six are mentioned briefly as specialized sourcing procedures. Four are treated in some detail because they are practiced extensively and involve a significant section of the private economy. They are unsolicited proposals, solicited noncompetitive proposals, change orders, and regulated industry purchases.

Specialized Sourcing Procedures

Six limited sourcing situations will be discussed that are highly specialized. Two, leader company and specific acquisition, are relatively infrequent but employ sole sourcing or sourcing among a restricted group of potential suppliers. In each case, price is based on criteria other than market competition.

Leader Company Procurement

Occasionally the government, particularly the Department of Defense, needs to expand the number of sources for a specific complex item or system for which only a single source exists, usually the developer. A leader company procurement may be used, wherein a contract, or possibly a subcontract from the intended new producer, is directed to the sole source. Under the contract, the sole source provides all required assistance for the follower company to become a producer. The objective is to establish an additional, potentially competitive producer. This technique is discussed further under solicited noncompetitive proposals and is pertinent to the section on second sourcing.

Architectural and Engineering Services

A decidedly controversial procurement practice pertains to the selection of architectural and engineering firms for design and specification of public construction projects. The basic procedure has been delineated by statute (Public Law 92-582, October 27, 1972). It specifies:

1. Public announcement of requirements for A & E services
2. Discussions regarding "anticipated concepts and the relative utility of alternate methods of approach" with three or more A & E firms
3. Ranking firms in order of preference
4. Negotiation with the firm considered to be most qualified.

This procedure is controversial since no competitive pricing is allowed, although the government, after an unsatisfactory price negotiation with the most qualified firm, can refuse to award a contract and negotiate with the next most qualified firm. This procedure is considered by many to be appropriate for A & E services but is contested by others. Congress reconfirmed its policy on this matter in CICA by legislatively defining the procedure as a competitive one, thus ranking it equally with price competitive procurement.

Provisioned Item Orders

Under prime contracts for major end items of a repairable nature, a prediction of the need for spare parts is complex. It involves the general maintenance philosophy to be employed, including location and level of maintenance capability, level of repairability (piece part, subsystem), prediction of parts subject to failure, mean time between failures, mean time to repair, operational requirements to be encountered, and so forth. The selection and ordering of provisioned items is generally a combined effort of the end item contractor and the government support activity. It results in a list of provisioned items that, initially, and often for a longer period, is procured from or through the prime contractor. This area has been under fire since 1981 because of a succession of media reports detailing overpriced spare parts contracts. Congress chartered the OFPP in P.L. 98-191 to review and report on DOD procurement of spare parts. The OFPP study was completed in June, 1984.

In October, 1984, Congress enacted two new statutes that attempt to deal with the procurement of spares. They are P.L. 98-525, The Defense Procurement Reform Act of 1984 and P.L. 98-577, The Small Business and Federal Procurement Competition Enhancement Act of 1984. The two acts were similar in certain areas such as: (1) planning for competitive procurement of spares, (2) constraints on agency use of qualified products lists, (3) direction of procedures for challenging a contractor's proprietary data restrictions, (4) requirement for contractors to certify their prices (on commercially sold items), (5) prohibition of contractors unreasonably restricting subcontractors from making direct sales of property to the United States, (6) requirement for identification of supplies sold by prime contractors to the United States to which the contractor did not contribute significant value and for restriction of overhead allocated to such supplies, and, (7) requirement that executive agencies include in their personnel appraisal systems recognition for employee efforts to increase competition.

In addition to the above items, P.L. 98-577 includes provisions to encourage timely payments by prime contractors to their small business subcontractors. It requires the SBA to establish a breakout procurement center representative at each major procurement center in addition to other SBA representatives and to be afforded staff support adequate for effective breakout of items from large contracts for competitive procurement.

P.L 95-525 imposed a requirement for DOD to obtain

guarantees from major weapon system contractors on the conformity of such systems to the contract. Waiver of this requirement is authorized if its imposition would not be in the interest of national defense or would not be cost effective. Redelegation of the waiver authority is restricted so that it will not go below the assistant secretary level in a military department. Both of these statutes contain other provisions in addition to those mentioned.

Policy Directed Sources

Numerous public policy limitations on sources apply to federal procurements. These limitations are designed to aid or protect segments of the economy. They include:

1. Procurement of specified items from the Federal Prison Industries
2. Procurement of listed items from agencies for the blind and severely handicapped
3. Award of contracts set aside for minority or economically disadvantaged groups as selected under procedures of the Small Business Administration
4. Required source procurement for jewel bearings.

Chapter 18 discusses the socioeconomic policies in greater detail.

Foreign Military Sales Agreements

Under its program for sale of military items to foreign customers, the Department of Defense effects the domestic procurement of items to be supplied. In general, it employs normal procurement practices, but where the foreign customer requests production by a particular source and this is incorporated into the letter of agreement with the customer, the procurement will be source-restricted.

Specific Acquisition of Rights in Technical Data

Infrequently, circumstances arise in which the government procures the rights to existing technical data. Such an acquisition is from the data owner and occurs when unlimited rights are needed for reprocurement (on a competitive basis) of the items for which the data is essential. It is done when there is no suitable alternative, the data to be acquired permits competent manufacturers to perform the needed production, and the anticipated savings through competitive reprocurement will exceed the cost of acquiring both the technical data and the rights to use it. It is one of the approaches to second sourcing discussed below.

Unsolicited Proposals

Important segments of government programs are carried out as as result of unsolicited proposals. This type of proposal is the subject of FAR 15.5 and has been confirmed as appropriate by CICA. It is treated as a special type of procurement.

An unsolicited proposal is submitted by a private organization or institution without prior formal solicitation. It should be a complete, written offer by a contractor to perform research or study under either a contract or grant. The unsolicited proposal should form an adequate basis for evaluation of the merit of the proposed program as well as for award of a contract or grant. A submission should be identified as an unsolicited proposal, but the government should not automatically accept it as adequate. All unsolicited proposals should be acknowledged and receive expeditious processing, including a technical evaluation.

The submission of research proposals via the unsolicited proposal method is especially encouraged by government agencies that sponsor research and development work. Nevertheless, the unsolicited proposal presents certain problems which the government must consider. Since it is submitted without an agency's solicitation, the proposed work has not specifically been budgeted or planned by the agency. Thus, acceptance of the proposal must involve some replanning or reprogramming of funds.

A second problem area is the ability to employ unsolicited proposals to shortcircuit the normal competitive processes of the procurement system. This possibility results because contracts awarded as a direct result of an unsolicited proposal must of necessity be awarded on a noncompetitive basis. The term noncompetitive used in this regard requires explanation. The unsolicited proposal avoids formal competition but does not avoid having to compete for funds against other proposals and work efforts which an agency chooses to sponsor. Therefore, the term noncompetitive as applied to unsolicited proposals refers to the lack of a classical solicitation and competitive proposal selection process.

A third problem area is safeguarding restricted data which may be included in the unsolicited proposal. In many cases, the basis for the proposal may include trade secrets which are submitted to the agency in confidence. The data should be used only for evaluation of the unsolicited proposal.

The fourth area of significance to the agency is the evaluation of unsolicited proposals. Evaluation is a resource-consuming activity but is needed to determine the technical merit of unsolicited proposals.

These potential problem areas indicate the types of evaluations which must be carried out to determine whether a procurement should be awarded. The evaluation is basically a scientific or technical review to determine whether basic technical merit exists within the offeror's proposal. A proposal must have scientific merit to be considered for an award. Additionally, it must present a unique set of techniques, capabilities, experience, or facilities which the offeror is able to provide and the agency is interested in supporting. This characteristic is the key issue. Assuming the agency wants to fund proposed effort, uniqueness is the principal questionable area pertaining to the determination whether a contract should be awarded on a sole-source basis. It is a technical or scientific judgment and may be based on the technique or approach proposed, facilities necessary to the work, background knowledge and experience of the organization represented, proprietary data, or the personnel capabilities offered. In most cases, the key person whose capabilities are vital to the acceptance of the proposal is the principal investigator who has sponsored the preparation of the offer.

If it is determined that the proposal should be accepted as a result of the technical evaluation, funding support must be programmed, and a justification for non-competitive procurement must be prepared by the agency's technical sponsor of the project. That person is responsible for preparing and obtaining needed signatures on the required justification. Similarly, that person secures budget and funding support for procurement and prepares the procurement request.

Limited source procurement using unsolicited proposals is of strategic importance to many government agencies. It opens an avenue through which new ideas, innovation, and private parties without preestablished positions in the government marketplace can enter the market. To many small business firms, it has provided the foot in the door and initiated long-term contributions to government programs. Congress strongly encouraged small business participation in this innovative research by adopting the Small Business Innovation Development Act (P.L. 97-219). That act was effective on October 1, 1982, and required agencies that have large research and development budgets to reserve a portion of that budget for award of R&D contracts to small business. It required the agencies to establish an annual solicitation that identifies areas of interest which it would support out of the reserved funds. Ten agencies were part of this program in fiscal year 1983 and awarded contracts totalling $38.1 million. The process can also be important to large business and to large government programs, as the following vignette indicates.

Classic Success Story:
The XA4D-1 Aircraft

In 1950, the Navy expressed an urgent requirement for a high-performance, carrier-based jet aircraft with all-weather capability to deliver tactical nuclear weapons. Aircraft design and manufacturing capabilities at that time were such that a twenty-six to fifty thousand pound aircraft was considered necessary to satisfy the speed, range, payload, and all-weather capabilities called for in the operational requirement.

Mr. E. H. Heinemann, Chief Engineer of Douglas Aircraft Corporation, took a different view. He felt that a capable, light, simple airplane, minus the complexities of the all-weather capability, could be designed at about ten thousand pounds and for about one-fifth the cost. The Douglas corporate leadership agreed and supported independent development and design efforts.

A conference was held with Bureau of Aeronautics and Chief of Naval Operations representatives in March, 1952, at which Mr. Heinemann presented the Douglas proposal for the D-641, which Navy designated XA4D-1. As a result of the proposal, a study contract was let with Douglas in June to determine whether certain specifications could be deleted from the 1950 operational requirement and still meet a substantial part of Navy needs with the simplified approach being pursued by Douglas.

The Chief of the Bureau of Aeronautics concluded in July, 1952, that the Douglas design met Navy requirements better than any other in the foreseeable future. Under the conditions of urgency brought about by the Korean War then in progress, he authorized a negotiated development contract with Douglas for one prototype aircraft and nineteen test and evaluation aircraft. To meet the funding requirement, thirty-two A2D-1 aircraft authorized earlier for production by Douglas were cancelled and the funds reprogrammed to cover the XA4D-1 contract.[1]

In justifying the sole-source procurement, the Bureau of Aeronautics explained, "Although our new types are procured normally through design competition, it appears that in this case such a procedure would be unfair to industry." A later letter amplified the justification for the negotiated sole-source procurement:

> In order to hold a fair design competition based on the concept proposed by Douglas, the results of Mr. Heinemann's . . . original thinking as well as the results of his study contract would have to be made available to the rest of the industry. The time allowed to prepare proposals would have to be inordinately long to allow the other competitors to catch

up, or they would be at an impossible disadvantage. The specification would be written around the Douglas proposal, since this represents what we want. This obvious fact, plus the lead that Douglas already has, would make it appear to other contractors that the competition was being 'staged' to give an appearance of competition where none actually existed.[2]

The basic aircraft is only the tip of the iceberg regarding technical proposals. In the twenty years (1951 to 1971) after the development of the A-4 aircraft, a total of 1003 engineering change proposals (ECPs) were submitted by Douglas. Of these, 852 (82 percent) were in response to solicitation. The remaining 151 (18 percent) qualify as unsolicited proposals. Seventy percent of these unsolicited proposals were accepted by the government.

In addition to the ECPs, there were a total of 520 airframe changes (AFCs) submitted on the A-4 aircraft. Of these, 307 (59 percent) originated with the contractor as unsolicited proposals, with the remainder being responses to government RFPs.

Prior to 1961, according to Douglas estimate, about half of the ECPs and AFCs originated through unsolicited proposals from the contractor to improve the capabilities of the aircraft (uprated engine, improved avionics, etc.). A considerable portion of the expense for the engineering and development which went into these unsolicited proposals was passed on to the government in the form of overhead charges for other active contracts. Douglas reports that since 1961, the Naval Air Systems Command (then the Bureau of Naval Weapons) has been more strict in allowing overhead charges for engineering to support unsolicited ECPs and AFCs. The result has been to make this type of unsolicited proposal almost nonexistent.[3]

Solicited Noncompetitive Proposals

Prior position affecting procurement generally arises in two ways. The first occurs when the contractor holds rights, capital equipment, or technological/managerial knowledge derived independently. This becomes an important procurement matter when a need arises for which the contractor's capabilities are exclusive and essential. The other general situation is created by performance of government work, particularly development work, through which the contractor gains possession of technical data, technological equipment, and personnel expertise uniquely suited to the undertaking. In this situation, government sponsorship of initial phases of work is responsible for creating exclusive and essential capabilities. Such sponsorship is often necessary for major systems acquisitions.

Four stratagems which could overcome the effects of prior position (whether privately sponsored or government created) may be used. One is to duplicate the existing position by investment using an independent source to develop an alternative item. Another is to procure the rights and data from the existing source and solicit competitive offers. This may also require contracting with the original source for transfer of the knowledge and expertise to another source. (The existing source must agree to support the transfer.) A third stratagem is to secure a licensing agreement from the existing source, under which a licensee can produce the system. This stratagem requires an agreement to provide all necessary support to achieve technology transfer. Such an arrangement differs in legal effect from the second technique but is similar in practical effect since, in either case, a technology transfer of significant complexity is required. These stratagems are costly, and it is often unclear which is least costly. All three require duplication of an existing capability. Each of them, or a variation, may be available, but they require complex negotiation as indicated later under Second Sourcing. The fourth stratagem is to negotiate on a cost analysis basis to procure the required work from the source holding the prior position.

When a prior position situation arises, justification of limited source procurement is achieved in practice by preparation of a written determination and finding that explains why a competitive procurement cannot be carried out. In a broader context, however, government strategy is derived from an accommodation of two basic

objectives. One of these objectives is to employ competition directly to capture the least costly procurement.
This requires more than one competing source and might be
expressed as the immediate benefit objective. The other
basic objective is advancement of the interests of the
government and the public by encouraging innovation and
entrepreneurial risk assumption. This second objective
has a longer time horizon for securing benefits to the
government, but it has important corollaries. They are:
the private entrepreneur should be allowed to profit from
competitive advantage when innovative effort is successful, and rights to future benefits resulting from private
investment should be recognized. These two corollaries
seemingly work against achievement of the first objective
as stated above. Under the first three stratagems, both
the practical impact of the cost of duplication of the
prior position and the objective of encouraging innovation and entrepreneurial risk assumption must be weighed
against the immediate benefits of competition.

The second stratagem is to employ specific acquisition of rights. It is used infrequently by the government when analysis shows that benefits outweigh costs.
The second and third stratagems involve forms of leader
company procurement whenever they require contracts with
the original source for technology transfer support. The
third stratagem is known as directed licensing. Both the
second and third stratagems require agreement of the
prior position source and may be impracticable if the
technology transfer is of great complexity and its cost
outweighs potential economic benefits. Leader company
procurement has been employed primarily under emergency
or mobilization conditions. Directed licensing has been
applied by DOD program managers in several recent efforts
to obtain second sources.

The fourth stratagem is used extensively in government procurement. It requires internal justification of
the sole source decision but avoids overturning at public
expense the competitive advantage created by the prior
position. It is limited by the fact that the source must
cooperate in approaching the contractual agreement. However, it applies to either privately sponsored or government created prior position holders. It allows, in negotiations, for a balancing of interests of the two parties

through their agreement on price. Unfortunately, it may encourage inefficiency and excessive price offers. Ordinarily, existing sole source suppliers have little interest in government creation of alternate sources. As a consequence, some motivation may need to be applied to obtain full cooperation. One powerful influence is the government's willingness and preparations for using stratagem one--independent procurement of an alternative system.

The use of limited source solicitation is resisted by procurement policy which has now been strongly reinforced by CICA. Even under CICA, however, the Congress recognizes the need for it. For example, contracts for initial production of technical or specialized supplies may ordinarily be placed with the developer of the supplies. This situation is commonly encountered with new weapons development and with procurement of any complex system. Often the developer is the only source able to make efficient and timely use of the knowledge gained in development.

Second Sourcing

Second sourcing has been partially treated under solicited noncompetitive contracting. Three stratagems for generating second sources were identified. The effort to create an additional source arises because no second source--no competitor--is available. The techniques are only of importance when a noncompetitive, complex item is to be produced. Efforts to create an alternative source are largely limited to specialized high-dollar procurement. For the purchase of common items, competition in the economy ordinarily creates multiple potential sources. This is not the case for military production. Equipment and systems for military application tend to be nonstandard, highly complex, uniquely developed and expensive. Other areas of government procurement such as space and aeronautical research, atomic energy, transportation, and medical research are often equally specialized and complex. The civilian agencies differ because they seldom procure production quantities. Second sourcing is associated with production.

The decision to create a second source is an investment decision. It invariably requires financing the transfer of technology (including rights in data, production know-how, design philosophy, etc.) from one source to a second source. The investment is made when future benefits can only be estimated. The techniques for achieving this, while cumbersome, have been reviewed. This discussion will be limited to identification of the objectives, barriers, and facilitators of second sourcing. Balancing these factors is a challenge to program and procurement managers because information on future outcomes is frequently speculative.

The principal objectives in seeking a second source are:

1. To secure cost reduction in future procurement by creating competition
2. To increase production capacity, particularly in terms of production rate per unit of time
3. Mobilization and/or security considerations such as:
   a. geographic dispersion of production facilities
   b. qualification of multiple sources respecting specialized technologies.

The principal elements that facilitate or increase the advantages of second sourcing are:

1. High, long-term production needs
2. Low or inadequatae capacity of current producer
3. High potential for commercial use.

Of these advantages, the most compelling is a government requirement for substantial long term production. This promises some pricing advantages of competitive reprocurement and is attractive although difficult to quantify. If requirements are short term, even if substantial, the benefits of second sourcing cannot be realized because of the time required for qualification of the new source. Of similar importance is inadequate production capacity of the current producer. When requirements exceed existing production capacity, the necessity for an additional source is evident. Timing remains a problem since inadequate production rates cannot be increased until the new source is qualified.

High potential for commercial use provides incentive for the developer to promote second sourcing since gains from royalties, in addition to production, can be substantial. This potential encourages licensing. Unfortunately, most government production is of items that have limited commercial value.

Barriers to second sourcing are substantial, but may be overcome. Principal barriers are:

1. High technical complexity (technology transfer difficulty)
2. High or unusual capital investment requirement
3. Existence of critical proprietary data
4. Long production lead time
5. Complexity in contractual commitments
6. High security limitations
7. Existence of sole source subcontractor
8. High level of logistics support.

The incidence of these barriers is interesting. They tend to be present under the particular circumstances (single source situations) in which second sourcing may be needed. For example, highly complex items are the kind for which a single source emerges, yet high complexity is a barrier to technology transfer. Similarly, high and unusual capital investments are often associated with creation of a single source, but that type of investment discourages competitors--or forces the government to finance additional capital items. Proprietary data may also be the basis for a single source situation but adds to the resistance of that source against creating a competitor.

Long lead time in advance of production discourages second sourcing because it increases the cost of preproduction activity for the new source and delays opportunity for earnings from production. Again, the technologies that give rise to sole source also tend to generate difficult and lengthy start up periods. In like manner, contractual complexity--especially requirements for guarantees such as reliability improvement warranty--tend to discourage second sources because risk is increased.

High security limitations discourage second sourcing

since the objective is to limit distribution of information. Sole source at the subcontract level defeats the competitive attraction of second sourcing, unless the technique can be applied at the subcontract level. The final area is logistics support. New sources tend to create new support requirements by adding to the number of inventory items that must be managed. If the second source provides a completely interchangeable item, this problem should not arise, but complete interchangeability is difficult to achieve.

Factors such as these have not prevented second sourcing activity. DOD projects such as the F-107 engine for the Cruise Missile, the Referencing Measuring Unit and Computer/Inertial Navigation Element (RMUC/INE) for the Cruise Missile, and the AN/ALQ-165 Airborne Self-Protection Jammer (ASPJ) have implemented second sourcing programs.

Change Orders

Limited-source strategy includes procurement action by modification of existing contracts. Large sums are involved in this type of action, nearly all awarded on a noncompetitive basis. Procedurally, this type of procurement activity is treated as contract administration, but it accounts for a major part of the workload of government procurement personnel and in some programs, has accounted for dollar awards exceeding the value of original contracts.

The change order differs from the solicited proposal primarily because it is based on an existing contract. Under existing contracts, additional work can be procured without a solicitation document, if the added work is related to technical changes, changes in government property, or work suspension. Clauses included as standard provisions of the contract provide for these actions by authorizing unilateral directions by the government. These clauses enable work to be initiated rapidly, but they are normally source limited because the work required is integral to the existing contract. Strict interpretation of the change clause reveals that all such changes should be within the "scope" of the contract, that is, require work that is within the basic objectives and understandings associated with the unchanged contract.

There are also new procurement actions which make additions to the scope of existing contracts. Frequently this type of modification is an addition to the quantity of items procured. Some of these actions are accomplished by means of option provisions; some are simply new requirements. For additions to the scope of existing contracts, the government's internal process is a new procurement with appropriate justifications (for example, a justification for noncompetitive procurement). For the contractor, the action is simply an addition of new business.

Most procurement by modification is initiated by change order as authorized by the changes clause of the contract. That clause provides not only for unilaterial changes by the contracting officer, but for equitable adjustment of the contract to reflect the changed requirement. This clarifies the critical features of the change clause. Under it, the direction to make a change is likely to be an initial action without final price agreement, followed by proposal, evaluation and negotiation to adjust the terms of the contract. This allows the change to be carried out swiftly but without the moderating influences of the solicitation, proposal, negotiation, and award cycle. It also allows the pricing process to be treated independently of the performance of work and, potentially, subsequent to its performance.

One consequence of this is increased managerial flexibility for the government. It allows rapid response to changing conditions or new information. This increased flexibility carries with it increased responsibility to exercise judgment. A complement to the buyer's increased flexibility is the potential for entrepreneurial contractors to market change proposals. While the decision to make a change belongs to the buyer, responsibility must also be assumed for evaluation of its need. Evaluation should consider that changes also increase the contractor's sales base.

The effects of procurement by modification or change are summarized in Chart 14-1. The chart shows the contractual effect of particular types of modification

CHART 14-1

MODIFICATION AND CHANGE
UNDER GOVERNMENT CONTRACTS

ADMINISTRATIVE CONSEQUENCES OR PROCEDURE	TECHNICAL DIRECTION (TD)	CHANGE ORDER (CCN)	NEW PROCUREMENT (AMENDMENT)
RELATION TO CONTRACT INTENT	WITHIN SCOPE	WITHIN SCOPE	NEW SCOPE
RELATION TO CONTRACTOR'S ORIGINAL OBLIGATION TO PERFORM	WITHIN REQUIREMENT OF SPEC WITHOUT CCN	NEW OBLIGATION IS INCIDENT TO CHANGE IN CONTRACTUAL SPECIFICATION	NEW ITEM OR QUANTITY, ALTERATING BASIC OBJECT OF CONTRACT (CARDINAL CHANGE)
ADMINISTRATION	SIMPLE	FORMAL	FULL CONTRACTUAL ACTIVITY
FUNDING	NONE	USUALLY AN INCREASE	INCREASE
TIME DELAY: ORDER TO START WORK	NONE	DAYS	WEEKS OR MONTHS
INITIATION	DISCUSSION AND LETTER	UNILATERAL CCN	TWO-PARTY AMENDMENT
CONTRACTUAL FOLLOW UP	NONE IF PROPERLY ISSUED	NORMALLY TWO ACTIONS: CCN AND TWO PARTY MODIFICATION	ACTION COMPLETED WHEN AMENDMENT IS ISSUED

action in relation to seven categories of administrative considerations. The three types of action shown differ substantially. An important difference is the time delay between issuance of the order and the initiation of work. Clearly, the fastest way to get things done is to use technical direction. Technical direction may be defined as directive or consultative communication by the contracting officer's technical representative (COTR) with the contractor's managerial or technical personnel. A technical direction, however, should not be used to effect any form of procurment action, since the authority to direct a contractor does not include the contracting officer's authority to obligate the government for additional work. Nevertheless, technical directions do alter or influence methods of performance. The contract change order, however, differs entirely. It is a document issued by the contracting officer and obligates the government for the costs pertinent to work which is ordered under the change notice procedure. It is a more lengthy procedure but substantially faster than amendment of a contract for new procurement purposes.

Regulated Industry Purchases

The government buys large quantities of utility services from hundreds of concerns, both public and private, virtually all on a limited source basis. In 1983, this category of procurement, government-wide, totaled $3.8 billion (see Table 13-1). These procurements are exempt from normal policy requiring competitive procurement, because, in nearly all cases, the provider holds the sole franchise to serve the area in which the services are rendered. There are circumstances where a choice between utility companies exists and warrants some source studies and negotiations.

In addition to the limited sourcing of utility services, there is seldom any negotiation of prices. The services are acquired at rates established by the source. This practice is based on the fact that in nearly all cases, utility rates are subject to public regulation. The rates are normally reviewable and determinable by the local public authority as are accounting and other practices of the companies. On this basis, the federal agencies are able to acquire services without demanding cost and pricing data which, under the Truth in Negotiations concept, they would otherwise be required to obtain.

Thus, the procurement of services from regulated industries is an important but highly specialized and noncontroversial subset of the limited source strategy.

Notes

[1]This ended the life of the A2D-1, a counter-rotating turbo-prop aircraft which never went into production as a result of the XA4D-1 decision.

[2]Bureau of Aeronautics letter Aer-AC-31 of 21 August, 1952. Subj: New High-Performance Attack Airplane, Model A4D-1; Report of.

[3]This vignette by David B. Miller, Captain, U.S. Navy, was written as part of a research report while a student in one of the author's classes, April, 1971. It was previously published in: Stanley N. Sherman, Federal Procurement Principles, Text and Readings, the George Washington University, Washington, D.C., 1972, p. 13-2.

15 Technological/ Conceptual Strategy

The focus of this chapter is acquisition of major systems, a subject that occupies center stage in most discussions of government procurement. Attention is given to major systems because they represent large commitments of national resources, and because most of them grow in cost after they are initiated. Projects in this category are among the best known government undertakings and include the Space Shuttle, the Trident System, and the Air Launched Cruise Missile. There are hundreds of others, most of them a part of the defense programs.

A General Accounting Office report, "Status of Major Acquisitions as of September 30, 1982," published in September, 1983, listed 444 major acquisitions with a total acquisition value estimated to be $842.36 billion. Sixteen executive agencies had at least one such project and seven agencies were sponsoring fourteen or more. One hundred seventy-three of the projects were in the Department of Defense. These projects represent a truly significant part of national resource expenditures. In the Small Business and Federal Competition Enhancement Act of 1984, Congress defined major systems as ones:

1. In DOD, with R&D estimated cost greater than $75

million or with a total procurement cost greater than $300 million

2. In civilian agencies, with total expenditures greater than $750 thousand. (Civilian agency heads are allowed some flexibility in designating a system as major.)

Regarding the civilian agencies, this definition is substantially lower than that used by GAO ($50 million). As a consequence a listing for 1984 and later would probably include more civilian agency sponsored projects than the cited report.

Management of major systems acquisitions receives much attention from every new administration and is regularly modified as new management teams occupy the lead positions. The problems associated with such undertakings are relatively consistent and include: funding--the amount, its timing, responsibility for increases; performance--whether the system will do its assigned job; schedule delay--the impact of delay and responsibility for it; competition, especially the lack of it.

Reference to major acquisitions occurs at several points in this book. Chapter 8 treats the basic concepts of project management, comparing it with functional management and indicating its dominance in major acquisitions. Chapter 10 contains a discussion of setting objectives and securing resources. This discussion puts the concept of mission analysis and needs determination into perspective with the more routine initiation of purchase action which is part of normal agency operations. It also summarizes factors to be considered in procurement planning.

Three elements are reviewed in Chapter 11. One is the model of the major system acquisition cycle (Chart 11-3). The implications of that model will be examined further in this chapter. Also in Chapter 11, a brief discussion of four general strategies pertinent to procurement are presented, one of which is technological/conceptual strategy, a title used by the author to characterize the nature of the competitive process by which sources for major systems acquisitions are selected. We shall now expand on that subject, attempting to show more fully the integration of acquisition and procurement

strategy. Finally, Chapter 11 discusses the interrelationships of five cyclical processes vital to government
procurement planning, funding and execution. Technologi-
cal/conceptual strategy depends upon the leadership and
decisions pertinent to all five cycles.

Any examination of major systems clearly shows that
most projects, and the largest projects, are for military
systems. While space systems, nuclear projects and some
automation projects approach the magnitude of many
weapons systems, the predominant experience is in DOD.
While that predominance is recognized, the discussion
herein seeks a generic approach to overcoming the problems, rather than an examination of the details of each
agency's management approach. The final section of this
chapter briefly examines the DOD system.

The basic problems of major systems acquisition
management are related to the issues of transition from
phase to phase, magnitude of resources, and competition.
The systems tend to be conceptually complex and to
embrace technological advances. Early phases in their
development create new processes, designs, and test or
qualification procedures. These early phases prepare the
foundation for subsequent phases and provide the organization performing the work with a knowledge of the system
that is extraordinarily difficult to transfer. Because
of the technological transfer problems, major systems
evolve into limited source procurement actions as they
progress to later phases of effort. Much of the turmoil
associated with major systems derives from this limitation of source when establishing new contracts for follow-
on work. Any indications of shortfall in performance,
delay in delivery, or cost growth complicate decisions
concerning the next stage of the project.

Overview - Technological/Conceptual Strategy

Programs that are conceived to meet new missions or
goals in our advanced economy often require new technolog-
ical/conceptual approaches. Challenges may be presented
that demand creation of a new systems solution. Devising
new systems requires consideration of the totality of the
environment and comprehensive interpretation of its treat-

ment. The problems are complex because the needed solutions are not apparent. They may require new technology and institutional change. Major programs of this kind require the formation of teams that ensure the application of all requisite disciplines. These are formed through organizational combinations brought together under a structure of contracts. Neither the classical competitive nor the limited source strategies are adequate for procurement of this type.

The technological/conceptual strategy provides a basis for the procurement process to assemble, in a competitive mode, the resources to create the needed system. The strategy differs from classical competitive strategy principally because the buyer does not specify the requirement as a system solution. Instead, the buyer (government) delineates its mission and goals plus operating constraints, program cost expectations, and circumstances surrounding their achievement. These elements are set forth in a solicitation calling for organizations to examine the mission and goals and to perform technological/conceptual studies and designs. The solicitation expresses the buyer's expectation of supporting, through contracts, several stages of work through which alternative system concepts are narrowed periodically, until the final system decision is made. Contracts for the initial phases of conception and design are awarded to more than one competitor. Each supported source, working independently, competes for ultimate selection as the systems provider. Selection of sources for contractual support is based on quality of the technological/conceptual approach. Subsequently, selection of the systems provider is based on evaluation of the alternative systems solutions considering all factors relevant to the mission. The first clear enuniciation of this procurement strategy was made in 1972 by the COGP.[1] The commission's concept was made into policy when the OMB issued Circular A-109. Chart 15-1 illustrates the process including the concept of narrowing alternatives over time.

Although this strategy first appeared in the commission's report in 1972, many elements have been applied to large undertakings throughout the post-World War II period. The commission's contribution was its synthesis of many facets of program and procurement planning into an overall major systems acquisition process. The commission stated its approach and its perception of the problems it sought to overcome in this quotation:

> Unlike many past studies that were constrained to deal with segments of the acquisition process, our study benefited from having an exceptionally broad Congressional charter to examine system acquisition and to make recommendations for its improvement.
>
> As a result, the Commission chose to take an integrated view of the acquisition process, covering all the basic steps from the initial statement of a need to the eventual use of a system. The report concentrates on the way the government organizes policies and procedures to accomplish these basic steps. It also deals with the problems caused by the vested interests and motivations of the principal organizations in the roles they most often play in major system acquisition, including:
>
> > Contractors who are over optimistic in their estimates of system cost, performance, and delivery date and who make contractual commitments according to those estimates in order to win program awards.
> >
> > Agency components, like the military services, that reinforce contractor optimism to gain large-scale but premature program commitments in order to meet their obligations to provide modern operational capabilities and to preserve their stature and influence.
> >
> > Agency heads who do not have effective means of control in discharging their responsibilities for coordinating components and programs in the face of severe bureaucratic pressures.
> >
> > Congress and its committees which have become enmeshed at a detailed level of decisionmaking and review in attempting to fulfill their responsibilities. This disrupts programs, denies flexibility to those responsible for executing programs, and obscures Congress' view of related higher order issues of national priorities and the allocation of national resources.[2]

The commission's recommendations were implemented by OMB Circular, A-109. Subsequently, the Department of Defense and other agencies have modified their management instructions to implement the new concept as policy.

Major systems acquisition is a complex and controversial field of activity. It is an area in which decision processes, in addition to being qualitative, must commit large amounts of resources well in advance of assured success of the enterprise. The thrust of the commission's recommendations is that, for this kind of acquisition program, government should place on industry a major technological/conceptual responsibility while imposing on itself a burden of disciplined and rigorous definition of its operational and mission needs.

Technological/conceptual strategy makes industry and institutional innovators a part of the requirements determination processes in systems acquisition. These processes are the part of procurement most critical to mission success. It is in these stages, far in advance of issuance of a solicitation for the large systems acquisition contract, that the key management, technical, and sourcing decisions are made. The intent of this strategy is to bring the full technological and conceptual resources of our economy into the formulation of these decisions in a fully competitive mode.

Historical Techniques for Securing Competition in Complex Acquisitions

The technological/conceptual strategy is a departure from four distinct types of competition which have been practiced in various forms for technologically sophisticated acquisitions. These are: conceptual design, preliminary design, engineering design, and production design.

Of these, the COGP preferred use of conceptual design competition because it believed that design latitude for the contractors is essential to meaningful competition for large, complex undertakings. It also sought to encourage competitive offerings by contractors of unique information for evaluation and to encourage innovativeness. It believed these objectives could be achieved best under a system that fosters the independence of competitors as they generate their proposals. As part of this, the commission sought a widening of the technical distinctions between new systems proposals responsive to agency need. This approach provides a more meaningful choice for the agency when selecting its operational system. Technological/conceptual strategy is built on this foundation.

The concept of using preliminary design competition is less desirable than conceptual design because of the preexistence of a singular conceptual solution to the need. Nevertheless, it would be preferable to engineering design competition because it leaves independent system design groups in competition both within the agency structure and within industry.

Competition for major systems contracts has been primarily based on engineering design competition. When using this approach, the government agency prescribes the major design features and performance requirements of the system. Competitors respond with offers to meet system performance parameters while following the major features of the prescribed system. Price and qualitative assertions of the competitors are the primary bases for award selection. This technique is embraced by classical competitive strategy and remains predominant in source selection for projects not classified as major systems acquisitions. Beyond that, practice and policy are not entirely compatible, and in some cases, the actual competitive procedure used for major systems today may fit more closely the engineering design approach than technological/conceptual strategy.

The fourth type of competition may be pertinent to follow-on production. It suggests that production quantities of systems could be acquired competitively subsequent to firming up and proving out the production data package for the system. This competition would be based on price. Some of the difficulties associated with it are discussed in Chapter 14 under Second Sourcing.

Technological/Conceptual Strategy in Brief

Under the technological/conceptual strategy, if performed in accordance with the commission report, contractual relationships would be structured to reduce the amount of risk assumed by contractors during the early formulative stages. The early contracts would be short-run, fixed-dollar agreements to solve specified elemental problems associated with a competitor's system concept. The contractor would be committed to solve such problems, reduce uncertainties, and produce validated test results, but the magnitude of risk assumed would be limited by the period of time contractually allotted.

Additionally, the strategy embraces a concept of sequential decisionmaking. This would establish decision points in the evolving system where the agency head could reorient effort based on revised agency needs or unpredicted technical events. Substantial competitive motivation from this technique would bear on the design teams through each short-term period, because the government executive would have authority to reprogram funds as he determines which efforts warrant continued support.

Use of technological/conceptual strategy encounters an additional risk that is primarily derived from the nature of the bureaucracy. The strategy demands greater effort during early planning stages of a program and delays the adoption of a systems configuration. Thus, it lengthens the period during which major commitments of resources must be made prior to existence of proven systems prototypes. During this period, challenges of the undertaking may arise, and support for development and production is more difficult to generate. Nevertheless, the strategy should also reduce the time and effort from the prototype to the operational stages, and it creates an alternative system, giving management a true choice at the key decision points.

Technological/conceptual strategy reduces buyer direction of contractor activity. The system buyer would require each competitor to independently conceive the solution to customer needs. Furthermore, the competition would be on a technological rather than a price basis. (However, program cost, especially life cycle cost, would be a design consideration. In this sense, price would continuously influence each competitor.) A part of the concept (not yet implemented and not a part of A-109 policy) is to extend competition to the bureaucracy by establishing an internal design group to interact with each contractor team. Each of these groups, supported by contractor teams, would seek approval of its system at the agency head level. This plan is oriented toward presenting management with distinctive alternatives for meeting the agency's need.

Specific Elements of A-109 Policy

As was indicated in Chart 11-3, the concrete steps in the major acquisition cycle are the specified points at which the agency head must make an approval before proceeding with subsequent phases of the acquisition cycle. The first of these decision points is identified as point number 1 on Chart 15-1, the point at which the agency approves a defined mission needs statement. This agency head approval is a final step in the evaluation and reconciliation of needs which agency personnel have derived from their continuing mission analysis. The mission analysis activity is a required part of the A-109 policy and includes a continuing analysis of mission capabilities and technological opportunities. Mission analysis could result in identification of a deficiency in agency capabilities indicating a need for an acquisition process. It could also identify new technological opportunities which indicate that the agency should establish a new capability. The preparation of a mission needs statement would follow these conclusions.

If the agency head approves the proposed mission needs statement, the work of generating systems concepts begins. Responsibility for the undertaking is assigned to an organizational entity within the agency, but additionally, responsibility for the new systems acquisition is placed under a program manager as quickly as possible after the decision to proceed. For example, Naval Material Command might be the entity, Trident, the program. Contractual action focuses on an RFP to explore alternative system design concepts. Programming and budget activity focus on OMB/congressional support. During this period, the agency and the program manager are obligated to consider alternatives to acquisition of a new system, particularly modifications which are less expensive and more certain to achieve technical objectives on time.

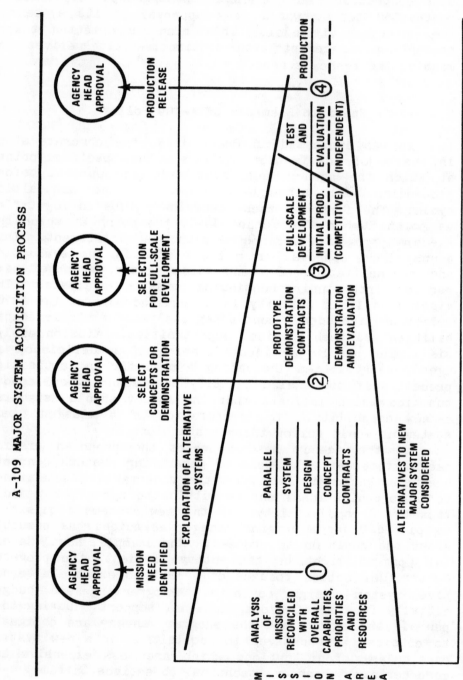

CHART 15-1

A-109 MAJOR SYSTEM ACQUISITION PROCESS

One of the initial principal tasks of the program manager is to prepare an acquisition strategy. The intent of the formal strategy document is to ensure that the program office has fully considered the acquisition process which they are about to enter. This thinking-through process is intended to bring about an objective appraisal in an effort to find the most economical, effective and efficient manner in which to proceed.

The objective of the initial contracting efforts associated with the alternative systems exploration is to cause the contractor to examine his systems concept and to identify risks and uncertainties associated with it. The initial contracts are expected to be parallel short-term arrangements in which competitive technological/conceptual efforts ensure the responsiveness of the system's design concepts to the mission need. Efforts to reduce risks of the systems approach are aggressively pursued.

A central part of this initial phase of work is the design of the solicitation for parallel development contracts. The solicitation should be expressed in terms of the mission need identified earlier and approved by the agency head. A mission need type of statement avoids specifying the systems solution and allows the contractor freedom to propose the technical approach, design features, subsystems, schedules, and costs. The expectation communicated in the solicitation is that trade-off studies will be made to present the competitor's best concepts. The key point of this procedure is to ensure that industrial innovativeness and competiveness are not constrained by predetermined equipment and/or systems solutions. During performance of the parallel contracts, a continuous review and evaluation of the contractor's efforts is carried on by the program manager. While this review must be intensive, the government program office is to avoid constraining the contractor's activity in any way that would restrict innovativeness.

Conclusion of the parallel contract phase is reached when there is progress that indicates a move into the competitive demonstration phase is prudent. Since competitive demonstrations will involve development of prototype systems or subsystems, the decision to move into that phase of effort involves a substantial additional commitment of agency resources. Therefore, the approval of such a move is an agency head decision, identified in Chart 15-1 as decision number 2. Competitive demonstration contracts are an extension of work begun in the prior phase under the parallel short-term contracts. However, the orientation shifts from proof of concept to demonstration of mission performance against criteria set forth by the agency. To the extent feasible, the demonstration is performed under operational test conditions. Depending upon the individual program condition, the competitive demonstrations may be of subsystems rather than a complete developmental model or prototype. Therefore, the exact operational test conditions must be set specifically for the program. Contractors are expected to be able to estimate life cycle cost of their respective systems given factors specified by the agency. The competitive demonstrations lead toward agency head decision point number 3. That decision point is the authorization of full scale development for a selected system or conceivably for a continuation of more than one competitive system into full-scale development. Critical to a decision to go ahead with full scale development are:

1. Demonstration of system performance using the contractor's systems concepts measured against mission and program objectives
2. Assessment of risk and uncertainty which remains unresolved at the time of the decision
3. Projection of acquisition and ownership costs
4. Evaluation of the contractor's capacities, technical capabilities, and managerial and financial resources in light of program objectives.

Full scale development starts with the contractor's developmental model or prototype subsystems, completes the full scale system, and puts it through the production engineering transition processes. It requires an initial production quantity for test and evaluation under environmental conditions and at performance levels expected to be experienced under operational conditions. Testing of these units is to be done by an independent agency, one that is independent of the procuring agency's development and user organizations and of the contractor.

A decision to proceed into full scale production is

decision 4 on Chart 15-1. It is pertinent only for the type of major systems acquisition which involves production. The concept of the A-109 policy is intended to address, as well, systems other than ones that would go into production. Specifically, its use is intended for one-of-a-kind construction projects, installation of ADP systems, development of software systems, and other undertakings involving major resource commitments of an agency. The practicability of such applications remains unclear at the time of this writing.

DOD Acquisition Policy Developments

The major systems acquisition process as defined in OMB Circular A-109 was developed largely as a response to problems with defense acquisition programs of the 1960s. As a result it sought to reduce problems with production of military systems. Nevertheless, the commission felt their concepts to be pertinent to other major systems acquisitions. Substantial difficulty in implementing the policy has been experienced in both civilian and defense agencies.

No agency approaches the depth of experience in major systems acquisition found in DOD. Ten years before OMB Circular A-109 was issued, DOD had segmented its acquisition cycle into four phases known as concept formulation, contract definition, full scale development/production, and system operation. The cycle didn't identify mission/needs analysis or the role of the agency head as decisionmaker at key points. Both may have been present but were not explicitly required. In 1969, DOD revised its approach under the leadership of Deputy Secretary of Defense, David Packard. Mr. Packard instituted formal secretarial approvals at three points in the cycle known as milestones. The phases became known as concept formulation, validation, operational systems development, and production. The first agency head decision, Milestone I, occurred prior to entering validation. It committed the agency to support prototype development and testing. The second decision, Milestone II, committed the agency to full scale development including operational systems development (transition through production engineering).

CHART 15-2

DOD MILESTONE DECISIONS AND ACQUISITION PHASES

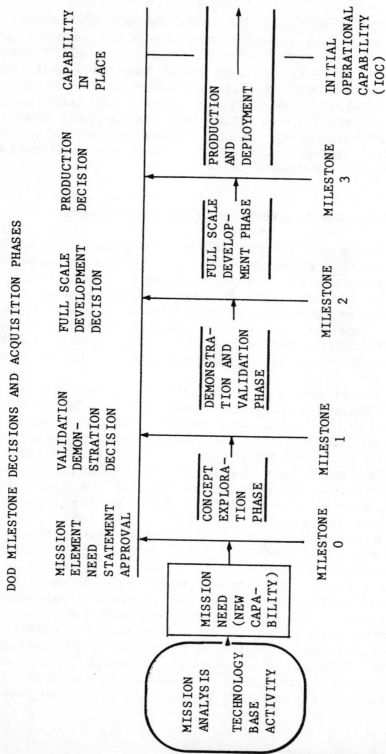

The third agency head decision approved production.

Mr. Packard also established the Defense Systems Acquisition Review Council (DSARC) assigning it responsibility for conducting milestone reviews for the secretary. Recommendations on milestone decisions emerge from these reviews. At that point, however, the DOD acquisition process still did not include a mission needs phase or decision milestone. That phase was added as a result of OMB Circular A-109. The result is four milestones beginning with Milestone 0 (see Chart 15-2).

Further revision of the DOD acquisition process under Deputy Secretary Frank Carlucci in 1982 modified the management approach to major acquisition decisions. Milestone 0 continued as DOD's mission needs determination but became a part of the planning, programming and budgeting process. It is analogous to decision point 1 on Chart 15-1. Milestones II and III are subject to a (DSARC) review. These are analogous to decision points 2 and 3 on Chart 15-1.

Notes

[1] Report of the Commission on Government Procurement, Volume II, GPO, Washington, D.C., 1972.

[2] Ibid, p. 69.

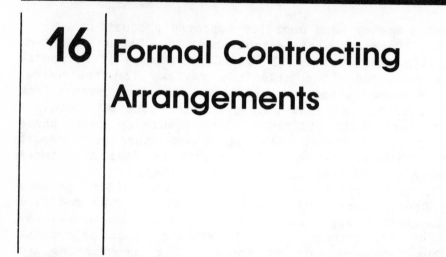

16 | Formal Contracting Arrangements

Familiarity with the range of contract types is important to effective procurement management. This chapter attempts to provide knowledge of the kinds of arrangements available as well as insight into the criteria that influence decisions. The chapter begins with some illustrations of problems created by questionable decisions on contract type. It explains the principal functions served by the formal instrument and the need for alternatives. Classification of contracts is then discussed which leads to an analysis of the principal features of the several types of contracts. Utilization statistics are also presented. Finally, the chapter examines the process of selecting contract types and details a number of criteria for making the decision as reported by procurement managers from both industry and government.

Procurement defines business relationships by establishing contracts. Its objective is to structure contracts to encourage successful projects. Whether that objective is achieved must, unfortunately, be measured by outcomes. Take, as an example, General Atomic's gas reactor project at Fort St. Vrain, Colorado. It makes good after-hours reading for frustrated project managers of high technology acquisitions. Management at General Atomic moved rapidly from their successful pilot reactor

to sell full scale power plants. They contracted to con-
struct the one at Fort St. Vrain on a fixed price basis
and promised on-time delivery of power at specified cost
levels. That was in 1967. By 1975 they had lost a billion dollars.[1] By 1980, full scale operations had not
yet begun.

General Atomic wasn't the first to learn that contracts are powerful tools. All manner of business relationships are created through their use. As an instrument for drawing together resources to perform work or as
a means for exchange of assets, the contract stands alone
in flexibility. It can be oral or written, some may
exist for hours, some for years. The monetary value may
range from insignificant amounts to billions of dollars.
It can be created in moments or through days and months
of interaction between the potential parties. While the
tool itself is ubiquitous, each contract is unique with
respect to terms and conditions, values, parties, objectives, and outcome. Contracting experts might argue that
General Atomic shouldn't have fixed the price as early as
it did in the construction of a full scale, new type
reactor.

Contract Type Historical Notes (1960-1980)

Type of contract has not often been a major issue in
private or public procurement, but it is important to the
success of large undertakings. A brief history, drawn
from public sector contracting, should help to give perspective to the matter.

During the late 1960s toward the end of the tenure
of Robert S. McNamara as Secretary of Defense, several
major projects were exhibiting acute financial distress.
Mr. McNamara objected to the use of cost type contracts
which had become fashionable with procurement of technologically advanced weaponry during and after the Second
World War. Such procurements often included, in addition
to production, the design and development of the required
system. Mr. McNamara's policy was expressed by _Business
Week_ as follows:

Originally, McNamara balked at the cost-plus-fixed-fee award so common in the 1950s. He considered this the least efficient type of procurement because it not only reimburses contractors for all allowable costs, but guarantees them a profit whether their performance is good or bad. Therefore, he restricted such contracting largely to exploratory projects where technical uncertainties abound, and where no meaningful measure of performance can be established in advance.

McNamara preferred firm fixed-price contracts because they force the government to prepare precise work statements at the outset, and motivate contractors to minimize cost overruns and schedule slippages to protect a profit that only good performance can bring.[2]

While it is questionable whether any type of contract "forces" particular behaviors on the parties, the general policy was clear. The secretary himself made the following comment:

Since 1961, we have made many significant improvements in managing Defense acquisition programs and in procurement policies. The cost-plus-fixed-fee environment of earlier years has been replaced by tighter management--both on our part and that of our contractors--as exemplified by the introduction of more intensive competition, more extensive use of incentive and fixed-price contracts, and greater contractor investment in plant and equipment.[3]

Regardless of these statements, problems of great magnitude involving cost, schedule and technical issues arose during several major acquisition projects which were on a fixed-price or fixed-price-incentive basis.

The problems encountered by C5A, Cheyenne Helicopter and other large acquisition projects of the 1960s gave rise to numerous studies including that of the Commission on Government Procurement commissioned by Congress in November, 1969.[4] A clear reversal of the McNamara policy occurred on May 29, 1970, when Deputy Secretary of Defense, David Packard, issued a memo that stated in part: "In all our contracting, the type of contract must be tailored to the risks involved." Mr. Packard intended the type of contract to be appropriate for the job. Subsequently, the Armed Services Procurement Regulation (renamed Defense Acquisition Regulation) was revised to amplify treatment of contract type selection. The FAR Part 16 now covers this subject matter.

Function of Contract Types

The type of contractual instrument serves several purposes of the procurement manager. Probably the most basic is to serve as evidence of the agreement. In effect the contract establishes a baseline for future reference, if the parties discover later on during performance that problems of interpretation of their agreement have arisen. This evidentiary function is not related only to legal or litigation problems although it can be important during resolution of disputes. More importantly, for long term contractual relationships, the parties need to be able to refer to the document which recorded their common understanding at the time that they entered into the agreement.

Related to the evidentiary function, the contract should also be designed to facilitate modification of the agreement as time passes. The reason is that contracts are static. They express the intent of the parties as it is best understood at the time of entering into the agreement. Unfortunately, as work progresses, the original intentions usually require alteration on the basis of subsequent events or the development of greater understanding of the purposes of the undertaking. Some of the modifications that routinely arise in long term contracts are changes in design or schedule, increased understanding of technological problems, and revision of the buyer's specific needs or objectives. The need to update for these kinds of purposes generally is a function of time. Change is incessant in the real world of performing contractual responsibilities, but contracts do not change without explicit effort on the part of the parties.

The contract plays a role in performance of required work, either facilitating or inhibiting progress. As a

consequence, the contractual instrument should be designed with care so that it will facilitate, not inhibit.
Contract parties have a perception of their responsibilities and the risks associated with them, as they apply
their effort. The ease or difficulty of accommodating
change within the scope of contractually stated objectives becomes important to constructive interaction
between the parties.

The contract provides for payment to the supplier
for work performed. The formal instrument is almost
essential in larger organizations as part of the documentation for processing invoices. In addition, it sets up
the basis upon which payment is made. In the firm-fixed-
price contract, the basis is price. In the cost-reimbursement contract, cost incurrence in pursuit of the
specified work is the basis. Throughout the range of
fixed-price, incentive, and cost types of contracts, the
instrument also sets forth the basis for payment of
profit or fee to the performer.

In many respects, the most important function of
proper contract design is motivation of the contractor.
Motivation is the fundamental basis for the incentive
contract and is the root of the general preference for
firm fixed-price contracts. The source of motivation in
contracting is the payment of profit. In designing a
contract, the objective is to structure the instrument so
that the performer obtains greater profit for achieving
higher levels of buyer satisfaction. The several types
of contracts which are designed on the basis of pricing
arrangement specifically address this issue. Each of the
several pricing arrangements provides a unique method for
determining, in the final analysis, how much fee or
profit will be paid to the performer. In general, the
determination of those sums is based upon the outcome of
performance as it relates to the expected performance as
outlined in the original contract instrument.

The Need for Alternative Types of Contracts

The most common type of contract is the one with
which all purchasing managers are thoroughly familiar.
It is the firm-fixed-price contract. The ordinary pur-

chase order, when executed by both parties, is an example. Under it, each party performs specified duties.
Contracts are enforceable by court action if necessary,
but in the ordinary business relationship, both parties
perform their duties without recourse to litigation. For
most purchases, no particular thought is given to the
exact type or form of the contractual relationship. Nor
should much attention be paid to the contract type for
routine purchasing circumstances. However, there is a
need for purchasing managers to be thoroughly familiar
with the range of choices available to them under circumstances requiring a more sophisticated relationship
between the parties than that provided by the firm-fixed-
price contract. The structure of a contract becomes
critical when:

1. The purchasing manager seeks to acquire nonstandard
   supplies or services, and the period of performance
   is likely to be long term, during which the two
   parties must have a working relationship that facilitates updating or modification of the relationship.
2. The proposed undertaking involves a large sum of
   money coupled with a high degree of complexity in
   the technological effort required.
3. The immediate undertaking leads towad substantial
   follow-on contractual opportunities in which the
   purchasing manager may wish to seek competition.
4. The performance of the undertaking is risky because
   of technological or other sources of uncertainty,
   and some sharing of that risk between buyer and
   seller is necessary.
5. The circumstances of the purchase action are such
   that the buyer seeks to obtain performance cost data
   from the supplier.
6. The buyer's objectives in entering into the contractual relationship include the reduction of inventory, the simplification of ordering procedures, the
   reduction of the cost of repetitive purchasing
   processes and other logistics goals.

Alternatives Available
to the Purchasing Manager

Choosing the best type of contract for a situation in which other than the firm-fixed-price contract is indicated can be a complex process. This complexity begins with the necessity for each party to assess its independent objectives and to approach the common goals sought in the contract as negotiable items leading to the final agreement. Each party starts with a set of objectives which must be accommodated to those of the other party. Of particular significance is the large number of alternatives from which a choice can be made. The choice is more complex than simply choosing from among twelve to twenty different types of contracts. The real task is to select from an unlimited number of varied terms and conditions which might be included in any of the contract types. The combination of available features is particularly large in the area of incentive arrangements. Let us examine some of the alternatives.

Bases for Classifying Contract Types

Comparison of contract types is aided by classifying the alternatives. One basis, form of acceptance, distinguishes contracts calling for completion of a specified objective from those that finance services of a continuing nature. The second basis, logistics needs, facilitates repetitive ordering and inventory minimization. The third basis and the principal method of classification is by pricing arrangement. Under this method, several contract types are known by techniques used to finally determine the cost, profit and/or price to be paid upon completion of the contract.

Form of Acceptance of Work

Contracts may be written on a term or completion basis. These are distinguished by the basic obligation assumed by the performer, that is, whether the performer is obligated to complete a specific, defined, and measurable end objective--or to apply efforts and resources in the pursuit of an end objective which in itself is beyond the completion of the contract. End objectives of buyers are not necessarily achieved coincident with the completion of a specific contract. Instead, a contract may provide for a period, or term of service. For example, in the purchase of services of a routine nature, such as maintenance, it is evident that services are continuous and do not come to completion at the end of any given contract. In this case, a new contract or an extension of the existing contract is necessary for continuation of performance. That type of arrangement is quite different from a construction contract wherein the builder undertakes the construction of a specific building, and upon both completion of the building and buyer acceptance, the work contracted is considered complete and coterminous with the expiration of the contract. The essential point underlying this observation is that the nature of the performer's obligation to the buyer is very different under a completion contract than under a term contract.

Another example of this distinction is found in the area of research. Many research undertakings are initiated under a contract which recognizes that the performing research party will apply his or her best efforts to the investigative process during a specified period of time. But at the outset, the parties recognize that the probable total extent of the research necessary for fruition of the project is likely to go far beyond the end of the initial contractual instrument. Thus, in many cases, the research effort is contracted on a term basis rather than a completion basis. As a consequence, the pricing arrangement and the funding of the contractual instrument are based upon measuring input to performance rather than output resulting from it.

In most R&D contracts, the buyer expects to have, at the end of the initial contract relationship, a working prototype of the system. Thus, the buyer of a new technological device (for example, a numerically controlled machine, newly designed to achieve greater rates of production and fewer defective products than had been previously achieved) will expect the performer of the R&D work to meet a delivery schedule by providing a new machine that will achieve all specified objectives. This

distinction between term and completion type contracts is
not dependent upon the pricing arrangement. When we
examine the fixed-price contract types, we find both term
and completion fixed-price contracts; in examination of
cost-type contracts, we find both term and completion
cost type contracts.

Logistics Needs

Logistics needs that can, in part, be met through
appropriate contract mechanisms include inventory minimization, standardization and simplification of inventory,
consolidation of ordering and shipping, simplification
and reduction of repetitive document generation, and
improvement of ordering and delivery elapsed time requirements. These objectives, plus some potential price
savings, can be achieved through application of arrangements known variously as corporate agreements, blanket
purchase orders, systems contracts, open end contracts,
basic ordering agreements, and indefinite delivery
contracts (including requirements, indefinite quantity
and definite quantity contracts). Each of these techniques is designed to systematize, perhaps to automate,
purchase of categories of materials and services that are
used on a continuing basis. Normally there will be a
separate agreement for each category of need, and a wide
variety of individual arrangements is encompassed by the
techniques.

Pricing Arrangement

The following discussion assumes, in each case, that
performance is carried out without impossibilities,
delays, repudiations, interferences, changes or any of a
variety of events that result in subsequent negotiations
that modify the agreement or the performance obligations.
That such events occur regularly is recognized, but
discussion of them is a separate and complex issue which
will not be treated at this time.

Fixed-Rate Contract Types as a Group. The fixed-
rate contract differs significantly from the firm-fixed-

price contract in part because the final amount to be paid to the performer is not determinable until performance has been achieved. Furthermore, the fixed-rate contract is not comparable to the cost type contract because final payment of the contract is not dependent upon the level of costs incurred by the performer. The fixed-rate contract type is distinguished by the establishment, at the outset of the contract, of a reimbursement rate for direct labor applied to the work. For example, if the contract requires the performance of engineering analysis, a rate will be specified in the contract for reimbursement to the contractor for each man-hour (or each man-day) of engineering analysis effort which the contractor applies to the job. The fixed rate is inclusive of direct labor cost, overhead charges, general and administrative or selling expenses, and profit. All of these elements of the cost of delivering the engineering services are summed, and a rate for reimbursement to the contractor is agreed upon by the parties. The buyer must observe and monitor the contractor's performance as the work progresses in order to verify that the delivered services are acceptable.

There are two types of fixed-rate contracts. One is the labor hour contract in which the only provision for reimbursement of the supplier is the reimbursement rate for direct labor applied to the job. The other is the time and materials contract which, in addition to the fixed rate, includes a provision for the delivery of materials at cost. Ordinarily the provision of material is severely limited in a fixed-rate contract, but the time and materials arrangement provides for the reimbursement process.

Fixed-Price Contract Types as a Group. The fixed-price group of contracts contains a fairly complex structure of potential arrangements. They are (1) the firm-fixed-price contract, (2) the fixed-price-incentive contract, (3) the fixed-price-redeterminable contract, (4) the fixed-price with economic price adjustment provision contract, (5) the fixed-price-level-of-effort-term contract, and (6) the fixed-price-incentive contract with multiple incentives.

The firm-fixed-price contract (FFP) should be compared with all of the others. It is a contract in which the party who is the supplier is a guarantor of successful performance of the requirements set forth in the contract, including accomplishment within the contractually specified delivery date or period of performance. Under FFP, the supplier becomes financially responsible for successful performance without any right to subsequent change in the specified contract price and schedule. In return, the buyer in a firm-fixed-price contract is obligated to make payment of the fixed price as specified in the contract without regard for the actual cost of performance of the work. This is a very simple relationship, one in which the supplier, working independently and under his own management direction, is provided the financial incentive to perform efficiently. If able to perform at less cost than originally anticipated, the contractor secures as profit, 100 percent of the costs saved. The buyer, on the other hand, is able to plan with the confidence that needed supplies will be delivered, on time, at the cost which has been defined in the contractual relationship. None of the other contract forms accomplish this fundamentally simple set of relationships.

The fixed-price-incentive (FPI) contract is distinguished by its inclusion of a sharing formula, whereby the performer is paid more profit if performance is completed at a cost below the expected (target) cost agreed upon in the contract. Conversely the contractor is paid less profit if cost at completion exceeds the agreed upon target cost. The ratio of reward or penalty is controlled by the formula stated in the contract. For example, the buyer may assume 75 percent and the seller 25 percent of decreases or increases in cost of performance (as compared with target cost). The fixed-price-incentive contract retains the fixed-price concept, because it includes a ceiling price which limits the buyer's obligation regardless of cost of performance.

A fixed-price-redeterminable (FPR) contract avoids the inclusion of a sharing formula, yet leaves the final negotiation of price until performance of work has proceeded to the point at which costs of performance are well enough known to predict (and negotiate) the final cost and price necessary for completion of work. The redetermined price is set forth in the contract when negotiated. Historically, the FPR contract was important to large government projects, but it has fallen into disuse in favor of incentive contracts. The principal advantage of FPR contracts was to delay price determination until some cost data could be generated by performance. This approach allowed a firm price to be set prior to completion of performance. Its advantages were offset by administrative complexities in negotiation and lack of confidence that it motivates efficient performance.

Fixed-price contracts with economic price adjustment provisions provide for price adjustment upon the occurrence of specified changes in cost or price factors set forth in the contract. The factors may be labor or material price indices or changes in industry-wide price levels. The factors selected should be exogenous variables not controllable by the management of the instant contract. This type of contract is designed to shift risk of price or cost inflation from seller to buyer.

The fixed-price-level-of-effort-term contract (FPLET) embraces the concept of term contracts. It is normally limited to research undertakings of limited scope in which progress toward a technological achievement, not completion, is sought. The contract permits firm budgeting of the contractor work plan and minimizes administrative oversight activity associated with performance. A high degree of confidence in the technical skill and dedication of the performer is necessary for this type contract.

Multiple-incentive contracts (MI), whether fixed-price or cost type, increase the complexity of negotiation and administration of the contractual relationship to its maximum. Whereas the FPI contract uses one independent variable (cost) to govern the amount of incentive profit to be paid, the multiple incentive contract may employ several variables: performance, schedule and cost. The modeling of such contracts is difficult and the impact of trade-off decisions is even more difficult to discern. Nevertheless, the contracts attempt to provide motivation, in a monetary sense, to the supplier for achieving maximum performance toward buyer objectives.

Cost versus Fixed-Price Contracts. The most fundamental distinction between types of contracts is the

difference between a fixed-price and a cost-type contract. The cost contract is established on the basis
that the customer will reimburse the supplier for costs
incurred by the supplier in attempting to perform the
obligations of the contract. This form of payment
requires the supplier to disclose cost records to the
buyer, and in the case of government contracting, to
submit books of records and accounts to the government
auditor to verify the amounts claimed for reimbursement.
This approach differs from that employed in the fixed-
price contracts discussed previously. In all of the
fixed-price types, the ultimate obligation of the buyer
to pay is based upon the price agreement of the parties
as set forth in the contract--not by the actual level of
the incurred costs. Nevertheless, as has been shown,
several of the fixed-price contract forms do require a
disclosure of the supplier's costs to the buying organization.

Under both the cost-reimbursement contract (completion format) and the firm-fixed-price contract, the obligations of a supplier to perform the work required are
essentially similar (with one distinction). In both
situations the supplier takes on the obligation to
complete the job in accordance with specifications and
within the time frame established by the contract. However, in a cost-reimbursement contract, the level of
accountability assumed by the supplier is significantly
reduced because the supplier is not a guarantor of the
estimated cost of performance. In effect, the obligation
of the supplier is reduced to the extent of applying
best efforts to performance with the objective of completing the contract in accordance with the agreement. The
difference is expressed best in terms of the assumption
of risks of the two parties. In the cost contract, the
buyer assumes most of the financial risks of nonperformance or delayed performance. In the fixed-price
contract, the supplier assumes most of the financial risk
of nonperformance or delay of performance. It is important to recognize that the contract arrangement is considerably more complicated than simply being either a fixed-
price or cost type of contract. The ultimate allocation
of risk between buyer and seller is determined not only
by the form of the contract but also by numerous possible

terms which may or may not be included in the contract, such as warranties and incentives. Additionally, the specifications of the contract are critical in the allocation of risk because the ultimate complexity and difficulty of performance depends on the specifications or other technical documentation which form a part of the agreement.

Cost Contracts as a Group. While all cost contracts are similar in requiring a disclosure of costs for the purpose of reimbursing the performing organization, the types of cost contracts are differentiated by the provisions for payment of fee or profit for work completed. The cost-no-fee (C-NF) contract is primarily used for research undertakings in which a university or other nonprofit educational institution is the performing party. The contract provides no sum of money over and above the allowable costs of performance. However, cost reimbursements that contribute to fixed and semi-variable costs may be of great benefit to performing institutions.

The cost-plus-fixed-fee contract (CPFF) is the predominant form of cost contracting usually applied when a private profit earning organization receives a cost contract. In the CPFF contract, the amount of fee is agreed upon as a fixed sum, not as a percentage, during negotiation prior to award. That sum is then payable to the performing organization upon achievement and delivery of a satisfactory end product. It does not vary in amount with the actual cost incurred by the contractor. The cost-plus-fixed fee instrument is of primary use when a substantial degree of uncertainty surrounds the performance cost of the contract effort. The source of uncertainty normally is derived from technological or producibility issues resulting in inability to discern cost of performance with a high degree of reliability in advance of the award of the contract. As a result we find that the cost-plus-fixed fee contract is used extensively for research or research and development work.

A cost sharing (CS) type of contract is also pertinent in many procurement situations when it is evident that the performing organization will gain substantial commercial advantage as a consequence of being funded for an element of work by the buying organization. While this contract type is not limited to government procure-

ment, the cost sharing idea is not ordinarily a popular
method of contracting from the point of view of the
performer and would only rarely be applicable for commercial relationships between private enterprises.

The cost-plus-incentive-fee contract (CPIF) operates
in a fashion similar to the FPI; however, CPIF differs
because a ceiling price is not established at the outset
of the contract. Instead, the ultimate cost limitation
remains unstated at the time of award, and limits are
placed on the amount of fee increase or decrease allowed
(fee floor and ceiling). As with FPI, the fundamental
incentive relationships can be varied by incorporating
independent variables in addition to the cost variable.
Thus, a cost type incentive contract may be designed as a
multiple incentive contract.

Contracts may take the form of an award-fee arrangement. Under the cost-plus-award fee (CPAF) contract,
assessment of performance is based on the buyer's subjective determination of the contractor's level of performance in relationship to that required by the contract.
The award fee contract provides no formula at all with
respect to final payment of profit to the performer. It
does provide reimbursement of costs by the buyer and
normally allows a minimum fee to be paid upon completion
of the duties of the performer. However, the minimum fee
in an award fee contract is agreed upon at a relatively
low level with respect to the total aspirations of the
performer. Over and above the minimum fixed fee for
completion of the job, the award-fee contract provides
that an additional sum may be paid from an amount established in the contract. The amount of the award fee is
made available for payment in the original agreement pending the buyer's periodic assessment of the seller's
performance. For higher degrees of performance against
the standards of the buyer, a higher award fee would be
allocated by the buyer at the time the award fee assessment is made. This system of incentive allows maximum
exercise of judgment by the contracting parties during
the performance period. It allows for changes in direction or modification of emphasis during performance and
permits payment of profit in accordance with the degree
of satisfaction that the performer is able to deliver.
The award fee contract is normally used only by govern-

ment agencies, but there could be circumstances in which the industrial purchasing agent may use an award-fee contract for establishment of particular contractual activities.

In summary, fixed-price incentives, cost-based incentives, multiple incentives and award incentives are available to the buyer depending on the circumstances which h/she wishes to address when the new contractual relationship is established.

Contract Type Utilization Statistics

Table 16-1 presents data on use of contract types in government procurement. The data, drawn from the Federal Procurement Data center Report covering fiscal year 1983, is useful in showing the predominance of fixed price contracts. Readers should recognize that the statistics are not broken out to show all the types of contracts. It is noteworthy that the proportion of cost type contracts in number of actions is only slightly more than half their proportion in terms of dollars. They tend to be larger contracts than most fixed price awards. Not shown by the table is the proportion of fixed price awards that were incentive contracts (thereby involving some flexibility in cost and price outcome).

The Process of Selecting Contract Type

Under FAR Subpart 16.1, contract type is a matter for negotiation, but in numerous interviews conducted by the author, it is clear that most agencies decide upon the contract type prior to issuance of an RFP. Furthermore, contract type intentions are set forth in the "acquisition strategy" document now required in connection with planning for major systems acquisitions. Under those conditions, it would appear that the decision on contract type is normally made prior to formal involvement of the potential contractor.

In practice, contract type is approached in several ways. It may be decided by top management. It could be decided in negotiations. The contracting officer or

TABLE 16-1

CONTRACT TYPES USED IN GOVERNMENT PROCUREMENT
FISCAL YEAR 1983[a]

Contract Type	Actions		Dollars	
	Number	%	(Millions)	%
Fixed Price	336,932	81.2	105,756	69.4
Cost	68,243	16.4	45,348	29.8
Time & Materials	6,807	1.6	901	.6
Labor Hour	3,180	.8	331	.2
Totals	415,162	100.0	152,336	100.0

[a]Table derived from "Total Federal Snapshot Report," (individually reported actions--excludes small purchase orders). Federal Procurement Data System Standard Report, Fiscal Year 1983, dated January 26, 1984, p. 17.

negotiator may make the decision in preparation of planning or negotiation documents. On occasion, an intended contract type is modified as a consesquence of events such as refusal of potential sources to respond to an RFP. Two instances of this were cited by interviewees. Frequently, the best contract type is evident to all participants and little or no discussion occurs. In a limited number of actions it may be predetermined by statute or regulation as in the case of energy related demonstrations financed by DOE in which a grant is prescribed by statute, and the DOE Assistance Regulations proscribe payment of fee under the grant.[5] Also, recent use of draft RFPs circulated to potential contractors for comment has, in some cases, provided information that influences the decision.

With respect to its impact on operations, the persons or groups principally affected by contract type are the government project or technical team, the contracting officer or negotiator and their counterparts working for

the contractor. Each of them must live with and administer the project under the conditions set up by the
contract. Nevertheless, several interviewees held that
the decision is rarely made through their interaction at
the negotiation table; rather, it is a policy matter and
is decided in earlier stages of planning. Contractor
interviewees found that their best opportunity to influence the contract type occurs in discussion with project
and policy level personnel of the government in advance
of RFP issuance. This was confirmed indirectly by government interviewees who indicate they keep channels of
communications open so that contractor ideas will be
available and expressed.

The power of individuals to influence contract type
depends in part on expertise and in part on the responsibilities vested in the office held. Technical uncertainty must be assessed by technically knowledgeable
persons. Assumption of risks, however, must be decided
by persons qualified and appointed to carry responsibility for the overall business risk. This applies equally
to sponsor and performer organizations.

Additional techniques cited by contractors for influencing contract type included submission of alternate
proposals, negotiation for insertion of risk allocation
clauses and where pertinent, submission of unsolicited
proposals in which type of contract is specified.

In some cases, contractor policy positions are as
specific as government positions, although they may not
be published. One respondent would object strongly to
any fixed price development contract. Another would
object to fixed priced software development. In both
cases, the concern expressed was with the degree of
unknowns.

Based on the interview data, it appears that contract type is not a major issue in most acquisitions, yet
it remains crucial to the interests of the parties. The
area of greatest sensitivity is fixed priced contracting
when development work is required. Interviewees in
government positions expressed concern with risk allocation as did contractor representatives. There appears to
be a consensus that high technology projects of the
government are best managed if the principal risks rest
with the government.

Criteria for Contract Type Selection

A few authors have attempted to establish criteria for selection of contract type.[6] Their efforts are helpful, but the dynamics of contracting warrant a periodic review of the problem. FAR 16.104 offers a list of ten factors used to approach the decision. Still, in surveying key personnel in the contracting community, the question of criteria elicited a spectrum of responses such as, "It's obvious 80 percent of the time," and "It's a crucial issue to me on every major acquisition." That diversity of view is partly accounted for by individual experiences and partly by the level at which the matter is considered. If one is thinking only of contract type in the sense of cost type versus fixed price, the alternatives are few. However, contract type, inclusive of formula and award concepts, multiple independent variables, ceiling levels, incentive slopes, and risk modifying clauses, presents the negotiator with an unlimited set of choices. It is in that context that the following criteria are developed. There are many choices, and every undertaking has some unique combination of objectives and circumstances which the contractual agreement should accommodate. The criteria proposed here are thought to cover most situations--all have been suggested by leading practitioners interviewed for this study as important--but they are not presented as an exhaustive list. Surely there are others that, in given situations, may govern the negotiation.

Current State of the Art. Together with the second and third items, current state of the art is the basis for determining the nature and scope of technological uncertainties associated with performance. These uncertainties are critical to proper selection of contract type. They are viewed as the principal source of risk in regard to achievement of program objectives. The current state of the art, if in equilibrium with the requirement, minimizes risk to be allocated between the parties. However, when elements of required performance mandate an advance from the current state of the art, the level of uncertainty increases, and the parties must carefully consider who assumes the risk that the advance might not be achievable.

Current Stability of the Technology. This criterion, viewed in concert with current state of the art, refers to rapidly evolving knowledge found in specific fields. It is a source of uncertainty with respect to acceptability of program achievements. In a changing state of knowledge, contractual specifications may fail to adequately express what performance is acceptable. This situation permits a moving base line to create an associated uncertainty respecting contract completion. As a consequence, it is a source of risk for allocation between the parties.

Nature of the Contract Specification. Again, this criterion might be viewed in concert with current state of the art. The technical documentation is expected to delineate which party is responsible for a particular effort and to establish criteria for acceptance of the performer's work. Uncertainty is increased when the contract documentation lacks clarity in either of these aspects. A low level of clarity could result from poorly drafted documentation or from the nature of the effort. For example, reliability and maintainability standards might involve sensitive judgments regarding the level of achievement, even though the acceptance standard may appear to be exact. If the nature of the work lends itself to exacting specification writing, and if the specification is clear regarding who performs specific effort, and clear as to acceptance criteria, uncertainty is minimized. Otherwise, the contractual risk allocation requires careful review of uncertainties.

Program Objectives. The emphasis, or prioritization, of broad program objectives such as schedule, cost and performance influences contract type. If limitation on program growth (in cost terms) is critical, the type of contract would move in the direction of the more advanced forms (the fixed price types). A similar implication arises from tight schedule objectives. These objectives, however, imply limitation of emphasis on technological achievement either by limitation on performance requirements or by movement toward risk adjusting contract provisions such as term type or level of effort clauses. The basic trade-off is cost emphasis or technological emphasis. Advanced contract types are consistent with cost emphasis and vice versa.

Program Importance. While all programs are important to the involved parties, the level of interest and
importance accorded to the effort by top management or
political decisionmakers influences the viability of
contract types. A necessity for increased visibility
implies greater levels of detail in technological and
financial reporting, greater facility in adjusting project plans, and in general, lower stability for execution
of effort. High levels of program importance, therefore,
would indicate movement toward the less advanced (cost
type) contract types. The reimbursability of costs tends
to facilitate the sponsor's expression of needs for information and other responses to special demands.

The need for maintenance of visibility over the life
of major programs is also a factor in use of award fee
contracts. The periodic "report card" in support of
award decisions stimulates intense interest in program
progress by top management of both parties. It continues
as a stimulative force over the life of the program, long
after the glow of newness is gone.

Program Stage. This factor is illustrated by para-
phrase of an interview: Conceptual study contracts generally go out as fixed price. We use them in following
A-109. Funding of these studies is limited by budget,
and contractors regularly overspend the allotted funds
and must absorb the costs. This is the business decision, but they do it to be ready for validation phase
contracts. There isn't much risk involved, since the
product of their efforts is their conceptual design and
approach to meeting the mission need of the agency. The
validation work will move to the CPAF contract, sometimes
in conjunction with an incentive fee feature, to encourage cost reduction. Full scale development will involve
a cost type contract. Generally, an award fee is used,
although for clearly defined and measurable performances,
multiple incentives are used. During the production
phase, FPI is the objective; however, delays occur
beyond the pilot and first or second production contracts
because of the lack of design stability. The multiple
incentive versus award fee issue is largely a question of
measurability of performance as opposed to its judgmental
quality.

Duration. Several sources of risk were associated

with duration by interviewees. Specific risks cited were: 1) possible termination for convenience; 2) inflation, particularly the amount of inflation pertinent to performance cost; 3) risk of a funding cut off in multi-year production; and 4) extent of warranties, particularly the number of production units over which design warranties might be extended. Each of these risks, if considered dangerous to the contractor, is a basis for movement toward less advanced contract types, or in the case of inflation, adoption of economic price adjustment clauses. Also, movement to fixed-price-incentive from firm-fixed-price is considered as a way to share the risk of escalation if there is likelihood of extensions of the performance period.

Motivational Factors. Each contract type conveys messages outlining ideas that the sponsor expects the performer to emphasize. However, the motivational force of contractual provisions may be limited by several circumstances. One of these is the possible isolation of contractual incentives from the performer's decision-makers. The contractual incentives for decisions which are desirable to the sponsor may not be perceivable at the level of the corporate manager who makes the decision. The translation of contractual provisions to workers is dependent upon the management policies of the performer. Another limitation is that the motivational force (the bait) in contracts (with two exceptions) is limited to profit dollars payable under the instant contract. As a consequence, other motivational forces may overwhelm the impact of contractual profitability outcomes. Examples of powerful non-contractual pressure are: reputation of the performer, maintenance of performer work force, amortization of performer facility investments (particularly in periods of overall decline in sales by the contractor), potential for winning new business, and overall corporate strategies regarding the future business mix.

The two contract types that may provide contractual motivational forces beyond the instant contract profit are award fee contracts, and contracts that provide for value engineering incentives payable for program cost reductions. The award fee contract is an exception only because of its periodic "report card" feature. Although

the amount of award fee available is limited to the
instant contract award fee pool, the impact of a good
report card versus a bad one may be an extremely powerful
motivational tool.   The value engineering incentive
differs in that it is strictly a monetary motivator but
is still exceptional, because it may offer the potential
of a profit return on future production savings which can
far exceed instant contract profit potential.

Past Performance of Contractor.   While past performance is best recognized as a factor in source selection, it can sometimes influence the selection of
contract type.   One agency which extensively uses CPFF
and CPAF contracts for services, prefers CPFF whenever a
contract is going to a contractor who has demonstrated
excellent performance.   This approach is applicable when
the extra motivation of the report card is unnecessary.
Conversely, for similar services from an unproven source
or one believed less effective in terms of the agency's
standards, CPAF is used.

Legal Constraints.   Contract type is not affected
substantially by legal constraints.   Statutory and regulatory limitations of fees on cost type contracts are not
an issue.   However, the statutory limitation on the
amount of cancellation charges payable for multi-year
contracts may constrain their use.   Where this issue is a
factor, three possibilities arise.   One is the use of a
cost reimbursable contract (so that cancellation risks
are not borne by the contractor) coupled with management
of the production process and subsequent awards, so that
cost savings based on production continuity are pre-
served.   However, the cost contract is difficult to justify if production could employ a fixed price contract.
Additionally, it forces the current budget to absorb the
entire start-up cost.   A second approach is to proceed
with a multi-year contract award even though cancellation
costs exceed the congressionally imposed dollar limitations.   This process is used when the nature and/or
urgency of the product eliminates the contractor's doubt
that subsequent year funding will be provided.   This
approach, however, places the risk of future program funding on the contractor.   The third alternative is to
revert to one-year production on a fixed price basis with
no explicit effort to reduce price by avoiding the rein-

currence of start-up costs.

Production Potential. In one case cited by an interviewee, a research and development contract was awarded on a firm fixed price basis under conditions in which development cost estimates were believed to be sound but uncertain. In that case, contractor willingness to use the firm fixed price arrangement was based on his confidence that follow-on production was assured, and that little or no likelihood existed of losing the entire production to other sources.

Contract Management Complexity. Complexity in contract management appears to be related to technological complexity, duration, and magnitude of the program. It is affected by the number of contractors and agencies involved, relationship of the immediate work to existing capabilities and plans, and management philosophy of key leaders. This factor can be crucial to contract type decisions. High complexity suggests less advanced contract forms.

Complexity discussions also brought out two facets of the management problem. One was the question of contractor responsiveness to program demands. The other was discipline or control over intervention in the work by government program personnel. The advanced contract type is believed to reduce responsiveness but may increase discipline. Fixed prices, tight ceilings, and steep incentive slopes, make critical the effective management of the performer and the use of keen discretion by the sponsor in oversight activity. Conversely, CPFF reduces criticality in administration. It is interesting to note that because of its "report card" procedure, the CPAF contract is believed by several interviewees to enhance both discipline and responsiveness.

Independence of Action During Performance. Independence of action is indicated by the level of interaction between sponsor and performer personnel while work is in progress. The level believed to be necessary at the time of contract formation is keynoted by the sponsor's technical management. The level of interaction should be assessed and contract type should reflect that relationship. In general, low interaction allows advanced contract types; high interaction is supported by the less advanced contract types.

Administrative Costs. The cost of administration of contracts plays a part in selection of contract type. The most advanced contracts (firm-fixed-price) require the least amount of administrative costs. Under these contracts, audit is not required, and oversight activities of the sponsor are minimized. The performer expects to provide minimal information services beyond specified deliveries. Conversely, all cost or incentive contracts require cost and technical reviews and assessment of status regarding the incentive. The award fee is believed to maximize administrative effort. Fixed rate contracts (time and material, labor hour) require regular administrative attention to ensure proper application of effort. Consequently, sponsoring agencies must assess their ability to carry on oversight work when less advanced contract types are selected.

Use of Government Furnished Property. Property furnished by the sponsor alters the appropriateness of advanced contract types, particularly when in combination with development effort. Use of GFP opens the relationship to complex assessment of suitability of the property to the work effort. In like manner, the availability of GFP for use by the performer may become an issue. Additionally, deficiencies in technical data may be difficult to assess. As a consequence, when an acquisition requires provision of property by the sponsor, the contract type may need to be adjusted to provide an appropriate level of interaction between the parties regarding the use of the property.

Availability of Cost and Pricing Data. All of the contract types except firm fixed price entitle the contracting agency's audit organization to review the actual costs of performance. Additionally, comprehensive technical, cost and management reporting systems are activated primarily for non-firm-fixed-price contracts. As a consequence, when an agency must obtain detailed information concerning performance, the contract type used most often falls into the incentive or cost reimbursable categories.

Accounting Systems. Principally in the case of small business, adequacy of the contractor's accounting system may be a factor in preferring FFP contracts. This was not viewed as an issue in very many situations.

Summary

The processes and criteria influencing contract type selection are evident only when the participants are fully aware of background factors, plans, uncertainties and communications expected during performance. The decision requires an acute sensitivity to the acquisition's requirements, the organizations and personnel involved, and special factors that affect risk and uncertainty.

Notes

[1]William M. Carley, "How Chaos, Bad Luck, Lost Gulf and Shell Millions on a Reactor," Wall Street Journal, February 25, 1976, p. 1.

[2]"Industry Fires Away at Fixed-Price Contract," Business Week, November 16, 1968, p. 94. Cited by Leonard Sapera, "A Study of the Defense Contracting Officer and Contract Type Selection," unpublished Masters thesis, The George Washington University, 1969, p. 67.

[3]Defense Procurement Circular #60, Memorandum from Secretary of Defense, April 1, 1968, p. 1.

[4]Public Law 91-129, November, 1969.

[5]P.L. 93-577, Section 14, cited by Aleta Caracciolo in "Selection of Contract Type," unpublished research report, The George Washington University, March 24, 1980.

[6]Seymour Herman, "How to Select the Right Government Contract," Business Management, Volume 22, July 1962, p. 54; Sapera, op. cit.; Aerospace Industries Association, "Type of Contracts and Their Selection," AIA, Washington, D.C., July, 1971.

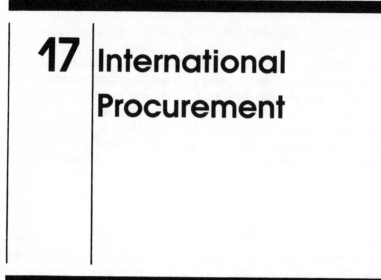

17 | International Procurement

Government procurement is a factor in the evolution of international trade relations. Governmental bodies in every nation are participants in the procurement process as buyers of essential goods and services. Their interest in procurement, however, similar to that of the United States government, extends beyond the mere acquisition of goods and services. They are also concerned with objectives such as economic gains and creation of jobs within their respective economies. Government procurement, therefore, naturally becomes the object of protectionist policies and practices such as those embodied in the Buy American Act of 1933.

Several aspects of international procurement which this chapter discusses are: 1) the Buy American Act, currently the foundation for U.S. policy and practice in this area; 2) the Balance of Payments program for minimizing the adverse flow of dollars incident to the combined effects of international military aid, development aid, and commercial transactions; 3) implementation of the Agreement on Government Procurement and its potential for enhancing the competitiveness of government procurement; 4) a comparison of the objectives and actual achievements during the first year (1981) of experience with the 1979 Agreement on Government Procurement; 5) special concerns raised by the transparency and government assistance challenges of the Agreement on Government Procurement, and 6) the evolving policy and practice associated with the North Atlantic Treaty Organization's (NATO) rationalization, standardization and interoperability (RSI) programs.

Most nations subscribe to the broad objective that barriers to international trade should be reduced and that free and fair trade become the norm. Ninety-nine states, including the United States, participated in the Tokyo round of Multilateral Trade Negotiations (MTN) initiated in September, 1973, under the sponsorship of the General Agreement on Tariffs and Trade (GATT). One area in which non-tariff trade barriers are substantial is government procurement. In general, governments, subtlely or otherwise, discriminate against foreign source suppliers in their procurement programs.

The Agreement on Government Procurement was signed in Geneva on April 12, 1979, as one product of the Tokyo round of MTN. It promises some reduction of existing preferential treatment accorded to domestic suppliers by the signatory governments. The hoped-for reductions are on a reciprocal basis for at least twenty signatory nations. (Nineteen nations signed the original agreement, but Israel has subsequently signed. Also, under the agreement benefits are extended to several Third World countries so that a total of 45 nations are currently listed as "designated countries.") The potential impact of the agreement on U.S. government procurement practices and the potential for increased sales in foreign markets by U.S. firms may be substantial. Realization of the potential depends on a number of other elements pertinent to international procurement. Numerous policies and practices in this area must be considered in light of several complex strategic trade and economic interrelationships. The effectiveness of the agreement, however, is probably influenced more by the balance among signatories of new export opportunities and of commercial advantages for each.

With respect to the United States' policy toward more visibility or transparency of government procurement to international competition, three distinct phases are discernable in the period from 1930 to the present.

These periods emphasize, first, job protection during the depression years; second, resistance to the adverse balance of payments beginning in the late 1950s; and third, renewed concern with cooperation among alliance members to strengthen NATO conventional force readiness beginning in 1974. This renewed concern was oriented toward offsetting the power of the Warsaw Pact military capability. The effectiveness of the agreement, however, is probably influenced more by the balance among signatories of new export opportunities and of commercial advantages than any other factor.

✓ Buy American Act

The Buy American movement in the United States Congress began about 1930. It was a result of rising national sentiment against protectionist policy adopted by other nations, in particular, the British Commonwealth of Nations which had adopted a buy British policy. It was further nurtured by the hard economic times the U.S. was experiencing. Congress' concern with these developments was first expressed by a buy American statute which was passed as an amendment to the War Department Appropriation Bill of 1932. That amendment required that only American products be purchased for use within the War Department. That precedent set up the legislative process that resulted in the Buy American Act. It was passed as Public Law 428 on March 3, 1933. A key provision in section 2 of the statute is:

> Only such unmanufactured articles, materials and supplies as have been mined or produced in the United States, and only such manufactured articles, materials and supplies as have been manufactured in the United States substantially all from articles, materials, or supplies mined, produced or manufactured, as the case may be, in the United States, shall be acquired for public use.[1]

That section of the statute was not applicable to articles, materials or supplies procured for use outside the United States, and it was not applicable to items which were not manufactured, mined or produced in the United States in sufficient and reasonably available commercial quantities of a satisfactory quality. Also, the statute provided for administrative discretion on the part of the head of an agency in determining whether the procurement of a domestic item would be consistent with the public interest and whether the cost of such a procurement would be unreasonable.

Section 3 of the statute was concerned specifically with construction contracting and treated it somewhat differently from the procurement of supplies and materials. Section 3 required that contracts for construction, alteration or repair of public buildings or public works in the United States include provisions that only domestic materials and supplies could be used in performance of the work. Also, Section 3 was explicitly provided with a penalty for violation--debarment for three years from participation in government procurement. As a result, the protective provisions of the act with respect to construction are more restrictive than its provisions with respect to supplies and materials for public use in general.

Section 4 was added to the act in 1949 as part of the National Military Establishment Appropriation Act of 1950. The intent of that modification was to clarify congressional intent with respect to the act. The amendment provided that those goods manufactured from domestic raw materials and those manufactured from foreign materials, when domestic materials are not available, would have equal benefit under the act. The modification did not resolve interpretation problems regarding "unreasonable costs" or "inconsistent with public interest" which had arisen. There were no guidelines with respect to those terms in the original legislation.

Interpretation of the imprecise language of the Buy American Act was improved on December 17, 1954, when the President issued Executive Order 10582, under which he prescribed uniform procedures for use by executive agencies in evaluating foreign bids. The executive order established that materials would be considered to be of foreign origin if the cost of the foreign products used in such materials constituted 50 percent or more of the cost of all products used in such materials. If the price of domestic origin material exceeds that of foreign material by 6 percent, including customs duties, its purchase was considered inconsistent with the public interest under the executive order. Alternatively, a domestic price which exceeds a foreign price by 10 percent, excluding duty, would be considered unreasonable. In addition, when the bid from the domestic source is made by a small business firm or a firm that will perform the work in a labor surplus area, an additional 6 percent differential would be applied, effectively creating a 12 percent preference for the small business and labor surplus area firms. Nevertheless, the executive order permitted the head of the agency to reject domestic source bids where the purchase would be inconsistent with the public interest or essential national security interests or would involve an unreasonable cost after application of the percentage differentials. Also, an important provision of the executive order is that it permits the head of an agency to set larger percentage differentials if he considers it appropriate.

Additional restrictions on foreign sources have been imposed by annual Department of Defense appropriation acts. They have restricted procurement of specific commodities and services in accordance with the Buy American Act, without regard to the application of differentials as discussed above. An important illustration of this is the type of amendment known as the Berry Amendment which has been a part of each military appropriation act since 1954. This type of amendment places restriction on use of appropriated funds for procurement of specific commodities or articles, namely food, clothing, specialty metals, cotton, wool, silks, and synthetic fabrics of foreign origin.

Implementation of the Buy American Act within each agency has been accomplished in the past by provisions in their respective procurement regulations. Since April 1, 1984, Part 25 of the FAR has covered this area. It is mandatory that all supply contracts, and service contracts when applicable, contain the Buy American Act clause unless the procurement is made under the Trade Agreements Act of 1979. The clause sets forth definitions of "end products," "components," and "domestic source end products." Under the clause, contractors are bound to comply with the provisions of the act and must agree to deliver domestic source end products, unless one of the pertinent exceptions is applicable. Other techniques that aid enforcement of the act are a requirement for certification of domestic origin to be made on payment vouchers, and certification by contractors of the percentage of foreign materials included in the products they are furnishing.

The principal exceptions to the application of the act relate to products that are not available within the domestic economy of the United States and to Canadian end products. The question whether or not a particular product is available domestically is determined by administrative decision, and a list of excepted articles, materials and supplies is compiled by each military and civilian agency head. A list of excepted items is published in the Federal Acquisition Regulation, Subpart 25.108, and agencies may make additions at the discretion of the agency head. In general, the excepted items include minerals, agricultural products, and animal products and their derivitives which are not found in, or are not native to, the soil and climactic conditions of the United States.

One of the most difficult areas in the administration of the act has been determination of the meaning of "domestic end products" as opposed to "foreign end products." In general, to be a domestic end product, a product must be an unmanufactured end product mined or produced in the United States, or an end product manufactured in the United States, and if it meets that requirement, it must be made up of components of which at least 50 percent of the aggregate cost must be domestic cost. This area is somewhat ambiguous because there is no precise delineation of which factors could be included as costs with respect to either foreign or domestic components. A substantial body of decisions has accumulated regarding these issues. The decisions of greatest importance are those made by the Comptroller General of the United States pursuant to protests that arise in connection with the award of government procurement contracts.

Balance of Payments Program

As a consequence of its commitment to maintain an overseas military presence subsequent to World War II, the United States began to accumulate an adverse balance of international payments resulting in an outflow of U.S. dollars and some depletion of United States' gold reserves. This development became evident by the mid-1950s, and by 1960, had reached a point where President Eisenhower announced a balance of payments directive which initiated restrictions on overseas military expenditures. That action was taken in November of 1960. It affected numerous aspects of military expenditures and included direction that procurement at overseas locations should be returned to the United States when the cost of supplies and services was less than 50 percent greater than the cost of the supplies procured from a foreign source. These procurement actions were not subject to the Buy American Act, since the use of the end items procured was outside of the United States. While procurement is only one aspect of the Balance of Payments program, it amounts to a significant additional restriction against award of government procurement to foreign sources. The lead agency in this action was the Department of Defense, since it was by far the largest procurer of overseas items.

Balance of payments programs were designed to protect the domestic economy without undermining the United States' international responsibilities. The basic goal was to achieve a reduction in overseas dollar expenditures while incurring an acceptable limited increase in budgetary costs of performing required undertakings. Efforts to control the adverse balance of payments involved numerous actions other than those pertinent to government procurement. They included temporary controls on overseas investments in 1968 and imposition of a temporary 10 percent import surcharge in 1971. Within the DOD Balance of Payments program, they included reduction of spending by military, civilian, and dependent personnel stationed abroad; use of excess foreign currencies when feasible in certain contract payments; reduction in military troop levels in allied foreign countries; reduction in employment of foreign nationals, and the establishment of barter and excess currency programs. The reductions in foreign procurement spending achieved substantial reductions in the adverse flow.

In addition to the foregoing, the balance of payments problem involved extensive restructuring of foreign military and economic assistance. These measures also restricted the federal procurement process so that it awarded contracts to domestic sources for acquisition of supplies to be provided in support of the international aid programs.

✓ The Agreement on Government Procurement

A potentially significant new development in government procurement became effective on January 1, 1981. On that date, the new Agreement on Government Procurement was implemented by Executive Order 12260, dated December 31, 1980, and under U.S. law by the Trade Agreements Act of 1979 (Public Law 96-39) signed by the President on July 26, 1979. Title 3 of that act implements the agreement for the United States. The basic objective of the new agreement and of the implementing legislation and executive order is to achieve equal treatment of foreign and domestic suppliers of designated nations, and to provide them equal opportunities (on a reciprocal basis in both magnitude and quality) to compete for contracts awarded by specified government entities. It represents a most remarkable reversal of more than fifty years of international trade and economic history.

A governmental entity is a government bureau or department specified in the agreement for participation in this new international understanding. While the potential for increased competition is great, with only twenty signatory nations, the initial effects will be limited. Under the agreement, each signatory has committed itself to lower the non-tariff barriers that have, until this time, significantly limited the opportunity of foreign suppliers to compete for purchases by the governmental entities of the signatory nations. These commitments depend on the reciprocity actually achieved. Opening of governmental purchases to worldwide competition will not come easily for any nation. Nevertheless, sales opportun-

ities for United States private enterprises were originally estimated to be increased by $20 billion per year.
In return, procurement by United States government agencies that would be opened to foreign competition was
estimated at $17 billion. The major barrier removed by
this agreement in the United States is the Buy American
Act of 1933. The balance of payments program is also set
aside for the designated countries. The nature of these
barriers has already been discussed in this chapter.

Prior to the effective date of this new agreement,
there have been a number of waivers and exceptions permitted under the Buy American Act in specific areas of U.S.
government procurement activity. However, the new agreement is the first generally applicable reduction of the
non-tariff barriers erected by the act. The implications
of the new agreement could be far reaching with respect
to the procedures of U.S. government agencies as they
carry out their normal procurement responsibilities.

A review of U.S. government procurement procedures
was conducted to ensure that procurement requirements are
made available to foreign sources in time for them to
compete. Time and distance complicate this matter. For
example, the Commerce Business Daily is the U. S.
government newspaper that publicizes all government solicitations over $10 thousand and awards over $25 thousand.
It is a valuable tool because it announces in advance
that an action is going to be taken. Under the revised
requirements in the Competition in Contracting Act of
1984 for publishing synopses in the Commerce Business
Daily, the synopses will fully meet the standards of the
Agreement on Government Procurement, which are a minimum
of thirty days between announcement of a procurement
requirement and the deadline for receipt of bids or proposals. This minimum time period provides a foreign
source with sufficient time to obtain the synopsis, and
subsequently the solicitation document, and to prepare
and submit its offer. One shortfall of the CBD in the
past has been its failure to provide enough time between
the publication of synopses and the date bids were due.

In the international procurement sector, terminology
is used that will be new to U.S. government buyers. For
example, in the U.S., IFBs and RFPs are standard, but in
international procurement, the solicitation is a tender.

The entire procurement process is referred to as a tender and under the International Procurement Code, there will be open tenders and selective tenders. It also recognizes the single tender, but that type of solicitation is not under the agreement since it initiates a sole-source procurement. Open tender is a procurement opportunity which is open to any party that would like to compete. Selective tender involves a prequalification process whereby the governmental entity that is issuing the tender can determine, prior to issuance of the tender, the sources it is willing to consider. Since both selective tenders and open tenders involve competition, they are compatible with the objective of the Agreement on Government Procurement, that is, to bring about equal opportunity to domestic and foreign sources.

Important exceptions to the new agreement include procurement of services. These probably comprise 27 percent of total government procurement. Supply procurement is the principal area that is included. Construction contracts are excluded. Set aside procurement (small business, minority business, and labor surplus area procurement) is excluded. Procurement for foreign assistance objectives and for national security purposes are not included. State and local governments are not subject to the agreement, as well as the Energy and Transportation Departments and some areas in the Department of Agriculture, principally agricultural support procurement. The agreement is not pertinent to small procurement. The threshold for applicability is set forth in terms of special drawing rights (SDRs), and it is pertinent to contracts that are in excess of 150,000 SDRs, which in terms of 1984 dollars approximates $160 thousand. Procurements less than that amount would not be covered under the agreement. The agreement does involve a requirement that suppliers certify the origin of their goods. The need for a certificate of origin continues, because with only forty-five "designated countries," there are still dozens of nonparticipating nations. The origin of the commodity remains important.

The U.S. trade representative makes interpretations under the agreement, and the Department of Commerce is responsible for its implementation. They must address several problems. One is the language problem. Two languages are recognized for synopses--French and English. As a result translation and communication services are likely to be needed for marketing activities. Other procedural elements such as those needed to qualify bidders have not been fully worked out. Another of the major problems is to familiarize U.S. industry with the new opportunities. There is a need for promotion and information services to domestic manufacturers. A key responsibility of the Department of Commerce is to monitor compliance with this new agreement by other nations. This is probably the most difficult area of all. Regardless of what the agreement says, what the people do is what counts.

Objectives and Potential Impact of
the Agreement on Government Procurement

The Agreement on Government Procurement must be viewed primarily as a commercial trade policy accord. Its implementation demands some change in government procurement practices and procedures and, potentially, largely increases the number of competitors who may seek contract awards. Consequently, the U.S. government contracting officer is directly affected by it and should become fully aware of its objectives and requirements. The importance of the agreement rests in part on its impact on sourcing of government purchases and in part on its effect on trade activity and policy. In the trade policy area it may have greater influence than other agreements of recent years. Examples of other agreements include the memorandums of understanding which have been established between the U.S. and several other NATO nations, and the "internal directives" by which the European economic community has required its member states to treat equally all firms within the European economic community in the award of public works contracts. The greater potential of the Agreement on Government Procurement results from its establishment of internationally recognized procurement procedures designed to create nondiscriminatory government purchase actions. In addition, the agreement has been established under the auspices of the General Agreement on Tariff and Trade (GATT). This status of the agreement gives the commercial community much greater assurance of a continuation of the policy by which their access to government procurements is assured. Additionally, it is conceivable that the scope of the agreement could be extended to include the major trading countries of the world.

While the agreement has a great deal of potential, the reality of its implementation is far more important to its expansion or continuation than the intentions of its sponsors. According to a July, 1984, report of the Comptroller General of the United States, its practical impact on government procurement activity and the opening of government procurement to international competition has been minimal. Table 17-1 provides a statistical summary of the results of the agreement during 1981, its first full year of operation. The table discloses vast differences between the estimates made by the negotiators at the time the agreement was established in 1979 and the actual opening of trade opportunities in 1981. It summarizes several realities which must be recognized when interpreting the usefulness of the agreement for the United States. On the optimistic side, the original estimates of annual volume at the time of the agreement in 1979 of 37.5 billions (total activity) in increased availability of government procurement to competition by foreign sources was exceeded by the total opportunities realized in 1981 of 46.3 billions. However, that sort of glowing conclusion must be tempered by the reality that very little action has occurred during the early implementing period. Furthermore, the true assessment of the agreement from the perspective of a signatory nation such as the United States must include assessment of its commercial value to that signatory nation. Table 17-1 reveals that the United States is the source of the entire increase of the actual total opportunity falling under the agreement. The other nations actually had a decrease from their estimates of 20.5 billions to 17.4 billions in the amount of government procurement they made available under the agreement. Of course these figures are reduced by the large number of procurements which fall under the agreement but for practical purposes are not covered, because they are for amounts less than the threshold level at which foreign sources must be

Table 17-1

Market Opportunities Opened to Nondomestic Competitors
By the Agreement on Government Procurement
1981 Data – Billions[a]

	Estimated Annual Volume at Time of Agreement (1979)	Actual Total Opportunities (1981)	Total Falling Below Agreement Threshold (150,000 SDR)	Total Covered by Agreement	Single Tender Actions	Total Open to Nondomestic Competitors	Actual 1981 Purchases Under the Agreement	Fuel and Related Products	Net Purchases Under the Agreement
Total of 19 Signatory Nations	37.5	46.3	18.1	28.2	6.0	22.2	3.51	3.0	.480
Total U.S.	17.0	28.9	9.0	19.9	1.9	18.0	3.3[b]	3.0[b]	.270[b]
Total of 18 Non-U.S. Signatories	20.5	17.4	9.1	8.3	4.1	4.2	0.210[c]	---[c]	.210[c]

[a]Source: United States General Accounting Office Report #GAO/NSIAD-84-117, dated July 16, 1984, pp. 12-17. The data used is subject to reporting deficiencies but is viewed as a good approximation by the GAO.

[b]Ibid. p. 17. (This data is estimated. Deficiencies in the U.S. data collection system are treated on pp. 46-48 of the GAO Report.)

[c]Ibid p. 15. (This data is estimated. Deficiencies in the EC data collection systems are treated on pp. 45-46 of the GAO Report.)

allowed to compete. The threshold is 150,000 special drawing rights. Therefore, the total available amount is reduced to the $28.2 billion indicated in the table. Furthermore, the value of procurement actions under the agreement must be reduced by the total value of single tender actions. A single tender is, in fact, a sole source procurement. Such actions are not required to be made available as competitive opportunities to any source other than the sole source. As the table shows, after these deductions have been made, the total amount of government procurement available to nondomestic competitors was $22.2 billion in 1981. Of this total amount the United States accounted for $18 billion, and the total of all non-U.S. signatory nations amounted to $4.2 billion. While these large numbers represent potential sales opportunities, the reality of the 1981 purchases under the agreement is comparatively unnoticeable. Procurement by the U.S. government of fuel and related products falls under the agreement, but such procurement would have been placed with foreign sources regardless of the existence of the agreement. Therefore, after deducting that amount from the total, the amount of purchases falling under the agreement, and which would not otherwise have occurred, approximates only one quarter of one billion dollars for the United States and somewhat less for the other signatories combined. This amount could grow substantially if the rules and rights established by the Agreement on Government Procurement become widely known. In its review of the early operations of the Agreement on Government Procurement, and particularly its search for reasons why the agreement appears not to have generated a great deal of new procurement opportunities, the General Accounting Office identified several business practices which were in violation of the agreement and yet effectively limited the actual amount of procurement available for nondomestic competitors. The practices identified are not unfamiliar even in the domestic market, since generally each of them is an effective means of limiting competition.

The principal competition-limiting practices are:

1. Single tendering. The single tender procedure allows the agency to solicit a sole source without public announcement of the procurement action. Since many

procurements are of necessity sole source in nature, it is extremely difficult to assess whether it is properly made under the rules established by the Agreement on Government Procurement.

2. Splitting contracts. In order to avoid competing a procurement nondomestically, a government agency can subdivide its procurement actions into separate contracts each of which would fall below the 150,000 SDR threshold.

3. Limiting design specifications. An agency can often describe the product which it is seeking in such a way as to limit competition from nondomestic sources. The use of detailed design specifications in the purchase description normally is an effective means of accomplishing this source-limiting practice.

4. Diversion of the purchase action. If a government agency which has been made subject to the agreement, objects to allowing nondomestic competition for a particular purchase, it could transfer the purchase responsibility to another government agency, one not subject to the agreement. This strategy would effectively sidestep the requirement for opening the competition.

5. Failure to disclose award information. Through the simple device of not announcing its award decisions and by not making a practice of debriefing the unsuccessful bidders, an agency is able to obscure situations where the foreign competitor should have won a competition in which the domestic bidder was actually selected.

The GAO does not explicitly state that foreign countries are engaging in the practices identified above. The fact that they have identifed them as a result of the study is indicative that they believe that to be the case.

Transparency

A great deal of emphasis has been placed upon the need for vigorous and effective enforcement procedures to be established by the United States in order to ensure that other signatory nations comply with the Agreement on Government Procurement. This matter is of extreme importance because the validity of the agreement for the United States is largely rooted in the question whether adequate commercial benefits result from the agreement. As a consequence the executive agencies must assume a responsibility for full monitoring of the agreement's compliance by foreign governments.

This objective of ensuring that compliance occurs is referred to as transparency. The Agreement on Government Procurement contains several provisions requiring the signatory governments to have a transparent procurement process. Basically, transparency means that procurements must be conducted in the open and in accordance with an agreed upon published set of procedures. The basic objective of transparency is to ensure that noncompliance cannot occur without disclosure. A significant part of the enforcement mechanism is to devise ways of discovering noncompliance behaviors. One mechanism is to call upon U.S. business firms who are dissatisfied with or feel inappropriately treated under the agreement to carry their dissatisfaction to the United States Embassy or commercial trade representative thereby involving the government in negotiation for fuller compliance. The need for monitoring transparency is a part of the responsibility of each signatory government and is vital to effective support of the agreement. The belief is strongly held that only effective and vigorous monitoring and enforcement of the agreement by the U.S. government can ensure that its interests in the opening of procurement opportunities for U.S. firms will occur.

Method of Government Assistance

One of the problems with the Agreement on Government Procurement is that it is not self implementing. Its success depends on proper and widespread dissemination of information about its existence and the rights and benefits established by it. Additionally, success requires immediate access on the part of the domestic firm to information concerning specific procurement requirements of foreign tenders that draw on the field of activity in

which the firm is interested. The principal responsibility for ensuring the success of the agreement resides
in the Department of Commerce which is charged with its
promotion. Its activities include:

1. publication of pamphlets and brochures that convey
   information about the agreement to the public
2. establishing and conducting seminars for the United
   States business community on methods and techniques
   for participation in foreign government procurements
3. dissemination of notices of foreign government procurements through its already established trade
   opportunities program mailings.

The department also hoped to establish a secondary distribution of its trade opportunities notices (referral of
opportunities to third parties by recipients of the notices). It also hoped that the notices would generate a
number of domestic "multiplier" organizations--firms that
come into existence to train commercial service and trade
specialist personnel in the intracacies of the agreement.
        These plans by the Commerce Department were initi-
ated shortly after the enactment of the implementing
legislation in 1979. However, in February of 1982, the
International Trade Administration in the Commerce Department reorganized, and the Agreement on Government
Procurement disappeared from the conscience of Commerce
personnel.

✓ NATO RSI

        The historical conflict between protection of domes-
tic jobs and support for improved economic efficiency is
severely tested during adverse economic periods such as
depression or recession. Even during periods of relative
prosperity, the conflict of objectives is evident as
illustrated by intense bargaining during the latter half
of the seventies over the exact meaning and implementation of NATO RSI, or Rationalization, Standardization and
Interoperability. The concept of RSI is derived from a
set of broad objectives related to defense of the Atlantic Alliance nations. Essentially, RSI seeks rationaliza-

tion in securing maximum defense capability by pooling the national resources of the alliance. It also seeks the reduction of duplication of weapons systems with similar capabilities and an increase in interoperability between military forces of the alliance nations. To a large degree, the RSI objectives are implemented through government procurement.

While there are worldwide ecoomic and strategic effects of government procurement activity by the United States, throughout the decade of the seventies there has been a growing recognition that those activities strongly impact relationships among Western nations. Procurement finances economic benefits and technological progress. Of greatest impact are defense procurement and weapons development activities of the United States and its allied nations in NATO. In the negotiations over appropriate arrangements for the production of defense materials, economic interests of participant nations have become evident and sometimes dominant over strategic interests in efforts to achieve preparedness for the defense of Western interests. In recognition of this substantial problem, the Defense Department of the United States has initiated general policy developments favoring what has come to be known as NATO RSI. That policy movement and numerous agreements made under it preceded the Agreement on Government Procurement and deal with numerous complex transitional problems associated with defense procurement.

NATO standardization has been a goal since 1949. However, little progress toward that goal was made until the United States became concerned with the relative inadequacy of NATO conventional forces compared with those of the Warsaw Pact nations. The principal justification for standardization (and for NATO RSI) is military effectiveness. A secondary but important benefit of standardization is overall cost savings for the alliance. These justifications, however, are arguable since some experts believe neither justification is achieved through standardization. Substantial barriers to progress in the standardization of NATO forces arise because nations are not willing to make vital aspects of their security dependent upon other countries. Also, separate armaments development and production appeals to each of the member nations because they have: 1) significant differences in national perception of military requirements,   2) strong senses of national pride and prestige which are fortified by achievements in the defense sector,   3) pressures to maintain domestic employment and to obtain foreign currency exchange through military sales, and   4) a desire for increased influence in countries outside the NATO arena which is gained through agreements to supply arms.

An important step forward was made on July 14, 1976, when Public Law 94-361 was approved. Under that law, the policy of the United States stated that equipment procured for use of its personnel stationed in Europe under the North Atlantic Treaty should be standardized or, at a minimum, interoperable with equipment of the other members of the Alliance. Beyond that, the act required the Secretary of Defense to initiate and carry out procurement procedures that provide for the acquisition of equipment which is standardized or inter-operable with the equipment of the other NATO members, giving consideration to cost, functions, quality, and availability. The act also established the belief of Congress that progress toward standardization and inter-operability would be enhanced by expansion of inter-Allied procurement of arms and equipment within NATO. Additionally, Congress believed that inter-Allied procurement would be advanced through greater reliance on licensing and co-production agreements among the NATO signatories. Clearly, the Congress gave impetus to further development of NATO RSI. The congressional action was followed in March of 1977 by issuance of DOD Directive 2010.6. That directive established DOD policy and responsibilities for standardization and inter-operability of weapons systems and equipment within the Alliance. It supports cooperative defense equipment acquisitions and the development of equitable economic and industrial participation for cooperating nations. Development of more compatible doctrine and military tactics to improve the basis for increasing standardization and inter-operability were also supported.

To accomplish this, the DOD directive sets up three approaches. One is the authorization of general and reciprocal memorandums of understanding (MOU) within the NATO Alliance. The objective of MOUs is to encourage bilat-

eral arms cooperation and to provide for review of arma-
ment programs and trade. The objective of the reviews is
to enhance the efficiency of resource utilization. A
specific objective of the MOUs is to achieve waiver of
buy-national restrictions whenever possible. However,
since MOUs are not formally approved by Congress, they
represent understandings and nothing more.

The second approach is dual production. Under this
concept a nation that has already developed a military
system permits other nations to produce their system.
The objective is to avoid redundant development programs.
Several examples of dual production have been carried
out. For example, the F-16 fighter, one of the most ambitious co-production efforts ever attempted, employs European and Canadian dual production provisions. A similar
but reverse arrangement is U.S. dual production of European and Canadian systems. Examples of this include the
Roland Air Defense missile system, the MAG-58 armored
machine gun, and the 120 millimeter tank gun.

The third and more drastic approach is to establish
families of weapons. This concept refers to the development of new systems. Under this approach, the NATO
nations would negotiate in advance of initiation of development programs. The weapons system planning of the participating nations would be reviewed and aggregated by
mission area, and related or complementary weapons systems for defined mission areas would be assigned to participating nations for development as a family of weapons.
On the basis of that coordination, assignment of the
development of the respective equipments would be allocated, reducing duplication of effort. The first family of
weapons agreement was signed in August, 1980. It covers
air-to-air missiles allowing Europeans to develop an advanced short-range missile while the United States develops an advanced medium-range missile.

NATO RSI has also been advanced by negotiation of
bilateral MOUs covering reciprocal procurement of defense
equipment among the Allies. A number of these have been
signed. The MOUs are designed to increase competition in
systems acquisition through the technique of waiving buy-
national policies that otherwise would restrict the procurement process of the respective nations.

NATO RSI appears to be an attractive technique for

achieving an important cooperative posture for the NATO Alliance. Its future, however, is quite unclear at the time of this writing. Whether it will work in the military sense is arguable and the determination of whether, in the long run, it is a practicable means of reducing barriers to expanded trade between the involved nations, requires some extended experience. Additionally, the total economic savings that theoretically should accrue from this kind of interaction remain somewhat speculative. Nevertheless, the development is consistent with the trend indicated by the Agreement on Government Procurement. In both cases, the trend would indicate increased international competitive activity associated with a general lowering of barriers to foreign sourcing of government procurement. International arms cooperation encompasses political and economic consideration affecting both military and nonmilitary departments. As a minimum, it should ensure equitable treatment of U.S. industry and labor with regard to "buy national" policies and should conform to the U.S. arms transfer policy.

18 | Socioeconomic Issues and the Procurement Profession

This book has summarized the nature of government procurement, examined some details of its practice, attempted to place it in the context of its managerial contributions and environment, and analysed some processes and considerations associated with its current and future employment. Many issues, changing policies, and organizational practices have been lightly touched or omitted for space and time considerations. It is hoped that the topics covered are the major ones of interest to the reader. In this chapter, we shall examine certain features of socioeconomic programs, offer comments on government policy and practice respecting competition, suggest several qualities needed in procurement personnel, and speculate on the challenges and opportunities for achieving excellence and high professional standing for procurement personnel.

Socioeconomic Programs

At several points we have mentioned the effects of socioeconomic programs on procurement. The large number of these programs prohibits a detailed treatment at this time. In his recent dissertation on the burdens associ-

ated with socioeconomic programs, Richard Hampton enumerated fifty-two programs,[1] and in its draft proposal on
the NFPS, the OFPP listed forty-six.[2] The difference
in these listings results from the subdivisions of the
broad policies used by the authors. For example, small
business policy can be listed as one program or several,
since it includes procurement preference, subcontracting
preferences, mandatory subcontracting program requirements and within these, specific-policy implementing
procedures. It also includes nonprocurement programs
designed to foster small business development. At times
the Congress or the President adds to or modifies the
active programs. Enumeration of programs, therefore, is
not useful except for gaining a perspective of the many
specific objectives sought by the policies. Chart 18-1
is derived from the two sources mentioned. It organizes
the programs into the taxonomy used by Hampton.[3] The
taxonomy is valuable in identifying the general types of
objectives sought and in grouping the programs by those
objectives.

Certain conflicts arise because of socioeconomic
policies. While the programs themselves are designed to
benefit particular groups, many tend to adversely affect
other groups. An example of this is the minority contracting program. While it aids minority contractors, it
tends to divert business opportunities from other small
business concerns. Similarly, the Davis Bacon and Service Contract Acts provide wage and other benefits to
construction and service contract labor working under
government contracts. Simultaneously, they increase
procurement costs and create imbalances between pay
scales of government sponsored and privately sponsored
projects.

Socioeconomic programs represent a multitude of
program interests and objectives unrelated to procurement
objectives. Therefore, they receive substantial support
from protected or benefited groups but decidedly less
support from the program, user, and procurement groups
whose projects may be made more difficult, expensive or
time consuming. This is a matter of emphasis, not
necessarily one of opposition. It is rooted in the
increased complexity of the procurement process as the
demands to advance multiple independent objectives impose

CHART 18-1

SOCIOECONOMIC PROGRAMS

PROGRAM	AUTHORITY	THRESHOLD	PURPOSE
A. SOCIOECONOMIC PROGRAMS TO IMPROVE WORKING CONDITIONS			
1. Davis Bacon Act	40 USC 276a-1 to a-5	$2,000	Minimum wages, benefits, and work conditions for construction contracts
2. Service Contract Act	41 USC 351-7	$2,500	Minimum wages, benefits, and work conditions for service contracts
3. Walsh-Healey Act	41 USC 35-45	$10,000	Minimum wages, hours and work conditions for supply contracts
4. Contract Work Hours and Safety Standard	40 USC 328-332	$2,500	Eight hour day, forty hour week for laborers and mechanics on public works

Chart 18-1 - Continued

PROGRAM	AUTHORITY	THRESHOLD	PURPOSE
5. Fair Labor Standards Act	29 USC 201-19	None	Minimum wage, maximum hour standards for employees in commerce
B. SOCIOECONOMIC PROGRAMS TO FAVOR DISADVANTAGED GROUPS			
6. Small Business	15 USC 631-647	(1)	Promote contracting with small business
7. Minority Business	15 USC 631-647	(1)	Requires contracting and subcontracting with minority firms
8. Products of Blind and Handicapped	41 USC 46	None	Mandatory purchase of products made by blind and handicapped persons

_____

(1) a. $500,000 threshold for subcontracting plan requirements.

Chart 18-1 - Continued

PROGRAM	AUTHORITY	THRESHOLD	PURPOSE
9. Prison-Made Supplies	18 USC 4124	None	Mandatory purchase of certain supplies from Federal Prison Industries
10. Equal Employment Opportunity	EO 11246 EO 11375	$10,000	Prohibits discrimination, requires affirmative action
11. Employment of Handicapped	29 US 793	$2,500	Affirmative action for handicapped
12. Labor Surplus Area	PL 95-89 (Sec. 15 of Small Business Act) E.O. 12073	None	Preference to concerns performing in labor surplus areas
13. Disabled and Vietnam Veterans	38 USC 2012	$10,000	Affirmative action for disabled and Vietnam Vets
14. Required Source for Jewel Bearings	National Policy	$10,000	Preserves a mobilization base for jewel bearings

Chart 18-1 - Continued

PROGRAM	AUTHORITY	THRESHOLD	PURPOSE
15. Indian Self-Determination and Education Assistance	P.L. 93-638	None	Requires preference to Indian labor and Indian firms in carrying out programs for their benefit
16. Women Business Enterprise	EO 12138	$10,000	Promotes women-owned business
C. SOCIOECONOMIC PROGRAMS TO FAVOR AMERICAN COMPANIES			
17. Buy American Act	41 USC 10a-d	None	Provides preference for domestic material
18. Berry Amendment	Annual DOD Appropriation Act	$10,000	Restricts DOD from purchase of foreign food, clothing, textiles, and specialty metals
19. Preference for Domestic Hand Tools	Annual Appropriation Act	None	Restricts purchase of foreign hand tools
20. Acquisition of Foreign Buses	P.L. 90-500 Sec. 404	None	Restricts DOD purchase or lease of foreign manufactured buses

Chart 18-1 - Continued

PROGRAM	AUTHORITY	THRESHOLD	PURPOSE
21. Preference for U.S. Flag Vessels	10 USC 2631	None	Shipment of goods on U.S. bottoms
22. Preference for U.S. Flag Air Carriers	P.L. 96-623	None	Use of U.S. flag air carriers for personnel
23. Preference for U.S. Products for Military Assistance Programs	22 USC 2354(a)	None	Requires purchase of U.S. products for MAP
24. Prohibition of Construction of Naval Vessels in Foreign Shipyards	Annual Navy Appropriation Act Restriction	None	Prohibits construction of naval vessels or major components in foreign shipyards
25. Prohibition on Purchase of Non-U.S. Stainless Steel Flatware	Annual GSA Appropriation Act	None	Prohibits use of funds for purchase of stainless steel flatware not made in U.S.

Chart 18-1 - Continued

PROGRAM	AUTHORITY	THRESHOLD	PURPOSE
D. SOCIOECONOMIC PROGRAMS TO PROTECT THE ENVIRONMENT AND QUALITY OF LIFE			
26. Care of Laboratory Animals	P.L. 91-579	None	Requires humane treatment of animals in experiments
27. Humane Slaughter of Livestock	7 USC 1901-6	None	Purchase meat only from suppliers who conform to humane slaughter standards
28. Release of Product Information To Consumers	EO 11566	None	Encourage dissemination of government documents containing product information of use to consumers
29. Recycled Material	P.L. 94-580	None	Requires contractor certification as to use of recycled materials
30. Conservation of Energy	P.L. 94-163	None	Requires consideration of energy conservation in selecting contractors
31. Clean Air and Water	42 USC 1857	$100,000	Certification and agreement to comply with Act

Chart 18-1 - Continued

PROGRAM	AUTHORITY	THRESHOLD	PURPOSE
32. Occupational Safety and Health Act (OSHA)	29 USC 651-678	None	Requires contractor compliance with DOL regulation
33. Restriction on Conversion of Heating Plants in Europe	Anual DOD Appropriation Act	None	Prohibits use of funds to convert heating plants from coal to oil
34. Miller Act	40 USC 270a-d	$25,000	Requires performance and payment bonds on construction contracts
35. Copeland "Anti-Kickback" Act	18 USC 874 40 USC 276c	$2,000	Prohibits kickbacks from employees on public works
36. Maybank Amendment	Annual DOD Appropriations Act	None	Prohibits payment of differential by DOD to relieve economic dislocation
37. Covenant Against Contingent Fees	10 USC 2306(b) 41 USC 254(a)	$10,000 (Regulatory)	Prevents contingent fee payments

Chart 18-1 - Continued

PROGRAM	AUTHORITY	THRESHOLD	PURPOSE
E. SOCIOECONOMIC PROGRAMS TO ACHIEVE OTHER GOVERNMENT PURPOSES			
38. Purchases in Communist Countries	DOD Policy	$10,000	Prohibit acquisition of supplies for public use from some Communist areas
39. Balance of Payments	National Policy	$10,000	Reduce effects of overseas purchases on adverse BOP
40. Excess and Near Excess Currency	National Policy	$10,000	Preference in award to offerers willing to be paid in excess or near excess currency
41. Non-Use of Foreign Flag Vessels Engaged in Cuban and North Vietnam Trade	National Policy	None	Prohibits shipping any supplies on such vessels
42. Officials Not to Benefit	18 USC 43	None	Prohibits members of Congress from benefitting from any government contract

Chart 18-1 - Continued

PROGRAM	AUTHORITY	THRESHOLD	PURPOSE
43. Gratuities	10 USC 2207	None	Right to terminate a contract if gratuity was given to government employee to obtain it
44. Convict Labor Act	18 USC 436	$10,000	Prohibits employment of convict labor on government contracts
45. Duty Free Entry of Canadian Supplies	National Policy	$2,500	Further economic coo-peration with Canada
46. Procurement of A&E Services	P.L. 92-582	None	Precludes price competi-tion for A&E sevices

administrative procedures on the work force.

An important general area of conflict between procurement and most socioeconomic programs is competition.
Procurement as a profession is probably best known for
its propensity to seek competition. This is true whether
the buyer is governmental, industrial, or commercial.
Socioeconomic programs act to limit the competition otherwise available, and in this sense, conflicts with procurement objectives. Some examples of this are preferences
for small business and for American products, required
sources for specified items, and minimum labor pay levels
mandated for contractors. There are many others among
the programs listed in Chart 18-1. These requirements
differ in their impact. Some directly limit competition,
others limit the basis on which offerors can compete.
Overall, the socioeconomic programs impose burdens on the
procurement process that are significant yet difficult to
measure or quantify. Administration of the programs,
training personnel in program objectives, requirements
and procedures, and imposition of support requirements on
contractors all contribute to the burdens. This provides
no basis, however, for assessing whether the benefits outweigh the costs. For many of the socioeconomic programs,
neither benefits nor costs (burdens) appear to be measurable on objective bases.

Of the numerous programs, only a few have widely
observed effects on the procurement process. These are
led by the small business, minority business, and equal
opportunity and affirmative action programs and are
closely followed by the wage protections accorded to
construction and service contract labor. The buy American, labor surplus area, and affirmative action for handicapped programs have also been widely applied. While the
others listed in Chart 18-1 have less overall impact,
every program, in its particular area of application, is
significant for its costs and benefits to society in
general as well as its burdens on the procurement
process.

Since the small business programs appear to be the
most pervasive and most visable to procurement personnel,
an historical sketch of their development beginning in
1932 is included at this point. While socioeconomic
programs imposed on the procurement process can be traced

as far back as 1876 (preference for American sources of bunting), the major impetus for the policies was the depression of the thirties. Subsequent to that time, new fields of concern, such as environmental protection have emerged.

The legislative history of the Small Business Act is rooted in measures taken during the 1930s to overcome the adverse effects of the Great Depression. The Reconstruction Finance Corporation, created in 1932, was designed to aid large and small businesses. This attempt at an assistance program established the idea of aid to business, and although it was unsuccessful in court reviews, it gave impetus to the search for ways of effecting desired social and economic objectives through federal policy action. The idea of using the federal contract as an instrument of policy became significant during this period through mandatory insertion into contracts of requirements for contractors to pay wage minimums, give preferences to products made in the United States, observe child and convict labor laws, limit profit on construction of naval vessels and other measures.

The first legislation dealing specifically with small business was Public Law 77-603, passed July 11, 1942, creating the Smaller War Plants Corporation (SWPC). The work of this agency developed many of today's small business procurement policies and programs. One of its primary functions was to assist the small businessman in securing government prime contracts and subcontracts. It also established and maintained an inventory of small business production facilities. This inventory was used by government buying agencies and prime contractors in locating small business sources for products they needed. The SWPC also had the authority to make subcontracts with small business firms. Under this authority, the buying agency could contract with the SWPC for a required item; the SWPC could then award a subcontract for performance of the work to a small business. This placed the SWPC in a position to provide more assistance to the small business than if the contract had been directly with the procuring agency. Finally, when the small business needed financial assistance, the SWPC was able to make loans.

During its existence from 1941 to 1945, the SWPC

established a significant record of performance. Table
18-1 reflects the number of awards that it assisted small
business in obtaining. Although the agency was abolished
by executive order soon after the end of World War II,
the functions of the SWPC were continued through transfer
to other permanent agencies. Lending and prime contract
assistance were transferred to the Reconstruction Finance
Corporation, and the other functions were moved to the
Office of Small Business, Department of Commerce.

Congress again addressed the need for a specific
agency to assist small business during the Korean conflict. It recognized merit in the assistance rendered to
small firms during World War II by the SWPC and decided
to create a similar agency. In July of 1951, as an
amendment to the Defense Production Act of 1950, it
created the Small Defense Plants Administration (SDPA).
This agency was charged with helping small businessmen
obtain government contracts. It provided counseling and
information services and had authority to act as prime
contractor to procuring agencies, awarding subcontracts
to small business. One new capability that Congress
provided the SDPA was the authority to make competency
determinations, that is, to certify that a small business
firm had the capability to complete a contract. Such
determinations were issued in the form of "Certificates
of Competency" to the government buying agency. The
certificate of competency, or COC, was binding on the
contracting officer, that is, the small businessman's bid
could not be disqualified because the contracting officer
questioned the capability or capacity of the firm to
complete the contract. A competency review was usually
made only on firms that were low bidders on a procurement. Therefore, a savings to the government was possible if the firm was thought to be capable and was awarded
the contract. During the two years that the SDPA was in
existence, it issued 125 certificates of competency. One
weakness in the authority given the SDPA was that it had
no direct voice in the awarding of government contracts.
It acted only as an advisor to the contracting officer
and had no route of appeal if the contracting officer
decided not to follow its advice. Table 18-2 indicates
the scope of SDPA activity during its existence from
July, 1951, through July, 1953.

Table 18-1

SMALLER WAR PLANTS CORPORATION
November 1942 - November 1945[a]

Contracts Awarded Small Business	Number	$ Amount (Millions)
Prime Contracts	58,385	5,700.0
Subcontracts from Prime Contractors	52,000	30.6
Subcontracts from the SWPC	12	35.5

[a]Source: Addison W. Parris, The Small Business Administration, (New York: Frederick A. Praeger Co., 1968, p. 18.

Table 18-2

SMALL DEFENSE PLANTS ADMINISTRATION
July 1951 - July 1953[a]

Contracts Awarded Small Business	Number	$ Amount (Millions)
Prime Contracts	2,197	591
Subcontracts from Prime Contractors	759	19
Subcontracts from the SDPA	7	2

[a]Source: Small Defense Plants Administration, Seventh Quarterly Report of the Small Defense Plants Administration, (Washington, D.C.: Government Printing Office, 1953), p. 2.

By 1953 the defense requirements of the Korean War had been met to the point where the nation started moving in the direction of a peacetime economy. Congress felt that there was a continuing need even during peacetime for a separate agency within the government to carry out its policy of assisting the small business. Therefore, on July 30, 1953, it passed the Small Business Act (15 USC 631) and created the Small Business Administration (SBA), a new government agency whose purpose was, according to its basic charter, to assist and protect the interests of small businessmen and ensure that they are awarded a fair proportion of government contracts. The act abolished the SDPA as well as the Reconstruction Finance Corporation and provided for the assumption of most of these organizations' function by the SBA.

In 1958 Congress passed P.L. 85-536, an amendment to the Small Business Act, and added substantially to the original small business legislation. The paramount feature of this new legislation was that it recognized the SBA as a permanent agency and clearly recognized independent small business enterprise as a distinct and vital element of the national economy.[4] Further amendment of the act in 1961 added a requirement for major government prime and subcontractors to establish small business subcontracting programs.

One of the more significant recent amendments of the act was P.L. 95-507, passed on October 15, 1978. It established requirements for successful offerors in prime contract competitions to submit and negotiate a subcontracting plan as a condition of award of the prime contract. This applies to prime contracts that exceed $500 thousand ($1 million for construction). Requirements for the plan were established also. The contractor is required to have a program including percentage goals for the utilization of small business concerns and small disadvantaged business concerns in its subcontracting. The program requires prime contractors to delineate the effort they will take to ensure that small business firms have the maximum practical opportunity to compete for subcontracts. The prime contractor's plan must include a commitment to impose a similar program on large subcontracts (same dollar thresholds as for the prime contract). Failure of the contractor to comply with this plan "in good faith" is a material breach of contract.

The 98th Congress amended the Small Business Act to improve access to federal procurement information. Public Law 98-72, approved on August 11, 1983, substantially increased the public notification requirements for government procurement by requiring publication of notices (synopses) in the Commerce Business Daily, fifteen days in advance of the release of solicitations (thirty days when research and development work is to be procured). It also required a minimum of thirty days after publication before an order may be placed. These requirements were also included in CICA with certain conflicting rules which were subsequently resolved by passage of the Small Business and Federal Competition Enhancement Act of 1984 (P.L. 98-577). This act extended to forty-five days the period from publication of the notice to proposal/bid receipt for research and development procurement.

P.L. 98-577 also created a new advocate in the small business system. It required the SBA administrator to appoint a breakout procurement center representative (BPCR) at each major procurement center. This advocate is to become knowledgeable of the technical issues associated with provisioning of spare parts and to make recommendations leading to breakout, from major systems, of components for competitive procurement (presumably by small business).

P.L. 98-577 also limits use of prequalification procedures and imposes additional administrative steps associated with source restrictions derived from qualified product lists to ensure that competition in procurement is enhanced. This provision is also contained in an amendment to the Defense Authorization Act (P.L. 98-525). Both acts seek to overcome deficiencies in spare parts procurement that have been highlighted by numerous reports during the 98th Congress. A number of other procurement policies were introduced by these statutes. They are summarized in Chapter 14 under "Provisioned Item Orders."

Competitive and Noncompetitive Procurement

Table 13-1 confirms that nearly 65 percent of government procurement is awarded on a noncompetitive basis. This statistic seems incongruent with the historic emphasis on competition incorporated into procurement statutes and regulations and was a factor in passage of CICA, P.L. 98-577 and P.L. 98-525. Many reasons for the high level of noncompetitive action are discussed in Chapter 14. The extent to which competition is obtained by government buyers is of great importance and interest, and congressional action in 1984 has strongly encouraged it, but the most important question regarding it is not one of fact, but one of judgment. Would greater levels of formal competition achieve program objectives more effectively and do it more economically and efficiently? If that answer is affirmative, the question becomes, is it possible to increase the percentage of dollars awarded competitively?

The basic assumptions of our economic system indicate that buyers gain an advantage in almost any purchase situation if they have competitive offers from which to choose. Competition, however, is not adequately defined in terms of price. Competitive offers using different approaches to a problem frequently are based on the technical or management approach--not price. As the basis for decision, buyers often seek technological, qualitative, or schedule distinctions. The technological/conceptual strategy is one governmental approach to enhancing this type of competition. The whole field of competitive negotiations embraces the concept that non-price factors are a part of every competitive range and source selection decision. Both have been in effect for some time without significantly changing the statistical predominance of noncompetitive procurement.

Noncompetitive procurement implies that there is no choice between sources. The perception of no choice, however, depends on how one measures behavior. Government statistics are based on contract-by-contract reporting and each contract is catagorized as competitive or noncompetitive. This provides a short term viewpoint and disregards government rights to change its decisions at any time. The issue is complex because high dollar, follow-on procurements account for most noncompetitive purchases. Converting them to competitive procurement through second sourcing procedures is costly. It is entirely possible that the result (65 percent noncompetitive procurement) is a valid proportion considering the nature of the items bought by government. If so, the answer to the first question posed in this section is no, and the basis for the answer is the nature of governmental purchases. If the preponderance of government procurement dollars seeks to buy end items and services that do not lend themselves to competition (in the formal sense), then it would be uneconomical to significantly increase competitive procurement. That this is probably the case does not reduce the need for procurement professionals to seek competition, but it may indicate that arbitrary measures and increased administrative processes to obtain formal competitions are unnecessary and uneconomical.

Qualifications of Contracting Personnel

Although the trend in government policy is to increase regulatory requirements and investigation personnel in an attempt to cause improvements in procurement practice, an alternative that could potentially gain more for the overall benefit of the public is enhancement of personnel capabilities. Specific qualifications for appointment as contracting officers have never been delineated by the government. This has led to the absence of consistency in the ability of contracting personnel at all levels. While the procurement regulations mandate that persons be capable of sound judgment to be appointed, there is no operative standard for administration. Therefore, top management tends to reduce the importance accorded to the contracting officer position. This has prevented many contracting officers from engaging in the full scope of management interaction required to make the decisions necessary for major purchase actions. To date, little rigorous screening of applicants at the entry level and no priority for advanced educational achievement has been allowed. There is no formal ranking associated with contracting officers, and appointment is not clearly associated with any grade level or specific job classification. Employees may be drawn from a variety of skills--clerical, technical, or administrative. This situation needs review and change if government contracting is to overcome the negative image now given it by the public and contemporary management disciplines.

Based on the author's observation, qualifications for contract managers in the government should include business management and one or more of the following: industrial engineering, accounting, law and/or public administration. The level of educational attainment for buyers should include at least the baccalaureate degree. Appointment as a contracting officer should have a prerequisite of graduate education or substantial experience in procurement and completion of a sponsored series of continuing education courses and advance management programs. These programs should include issue studies specifically in the area of procurement and contracting. Since the power of contracting officers is to obligate the United States, and it is understood that the incumbent is authorized to take contractual actions, the responsibility of setting qualifications for the office should be decided by Congress or by a coordinated policy for the executive branch. Action in this area is overdue.

Professional Status of Buyers

Only a few occupations have achieved general recognition as a profession though many would claim to be professional. Others strive to become professional and procurement and contracting is one of these. Its people want to excel--they are concerned about the quality of their work. What specifically does this involve? First, we should establish the meaning of professionalism. Ernest Greenwood described the nature of a profession in the following quotation:

> . . . professions are distinguishable by possession of (1) a basis of systematic theory, (2) authority recognized by the clientele of the professional group, (3) broader community sanction and approval of this authority, (4) a code of ethics regulating relations of professional persons with clients and

with colleagues, and (5) a professional culture sustained by formal professional associations.[5]

This is an exclusive definition which few occupations could meet. A more pragmatic approach is expressed by the National Contract Management Association (NCMA). The NCMA considers the following to be prerequisites in attaining professional status as a government contract manager: thorough knowledge of the specialty; competent application of that knowledge; a sense of service to others over self (social responsibility); and a self-controlled, rigidly adhered to standard of conduct. A more succinct and perhaps most important thought is "professionals earn their designation by performance."[6]

This commentary is suitable and descriptive of the challenge facing buyers or contract managers as they seek broader acceptance of their occupation as a profession. Another criterion against which one might measure the professional character of procurement personnel is the quality of decisions those in the field must make. For example, are independent decisions made drawing on accumulated knowledge? Is there a "systematic theory" as referred to by Greenwood? Are decisions relied upon by clientele and the broader community? Is there a fiduciary relationship with clientele and/or the community as a whole? How often and how consistently must the answers be affirmative to grant the occupation the special stature of a profession? Firm answers seem unlikely, but the need for creative, ethical behavior is vital to the work.

Another approach to professionalism has been suggested by Kenneth Andrus.[7] He identifies five attributes of a profession as: knowledge, competent application of effort, social responsibility, self-control, and community sanction. These attributes are achievable and should be sought by persons in the field. One need not decide the status of the occupation to conclude that members of the work force must seek a professional level of performance as well as the recognition associated with professional stature.

More specific impetus for professionalism has developed for procurement personnel over the last decade. Ethical questions have arisen and productivity retrogression has surfaced, lending more pressure for reevaluation of the effectiveness of our production systems including the role played by the procurement function. People in the field need to consider this development and the opportunity it presents for revitalizing the identity of the field and improving its image. This can be done if they will reassess their mission and visualize the larger role of their work in achieving society's objectives as well as their organization's success.

Procurement managers have great potential for achieving productivity improvements. Their role is unique because they can enhance competitive forces in the economy through creative purchasing action. By seeking new supply sources, they are able to mobilize widely scattered capabilities and apply them to organizational objectives. These factors are vital to productivity gains because they are a powerful stimulus to economically aggressive behavior.

Government procurement personnel are continually buffeted between competing objectives, often ones defined by their contemporaries, by the media, or by higher levels in the bureaucracy. It is part of the environment in which they live. They can attack this problem by becoming better communicators concerning their function in the management of their agencies. Instead of quietly subscribing to the suggestion that procurement is a support function, they need to articulate its positive contributions. They must first recognize its importance and then find ways to inform their contemporaries in management. Professionals must become oriented to the overall objectives and environmental interfaces of their employers, placing procurement issues in perspective, and learning to think strategically in terms of the total system of which they are a part. It does no good to fully understand the mission of the procurement function if the mission of the entire agency is overlooked.

In summary, procurement managers, whether in government or private setting, should articulate their role more effectively to other members of management. To do this they must expose themselves to the larger objectives of the organizational system and become knowledgeable concerning external (environmental) pressures. They must then integrate the totality of objectives and determine courses of action that optimize the pursuit of agency (or corporate) mission. With this, professional stature will be enhanced.

Notes

[1] Richard J. Hampton, "Achieving Socioeconomic Goals Through the Federal Procurement Process," Doctoral Dissertation, The George Washington University, 1981.

[2] "Proposal for an Integrated Federal Procurement System," (Draft), Office of Federal Procurement Policy, Office of Management and Budget, July 31, 1981.

[3] Hampton, p. 19.

[4] U.S., Congress, Senate, Select Committee on Small Business, Small Business Programs, Policies, and Procedures of Government Agencies, Senate Report 2505, 85th Congress, 2nd Session, 1958, p. 26.

[5] Ernest Greenwood, "Attributes of Professionalization," ed. Howard Vollmer and Donald Mills, (Englewood Cliffs, N.J., Prentice-Hall, 1966), p. 9.

[6] Walter E. Willets, "Let's Get Rid of the Ribbon Clerks," Purchasing, October 1, 1970, p. 31.

[7] Kenneth R. Andrus, "Toward Professionalism in Business Management," Harvard Business Review, March-April, 1969, p. 50.

Appendices

Appendix 1

Categories of Services Regularly Publicized in the Commerce Business Daily[*]

A   Experimental, Developmental, Test and Research Work
H   Expert and Consultant Services
J   Maintenance and Repair of Equipment
K   Modification, Alteration, and Rebuilding Equipment
L   Technical Representative Services
M   Operation and Maintenance of Government-Owned Facility
N   Installation of Equipment
O   Funeral and Chaplain Services
Q   Medical Services
R   Architect/Engineer Services
S   Housekeeping Services
T   Photography, Mapping, Printing, and Publication
U   Training Services
V   Transportation Services
W   Lease or Rental (except transportation equipment)
X   Miscellaneous
Y   Construction
Z   Maintenance, Repair and Alteration of Real Property

[*] This listing indicates the categories of services actually procured by the federal government. It was prepared by sampling the CBD over a six-month period. All categories of procurement for which synopses of purchase actions appeared are included.

Appendix 2

Categories of Supplies, Equipment, and Material
Regularly Publicized in the
Commerce Business Daily*

10 Weapons
11 Nuclear Ordinance
12 Fire Control Equipment
13 Ammunition and Explosives
14 Guided Missiles
15 Aircraft and Airframe Structural Components
16 Aircraft Components and Accessories
17 Aircraft Launching, Landing, and Ground Handling
    Equipment
18 Space Vehicles
19 Ships, Small Craft, Pontoons, and Floating Docks
20 Ship and Marine Equipment
22 Railway Equipment
23 Motor Vehicles, Trailers, and Cycles
24 Tractors
25 Vehicular Equipment Components
26 Tires and Tubes
28 Engines, Turbines, and Components
29 Engine Accessories
30 Mechanical Power Transmission Equipment
31 Bearings
32 Woodworking Machinery and Equipment
34 Metalworking Machinery
35 Service and Trade Equipment
36 Special Industry Machinery
37 Agricultural Machinery and Equipment
38 Construction, Mining, Excavating, and Highway
    Maintenance Equipment
39 Materials Handling Equipment
40 Rope, Cable, Chain, and Fittings
41 Refrigeration and Air Conditioning Equipment
42 Fire Fighting, Rescue, and Safety Equipment
43 Pumps and Compressors
44 Furnace, Steam Plant, and Drying Equipment, and
    Nuclear Reactors
45 Plumbing, Heating and Sanitation Equipment

46 Water Purification and Sewage Treatment Equipment
47 Pipe, Tubing, Hose, and Fittings
48 Valves
49 Maintenance and Repair Shop Equipment
51 Hand Tools
52 Measuring Tools
53 Hardware and Abrasives
54 Prefabricated Structures and Scaffolding
55 Lumber, Millwork, Plywood and Veneer
56 Construction and Building Mataerials
58 Communication Equipment
59 Electrical and Electronic Equipment Components
61 Electric Wire, and Power and Distribution Equipment
62 Lighting Fixtures and Lamps
63 Alarm and Signal Systems
65 Medical, Dental, and Veterinary Equipment and
    Supplies
66 Instruments and Laboratory Equipment
67 Photographic Equipment
68 Chemicals and Chemical Products
69 Training Aids and Devices
70 General Purpose ADP Equipment Software, Supplies and
    Support Equipment
71 Furniture
72 Household and Commercial Furnishings and Appliances
73 Food Preparation and Serving Equipment
74 Office Machines, Visible Record Equipment
75 Office Supplies and Devices
76 Books, Maps, and Other Publications
77 Musical Instruments, Phonographs and Home-Type Radios
78 Recreational and Athletic Equipment
79 Cleaning Equipment and Supplies
80 Brushes, Paints, Sealers, and Adhesives
81 Containers, Packaging, and Packing Supplies
83 Textiles, Leather, Furs, Apparel, and Shoe Findings,
    Tents and Flags
84 Clothing, Individual Equipment, and Insignia
85 Toiletries
87 Agricultural Supplies
88 Live Animals
89 Subsistence
91 Fuels, Lubricants, Oils, and Waxes
93 Nonmetalic Fabricated Materials

95 Metal Bars, Sheets, and Shapes
96 Ores, Minerals, and Their Primary Products
99 Miscellaneous

*This listing indicates the categories of supplies, equipment, and material actually procured by the federal government. It was prepared by sampling the CBD over a six-month period. All categories of procurement for which synopses of purchase actions appeared are included. The codes listed are those used in the Federal Supply Classification System.

Appendix 3

Presidential Executive Order 12352

Federal Procurement Reforms

By the authority vested in me as President by the Constitution and laws of the United States of America, and in order to ensure effective and efficient spending of public funds through fundamental reforms in Government procurement, it is hereby ordered as follows:

Section 1. To make procurement more effective in support of mission accomplishment, the heads of executive agencies engaged in the procurement of products and services from the private sector shall:

(a) Establish programs to reduce administrative costs and other burdens which the procurement function imposes on the Federal Government and the private sector. Each program shall take into account the need to eliminate unnecessary agency procurement regulations, paperwork, reporting requirements, solicitation provisions, contract clauses, certifications, and other administrative procedures. Private sector views on needed changes should be solicited as appropriate;

(b) Strengthen the review of programs to balance individual program needs against mission priorities and available resources;

(c) Ensure timely satisfaction of mission needs at reasonable prices by establishing criteria to improve the effectiveness of procurement systems;

(d) Establish criteria for enhancing effective competition and limiting noncompetitive actions. These criteria shall seek to improve competition by such actions as eliminating unnecessary Government specifications and simplifying those that must be retained, expanding the purchase of available commercial goods and services, and, where practical, using functionally oriented specifications or otherwise describing Government needs so as to permit greater latitude for private sector response;

(e) Establish programs to simplify small purchases and minimize paperwork burdens imposed on the private sector, particularly small businesses;

(f) Establish administrative procedures to ensure that contractors, especially small businesses, receive timely payment;

(g) Establish clear lines of contracting authority and accountability;

(h) Establish career management programs, covering the full range of personnel management functions, that will result in a highly qualified, well managed professional procurement work force; and

(i) Designate a Procurement Executive with agency-wide responsibility to oversee development of procurement systems, evaluate system performace in accordance with approved criteria, enhance career management of the procurement work force, and certify to the agency head that procurement systems meet approved criteria.

Sec. 2. The Secretary of Defense, the Administrator of General Services, and the Administrator for the National Aeronautics and Space Administration shall continue their joint efforts to consolidate their common procurement regulations into a single simplified Federal Acquisition Regulation (FAR) by the end of calendar year 1982.

Sec. 3. The Director of the Office of Personnel Management, in consultation with the heads of executive agencies, shall ensure that personnel policies and classification standards meet the needs of executive agencies for a professional procurement work force.

Sec. 4. The Director of the Office of Management and Budget, through the Office of Federal Procurement Policy as appropriate, shall work jointly with the heads of executive agencies to provide broad policy guidance and overall leadership necessary to achieve procurement reform, encompassing:

(a) Identifying desirable Government-wide procurement system criteria, such as minimum requirements for training and appointing contracting officers;

(b) Facilitating the resolution of conflicting views among those agencies having regulatory authority with respect to Government-wide procurement regulations;

(c) Assisting executive agencies in streamlining guidance for procurement processes;

(d) Assisting in the development of criteria for procurement career management programs;

(e) Facilitating interagency coordination of common procurement reform efforts;

(f) Identifying major inconsistencies in law and policies relating to procurement which impose unnecessary burdens on the private sector and Federal procurement officials;   and,   following coordination with executive agencies,   submitting   necessary   legislative   initiatives for the resolution of such inconsistencies;   and

(g) Reviewing agency implementation of the provisions of this Executive Order and keeping me informed of progress and accomplishments.

                                        Ronald Reagan

The White House,
March 17, 1982

Appendix 4

STRUCTURE OF THE
FEDERAL ACQUISITION REGULATIONS

Subchapter A - General

Part 1 - Federal Acquisition Regulations System
1.1   Purpose, Authority, Issuance
1.2   Administration
1.3   Agency Acquisition Regulations
1.4   Deviations From the FAR
1.5   Agency and Public Participation
1.6   Contracting Authority and Responsibilities

Part 2 - Definitions of Words and Terms
2.1   Definitions
2.2   Definitions Clause

Part 3 - Improper Business Practices and Personal Conflicts of Interest
3.1   Safeguards
3.2   Contractor Gratuities to Government Personnel
3.3   Reports of Suspected Antitrust Violations
3.4   Contingent Fees
3.5   Other Improper Business Practices
3.6   Contracts with Government Employees or Organizations Owned or Controlled by Them

Part 4 - Administrative Matters
4.1   Contract Execution
4.2   Contract Distribution
4.3   Reserved
4.4   Safeguarding Classified Information Within Industry
4.5   Reserved
4.6   Contract Reporting
4.7   Contractor Records Retention
4.8   Contract Files

Part 5 - Publicizing Contract Actions
5.1   Dissemination of Information

5.2   Synopses of Proposed Contracts
5.3   Synopses of Contract Awards
5.4   Release of Information
5.5   Paid Advertisements

Part 6 - Reserved

Subchapter B - Acquisition Planning

Part 7 - Acquisition Planning
7.1   Acquisition Plans
7.2   Reserved
7.3   Contractor Versus Government Performance
7.4   Equipment Lease or Purchase

Part 8 - Required Sources of Supplies and Services
8.1   Excess Personal Property
8.2   Jewel Bearings and Related Items
8.3   Acquisition of Utility Services
8.4   Ordering from Federal Supply Schedules
8.5   Reserved
8.6   Acquisition from Federal Prison Industries, Inc.
8.7   Acquisition from the Blind and Other Severely
         Handicapped
8.8   Acquisition of Printing and Related Supplies
8.9   Reserved
8.10   Reserved
8.11   Leasing of Motor Vehicles

Part 9 - Contractor Qualifications
9.1   Responsible Prospective Contractors
9.2   Qualified Products
9.3   First Article Testing and Approval
9.4   Debarment, Suspension, and Ineligibility
9.5   Organizational Conflicts of Interest
9.6   Contractor Team Arrangements
9.7   Defense Production Pools and Research and
         Development Pools

**Part 10 - Specifications, Standards, and Other
         Purchase Descriptions**

Part 11 - Acquisition and Distribution of Commercial Products

Part 12 - Contract Delivery or Performance
12.1   Delivery or Performance Schedules
12.2   Liquidated Damages
12.3   Priorities, Allocations, and Allotments
12.4   Variation in Quantity
12.5   Suspension of Work, Stop-Work Orders, and Government Delay of Work

Subchapter C - Contracting Methods and Contract Types

Part 13 - Small Purchase and Other Simplified Purchase Procedures
13.1   General
13.2   Blanket Purchase Agreements
13.3   Fast Payment Procedure
13.4   Imprest Fund
13.5   Purchase Orders

Part 14 - Formal Advertising
14.1   Use of Formal Advertising
14.2   Solicitation of Bids
14.3   Submission of Bids
14.4   Opening of Bids and Award of Contract
14.5   Two-Step Formal Advertising

Part 15 - Contracting by Negotiation
15.1   General Requirements for Negotiation
15.2   Negotiation Authorities
15.3   Determinations and Findings to Justify Negotiation
15.4   Solicitation and Receipt of Proposals and Quotations
15.5   Unsolicited Proposals
15.6   Source Selection
15.7   Make-or-Buy Programs
15.8   Price Negotiation
15.9   Profit
15.10   Preaward and Postaward Notifications, Protests, and Mistakes

Part 16 – Types of Contracts
16.1   Selecting Contract Types
16.2   Fixed-Price Contracts
16.3   Cost-Reimbursement Contracts
16.4   Incentive Contracts
16.5   Indefinite-Delivery Contracts
16.6   Time-and-Materials, Labor-Hour, and Letter Contracts
16.7   Agreements

Part 17 – Special Contracting Methods
17.1   Multi-Year Contracting
17.2   Options
17.3   Reserved
17.4   Leader Company Contracting
17.5   Interagency Acquisitions Under the Economy Act
17.6   Management and Operating Contracts

Part 18 – Reserved

Subchapter D – Socioeconomic Programs

Part 19 – Small Business and Small Disadvantaged Business Concerns
19.1   Terms and Size Standards
19.2   Policies
19.3   Determination of Status as a Small Business Concern
19.4   Cooperation with the Small Business Administration
19.5   Set-Asides for Small Business
19.6   Certificates of Competency and Determinations of Eligibility
19.7   Subcontracting with Small Business and Small Disadvantaged Business Concerns
19.8   Contracting with the Small Business Administration (The 8(a) Program)
19.9   Contracting Opportunities for Women-Owned Small Businesses

Part 20 – Labor Surplus Area Concerns
20.1   General
20.2   Set-Asides

20.3   Labor Surplus Area Subcontracting Program

Part 21 - Reserved

**Part 22 - Application of Labor Laws to Government
        Acquisitions**
22.1   Basic Labor Policies
22.2   Convict Labor
22.3   Contract Work Hours and Safety Standards Act
22.4   Labor Standards for Contracts Involving
        Construction
22.5   Reserved
22.6   Walsh-Healy Public Contracts Act
22.7   Reserved
22.8   Equal Employment Opportunity
22.9   Nondiscrimination Because of Age
22.10   Reserved
22.11   Professional Employee Compensation
22.12   Reserved
22.13   Special Disabled and Vietnam Era Veterans
22.14   Employment of the Handicapped

**Part 23 - Environment, Conservation, and Occupational
        Safety**
23.1   Pollution Control and Clean Air and Water
23.2   Energy Conservation
23.3   Hazardous Material Identification and Material
        Safety Data
23.4   Use of Recovered Materials

**Part 24 - Protection of Privacy and Freedom of
        Information**
24.1   Protection of Individual Privacy
24.2   Freedom of Information Act

Part 25 - Foreign Acquisition
25.1   Buy American Act--Supplies
25.2   Buy American Act--Construction Materials
25.3   Balance of Payments Program
25.4   Purchases Under the Trade Agreements Act of 1979
25.5   Payment in Local Foreign Currency
25.6   Customs and Duties
25.7   Restrictions on Certain Foreign Purchases

25.8   International Agreements and Coordination
25.9   Omission of the Examination of Records Clause

Part 26 - Reserved

Subchapter E - General Contracting Requirements

Part 27 - Patents, Data, and Copyrights
27.1   General
27.2   Patents
27.3   Patent Rights Under Government Contracts
27.4   Rights In Data and Copyrights
27.5   Reserved
27.6   Foreign License and Technical Assistance
        Agreements

Part 28 - Bonds and Insurance
28.1   Bonds
28.2   Sureties
28.3   Insurance

Part 29 - Taxes
29.1   General
29.2   Federal Excise Taxes
29.3   State and Local Taxes
29.4   Contract Clauses

Part 30 - Cost Accounting Standards
30.1   General
30.2   Disclosure Requirements
30.3   CAS Contract Requirements
30.4   CAS Administration

Part 31 - Contract Cost Principles and Procedures
31.1   Applicability
31.2   Contracts with Commercial Organizations
31.3   Contracts with Educational Institutions
31.4   Reserved
31.5   Reserved
31.6   Contracts with State, Local, and Federally
        Recognized Indian Tribal Governments
31.7   Contracts with Nonprofit Organizations

Part 32 - Contract Financing
32.1   General
32.2   Reserved
32.3   Loan Guarantees for Defense Production
32.4   Advance Payments
32.5   Progress Payments Based on Costs
32.6   Contract Debts
32.7   Contract Funding
32.8   Assignment of Claims

Part 33 - Disputes and Appeals

Subchapter F - Special Categories of Contracting

Part 34 - Major System Acquisition

Part 35 - Research and Development Contracting

Part 36 - Construction and Architect-Engineer Contracts
36.1   General
36.2   Special Aspects of Contracting for Construction
36.3   Special Aspects of Formal Advertising in
        Construction Contracts
36.4   Special Procedures for Negotiation of Construction
        Contracts
36.5   Contract Clauses
36.6   Architect-Engineer Services
36.7   Standard Forms for Contracting for Construction,
        Architect-Engineer Services, and Dismantling,
        Demolition, or Removal of Improvements

Part 37 - Service Contracting
37.1   Service Contracts--General
37.2   Consulting Services
37.3   Dismantling, Demolition, or Removal of
        Improvements

Part 38 - Federal Supply Schedule Contracting
38.1   Federal Supply Schedule Program
38.2   Establishing and Administering Federal Supply
        Schedules

**Part 39 - Management, Acquisition, and Use of
     Information Resources**

Part 40 - Reserved

Part 41 - Reserved

Subchapter G - Contract Management

Part 42 - Contract Administration
42.1   Interagency Contract Administration and Audit
        Services
42.2   Assignment of Contract Administration
42.3   Contract Administration Office Functions
42.4   Correspondence and Visits
42.5   Postaward Orientation
42.6   Corporate Administrative Contracting Officer
42.7   Indirect Cost Rates
42.8   Disallowance of Costs
42.9   Reserved
42.10   Negotiating Advance Agreements for Independent
        Research and Development/Bid and Proposal Costs
42.11   Production Surveillance and Reporting
42.12   Novation and Change-of-Name Agreements
42.13   Reserved
42.14   Traffic and Transportation Management

Part 43 - Contract Modifications
43.1   General
43.2   Change Orders
43.3   Forms

Part 44 - Subcontracting Policies and Procedures
44.1   General
44.2   Consent to Subcontracts
44.3   Contractors' Purchasing Systems Reviews

Part 45 - Government Property
45.1   General
45.2   Competitive Advantage
45.3   Providing Government Property to Contractors
45.4   Contractor Use and Rental of Government Property

45.5   Management of Government Property in the
       Possession of Contractors
45.6   Reporting, Redistribution, and Disposal of
       Contractor Inventory

Part 46 – Quality Assurance
46.1   General
46.2   Contract Quality Requirements
46.3   Contract Clauses
46.4   Government Contract Quality Assurance
46.5   Acceptance
46.6   Material Inspection and Receiving Reports
46.7   Warranties
46.8   Contractor Liability for Loss of or Damage to
       Property of the Government

Part 47 – Transportation
47.1   General
47.2   Contracts for Transportation or for
       Transportation-Related Services
47.3   Transportation in Supply Contracts
47.4   Air Transportation by U.S.--Flag Carriers
47.5   Ocean Transportation by U.S.--Flag Vessels

Part 48 – Value Engineering
48.1   Policies and Procedures
48.2   Contract Clauses

Part 49 – Termination of Contracts
49.1   General Principles
49.2   Additional Principles for Fixed-Price Contracts
       Terminated for Convenience
49.3   Additional Principles for Cost-Reimbursement
       Contracts Terminated for Convenience
49.4   Termination for Default
49.5   Contract Termination Clauses
49.6   Contract Termination Forms and Formats

Part 50 – Extraordinary Contractual Actions
50.1   General
50.2   Delegation of and Limitations on Exercise of
       Authority
50.3   Contract Adjustments

50.4   Residual Powers

Part 51 – Use of Government Sources by Contractors
51.1   Contractor Use of Government Supply Sources
51.2   Contractor Use of Interagency Motor Pool Vehicles

Subchapter H – Clauses and Forms

Part 52 – Solicitation Provisions and Contract Clauses
52.1   Instructions for Using Provisions and Clauses
52.2   Texts of Provisions and Clauses
52.3   Provision and Clause Matrices

Part 53 – Forms
53.1   General
53.2   Prescription of Forms
53.3   Illustrations of Forms

Index

Acquisition categories, 43
Acquisition management, 20
Acquisition Management Information
    System (AMIS), 189, 194
Acquisition planning, 201, 231, 313
ADP
  applications in procurement, 180
  applications survey, 183
  government purchase rules, 77
  administration of contracts, 60
Advocacy, 57, 132, 360
Agreement on Government
    Procurement, 344, 351
  assistance, 359
  objectives, 354
  statistical results,
      first year, 355
  transparency, 358
Alternative systems, exploration,
    313
Analysis, price, 55
Anti-Deficiency Act, 37
Architectural and engineering
    procedure, 137, 285
Assistance programs, 29, 76
Auction bidding, 239, 256
Audit, 62, 72, 82, 114
Authority, delegation, 35, 65
Authority for procurement, federal,
    34, 70
Balance of payments program, 344,
    350
Best and final offer (BAFO), 268
Bid mistakes, 252
Bid processing, 248
Bid rejection, 251
Breakout procurement center
    representatives, 381
Budget execution system, 207
Buy American Act, 344, 346
Change order actions, 298

Classical competitive procurement
    strategy, 228
Clearance, contract, 52
Co-location organizational concept,
    94
Commerce Business Daily, 43, 121,
    130, 245, 352, 381
Commercial products, use of, 124
Commission on Government Procure-
    ment, 3, 100, 168, 217, 306
Communications during bidding, 247
Comparison, procurement, private
    and public sector, 6
Competition advocate, 132
Competition in Contracting Act of
    1984 (CICA), 118
Competitive negotiation, 127, 260,
    262, 271
Competitive proposals, 127, 138
Competitive range, 265
Complex acquisitions, historical
    approaches, 308
Comptroller General, 112, 134
Conflicts of interest, 42
Contract administration actions, 15
Contract management review, 58
Contract Disputes Act, 63
Contract type
  alternatives, 322
  historical notes, 319
  selection of, 333
  utilization, 333, 334
Contract types, classified, 324
Contracting officer
  authority, 35, 162
  limitations 36, 162
Contractor
  interrelationships, 277
  procurement systems review, 59
Correction of bids, 253
Cost and fixed price contracts
    compared, 329

Cost comparison, 105
Cost contracts, 331
Cost or pricing data requirements, 269
Criteria for selecting contract type, 336
Customer service actions, 16
Cycles, interrelated, 21
Data and record retrieval system, 13
Decisions of procurement managers, 163
Deliverable item description, 275
Design specification, 204
Designated countries, 353
Development, full scale, 314
Discussion requirements, 138, 241
Discussions
  cost and price, 280
  personnel capabilities, 279
  schedule, 277
  technical, 276
  terms and conditions, 274, 281
  written or oral, 267
Distributed processing, 179
  for contractual input (DPCI), 186
DOD acquisition policy, 315
Dual negotiations, 270
Ethical issues, 40
Excellence in procurement, 34
Executive Order 12352, federal procurement reform, 25
Expediting actions, 15
Extraordinary contractual adjustments, 62
Federal Acquisition Institute, 67, 168
Federal Acquisition Regulation, (FAR), 46, 103, 107
Federal procurement data center, 67
Federal procurement, scope and range, 26
Financing contract work, 212
Financing policy, 213
Firm-bid rule defined, 245
Fixed-price contracts, 327
Foreign military sales, 287
Formal advertising, history, 242, 260
Freedom of Information Act (FOIA), 38
Function of contract types, 321
Functional management, concepts, 170
Functional specification, 125, 205

Funding, incremental, 211
Funding processes, 209
General Atomic reactor project, 318
Generic procurement model, 220
Golden Fleece Award, 28
Government-furnished property, 278
Grant, definition, 30
Improper business practices, 40
Inspector General, 34
Integrated materials system, 9
Integrated system for procurement, elements, 100
Inventory policy, 14
Justification for noncompetitive procurement, 51
Leader company procurement, 284
Life cycle cost (LCC), 238, 258
Limited source strategy, 229, 283
Logistics functions, 10
Major systems acquisition model, 224, 225
Major systems acquisition
  process, 312
  significance, 303
Make-or-buy
  factors, 149
  government, 145, 152
  history, government, 153
  industry decisions elements, 146
Management improvement in procurement, 167
Management systems, contractor, 278
Managerial skills, perceptions, 164
Market research requirement, 122
Materials functions, 10
Materials management, 9
Matrix organization, 175
MILSCAP, 195
Mission analysis, 198
Multiple award schedules, 138
NATO-RSI, 345, 360
Negotiation
  authority for, 264
  competitive models, 271
  competitive proposals, 127, 138
  scope of, 274
  strategies in government, 261
Negotiator, organizational units, 54
Noncompetitive-competitive procurement, assumptions, 381
Noncompetitive procedure
  authority to use, 128
  strategems, 292
Non-price evaluation factors, 249

Objectives
  acquisition 197
  Agreement on Government
      Procurement, 354
  executive agency, procurement,
      24, 386
  materials management, 11
  of second source action, 296
  procurement management, 3, 22,
      29, 33
  procurement personnel, 386
Obligational authority, 208
Office of Federal Procurement
    Policy, 101, 103
Office of Management and Budget
  Circular A-76, 156
  Circular A-109, 311
Operations control, procurement, 56
Organization
  Environmental Protection Agency
      90
  Goddard Space Flight Center, 94
  Navy Material Command, 85
  of procurement, basis for 66, 74
Organizational conflicts of
    interest, 42
Parallel development contracts, 313
Payments, methods, 214
Pellerzi standards, 155
Performance specification, 125, 203
Personal-nonpersonal services,
    defined, 142
Physical distribution actions, 16
Planning for procurement, 20, 199,
    201
Policy development, 46
Policy directed sourcing, 287
Prenegotiation plan, 52
Price-directed strategy, 228, 238
Price order of preference, 249
Pricing data requirements, 269
Prior position, 292
Procurement
  a support function, 24, 386
  action variables, 15
  as a tool of management, 23
  executive, 169
  functions, 46, 73
  manager, defined, 160
  management, image, 165
  plan, 50, 122
  process, cyclical analysis, 230
  process, model, 218
  team, 200
  universally practiced, 5, 23

Procurement--Con't.
  work force, qualifications, 383,
      386
Procurement administrative lead
    time (PALT), 45, 120, 200
Professional status aspirations for
    procurement personnel, 363
Project management, 83, 170
  limitations, 176
Protest procedure
  Comptroller General, 134
  for ADP procurement, 136
Provisioned items orders, 285
Publication of procurement notices,
    130
Public Law 85-536, Small Business
    Act Amendment, regarding SBA
    permanency, 380
Public Law 85-804, Extraordinary
    Contractual Adjustments, 62,
    253
Public Law 87-653, Truth in
    Negotiations Act, 139, 265,
    269, 270
Public Law 90-23, Freedom of
    Information Act, 38
Public Law 93-400, OFPP Act,
    establishment of, 67
Public Law 95-224, Federal Grant
    and Cooperative Agreement Act,
    76
Public Law 95-507, Small Business
    Act, amendment regarding
    subcontracting plan
    requirements, 380
Public Law 96-39, Trade Agreements
    Act, 348, 351
Public Law 96-83, OFPP act
    amendment, 25, 31, 101
Public Law 97-177, Prompt Payment
    Act, 213
Public Law 97-219, Small Business
    Innovation Development Act, 290
Public Law 98-72, Small Business
    Act, amendment regarding
    procurement notices, 130, 381
Public Law 98-191, OFPP act
    amendment, 286
Public Law 98-369, Competition in
    Contracting Act, 22, 50, 57,
    65, 102, 113, 118, 179, 218,
    239, 240, 241, 256, 260, 264,
    265, 283, 288, 382
Public Law 98-525, Defense Pro-
    curement Reform Act, 286, 382

Public Law 98-577, Small Business and Federal Procurement Enhancement Act, 286, 360, 382
Publication of procurement notices, 130
Regulated industry procurement, 301
Request for technical proposal (RTP), 254
Responsible contractor evaluation, 250
Responsible source, definition, 139
Review
  legal, 53
  procurement action, 49, 58
Rights, specific acquisition, 288
Role of procurement, 4, 23, 30, 386
Rulemakers, federal procurement, 106
Sealed bid, criteria for, 240
Sealed bidding, 126, 138, 238, 260
  suboptimization, 255
Second sourcing, 295
Simplification
  regulatory, 124
  technical, 14
Small Business Administration, role of, 69
Small Business programs, historical sketch, 376
Small Business Innovation Development Act, 290
Socioeconomic
  policy, issues, effects, 365
  programs, listing, 367

Source exclusion, 129
Source identificaiton and planning, 57, 58
Source selection plan, 50
Spares procurement policy, changes in 1984, 286
Special policy agencies, 67
Specifications, types of, 202
Standardization, 14
Standards of conduct, 41
Statistics, government procurement, 16, 17, 18, 19
Strategies for procurement, 226
Subcontractors, co-contractors, 277
Supplier relations, 13
Synopses, 130
Sytem features, uniform federal procurement, 25
System Scoping Paper, assumptions, 32
Technical analysis, 55
Technical data rights, 288
Technological/conceptual strategy, 229, 305, 309
Training, responsibility, 48
Two-step sealed bidding, 253
Uniform federal procurement system, 25, 31, 160
United States vs Brookridge Farm, 242
United States vs Tingey, 70
Unsolicited proposals, 137, 288
Variables in procurement action, 15
Written or oral discussions, 267